THE BIBLE: Dogma, Myth, or Mystery?

alba house DIVISION OF THE SOCIETY OF ST. PAUL • STATEN ISLAND, N.Y. 10314

The BIBLE

Dogma, Myth, or Mystery?

BY FRANCIS V. MANNING

Nihil Obstat:

    Richard Sneed, O.S.B.
    Censor Librorum

Imprimatur:

    ✝ Victor J. Reed
    Oklahoma City, Okla. — August 31, 1966

The nihil obstat and imprimatur are official declarations that a book
or pamphlet is free of doctrinal or moral error. No implication
is contained therein that those who have granted the nihil obstat and
imprimatur agree with the contents, opinions or statements expressed.

Library of Congress Catalog Card Number: 68 - 15382

Designed, printed and bound in the U.S.A. by the Pauline Fathers
and Brothers of the Society of St. Paul at Staten Island, New
York as a part of their communications apostolate.

FOREWORD

In the mid-twentieth-century "change" has become more than a byword of our vocabulary; it has come to play a vital role in our daily lives. There is scarcely any domain of our existence which is exempt from its influence. Those whose temperaments are flexible or restless are inclined to greet the dynamism of the present age warmly and optimistically. Those whose tastes run more to the sure and stable tend to look upon our dizzily moving world with apprehension.

Although having its roots in another era, the contemporary approach to the Bible has nonetheless become very much a part of the rapidly evolving world of the present. Thus what is referred to by scholars as "biblical criticism" has been profoundly marked by the influence of diverse components of the scientific method of criticism which is received almost everywhere today with great favor. Inevitably, changes in interpretation of countless passages of the Scriptures, changes which at times reach startling proportions, have been suggested or in certain cases practically forced upon us by the results flowing from biblical research carried out across the past one hundred years or thereabouts. These changes, too, are welcomed with unreserved enthusiasm by some, and viewed with dismay by others. The significance of some of these developments will furnish the subject matter for the pages to follow.

The thoughts to be encountered here are not, for the most part, original. I have endeavored to select data from a number of the writings of respected Catholic biblical scholars, and to present it in reasonably digestible form. In some instances I have dealt at length with the opinions of certain Protestant scholars whose influence upon today's Catholic exegetes can hardly be overlooked.

If, from time to time, a somewhat original theme or proposition is introduced, or a departure from the center of the well-trodden path of orthodoxy seems to have taken place, it is not with the intention of indulging in novelty; rather, it is with the aspiration of stimulating further research into the inexhaustible riches of the Pleroma of the Mystery of God's Revelation.

When quotations are taken from original French texts, the translations are my own.

The Author

CONTENTS

INTRODUCTION

Reflections on Change

No one challenges the assertion that the twentieth century has witnessed changes unparalleled by any other comparable span of years in the history of mankind. Nor is there any question about the fact that the spirit of change has invaded every domain of life, whether it be science, or philosophy, or religion.

Because "change" is popular, however, this does not necessarily make it justifiable. Every change which significantly affects any area of our lives must be subjected to critical evaluation. An answer must be sought to the question: does this particular change contribute something of positive value, or is it a sign of disintegration?

Any number of more or less recent developments which have profoundly altered the pattern of our lives spring readily to mind: mass media communication (through newspapers, television, movies), jet transportation, atomic warfare, tranquillizers, the "pill." In the realm of biblical studies, archaeological discoveries, the uncovering of ancient manuscripts, and the emergence of new methodologies and perspectives in approaching Sacred Scripture, have been no less revolutionary in their effect.

While each of these developments must be objectively criticized, all of them are cast in an aurora of ambiguity: what is their real value? In themselves they represent technical advances enjoying the potential of contributing significantly to the enrichment of humanity. Yet, in the final analysis, everything hinges upon the way in which man uses what he has evolved. If he deploys his inventions and applies his findings in the right spirit, with the proper goal, their effect on the formation of human society will be positive and enduring; if man abuses the products of his creativeness and industry, however, the instruments he fabricates, the values he adopts, can destroy him morally and materially.

Everything that changes in this world, changes man himself. Hence, change is to be evaluated in terms of the man who is involved and in terms of his destiny. But the man who is involved is the supreme image and likeness of God in this world—at least that is his nature and his calling. This man, then, has the role of plunging into change, of mastering it, of purifying it of its elements of corruptibility, of seizing its dynamic value, and in love of channeling it to the Changeless, Pure Love.

* * *

Man was created to rule the created. He was given thought and volition as the tools of his conquest. But, more important, he was given a divine energy which was the only force capable of keeping in harmony the tremendous drives of his mind and will which, in turn, were to direct the expressions of themselves in the flesh. But somehow, in some mysterious way, man failed. He allowed the divine energy to slip from his grasp, and he died.

There came a Man to re-create the created. He was not merely in possession of the divine energy, he was one with it. In him was restored the force essential for harmonizing the powers of mind, will, and passion. In him alone was constituted, whether to be actuated antecedently or subsequently, the possibility of giving the proper direction to *change* in the world.

Mankind has experienced in its history, therefore, two of the most radical situations of change imaginable. In the first the intimacy of God is rejected; in the second the same intimacy becomes flesh, so that it can be scorned, rejected, never escaped, and ultimately embraced. In the second moment, the divine presence in man is assured, eternalized, through incarnate union.

Now these two situations of change have dominated the entire movement of time and the fluctuation of change in the universe as it involves man. They represent the utterances of two great acts of will, acts which transcend the boundaries of time: the stubborn No of humanity, and the obedient Yes of its Redeemer. In the one is contained the framework for the No of every child of man, the principle of all change in the direction of corruption; in the other is contained the possibility of an ever-increasing and intensifying assent, the principle of all change in the direction of an absolute Yes enveloping totally the living. Thus it constituted somehow, from the beginning, in the eternal plan of the Trinity, a tension between the possibility of disintegration and the possibility of perfection, a tension exerted on every element of the universe. At one pole there is sin, pulling in the direction of chaos; at the other pole there is the saving grace of the Redeemer, attracting from the outside and impelling from within, in the direction of the eschatological fulfillment of change, the achievement of the reign of God, through the Word who became man, through the Word in the Church, through the Church in God's world which must act as the servant of man whose destiny it is to give Christ's form to this world.

* * *

In the list of the attributes of God, it is customary to encounter that of immutability. To be subject to change is esteemed to be an imperfection, and, therefore, the divine nature which by definition must be all-perfect, has to be free from change. God is indeed "the Father of lights in whose Person there is no variation or shadow proceeding from movement" (James 1: 17).

The perfection of the immutability of God must, however,

be properly understood. It pertains to the purest and most complex kind of dynamism. God is changeless only because there is nothing in him except ceaseless activity, unlimited life, love unconfined by the slightest restriction. This is the essence of the uncreated, and in contemplating the changelessness of the divine, possibly we can better understand what change itself ought to be.

In the human sphere, in the order of the created, there is no dynamism, no activity, no life, no love, unless there is change. The less something changes, the more dead it is; the less someone changes, the more dead he is. As we have indicated, two directions of change govern the entire spectrum of alteration: change which perfects and change which corrupts; the change of a being evolving towards fulfillment, and that of an entity in the process of disintegrating. Change with positive value is marked by an increase of true, synthesizing complexity, yielding the strength which comes from close unity and coherency. Negative change is characterized by false complexity which is fostered by multiplication of disparate units fundamentally opposed to one another and tending to isolation rather than to the mutual interaction essential for oneness.

Every particular instance of change raises the question: does this witness to the presence of development or corruption, of intensified life or imminent death?

* * *

A most urgent issue, then, is where is the world of today in relation to the universal tension between chaos and the perfection of harmonic unity, between death and life? In which direction are we being led by the changes which we see around us in the world? To the committed Catholic the question poses itself in still more pressing fashion: where is the Church in reference to the tension between chaos and perfection, a tension which in reality is the struggle between sin and grace? Is *this* Church at *this* time responding to the utmost of its capacity to the imperative placed upon it by the Lord to bring about the universal Reign of God? Is it alive and vibrant, is it characterized by the positive

and energetic species of change essential to true development —
or is it infected by negative elements, the germs of pseudoevolution,
confusion, disorder, irrelevancy, stagnation, disintegration symp-
tomatic of a condition bordering on death?

The Catholic, of course, never allows himself to think in
terms of a dying Church, for he knows with the certitude of
divinely assured faith that "the powers of death shall not prevail"
(Mt. 16: 18). But, while unrelenting optimism and hope are
essential to the Christian viewpoint, the believer cannot afford
to forget that the Church is sufficiently complex and sufficiently
human to be both alive in principle and dead in fact, with respect
to its time and the issues which it is called upon to face. It is
never enough for the Church merely to continue. It is constantly
challenged to meet the needs of the "present" age, it is incessantly
summoned to change.

As has been said, our century is one of almost incredible
change. We cannot pretend that the Catholic Church of this
era has kept pace. But some might object "should it?" If the
changes which pervade the world are in actuality conducting man
along the path to self-destruction, is it the role of the Church
to become part and parcel of this type of "progress," or shouldn't
it resist?

In any event, the Church has been changing, and deeply so.
The changes have, until the last several years, been taking place
quietly; still, they have been significant and extensive enough to
lay the groundwork for the emergence of Vatican Council II.
The Council was not just the result of a spontaneous decision on
the part of the impulsive and beloved John XXIII. It was made
possible by the patient and assiduous work of leaders within
the Church, leaders in such fields as Scripture, Ecumenism, and
Liturgy, as well as by encouragement coming from our brothers
not of the Roman persuasion; it was the thorough, scholarly,
and tactful work by men such as these that created the atmosphere
of fresh air which took hold of John one day as he opened his
window high in the remoteness of the Vatican and decided to
let a breath of fresh air into the Church.

The Second Vatican Council, then, is not an abrupt rupture

with the trend the Church has been following throughout the last century; rather, it is the fruition of seeds planted across the years through the persistent and indefatigable efforts of those who have kept in the most intimate touch with the life dwelling within the Church.

The Church knows that she must be brought up to date. She knows that she cannot elude the touch of the spirit of change. She is also quite conscious that the companion of change is the danger of disorder and confusion. But the fact that she can count among her faithful many diligent sons of the quality of those who have made Vatican II a reality causes her to look to the future with confidence, despite the perils. Inspired by the very vitality of the Holy Spirit, the Church has no doubts that the changes she is introducing and will introduce bear witness to an evolution in the direction of the fullness of perfection to which she is called by Christ, and only incidentally reflect, as inescapable side effects, certain aspects of negative change.

Nevertheless, the suggestion that the Church needs to be changed, that she is not immaculate, that she might even in some vital areas be rather irrelevant, has shocked not a few of the members of the Body of Christ. Within the ranks of the fathers of the Council itself not infrequently voices of protest were raised; and the tremor going forth from the intimation that reform is in order has shaken to the marrow more than one of those who loyally fill the pews.

Fundamentally, the problem is that of the ambiguity of change: is it corruption or evolution? Evolution demands the crossing of thresholds; it presupposes a leap, a risk, the daring of the pioneer. There are those who are convinced that the risk is worthwhile, that in fact it must be taken, for the alternative is slow death. For them the changes urging themselves upon the Church are ineluctable and must be embraced, suffered, and fully implemented, whatever courage may be required, whatever price must be paid; there are others who see change as little more than surrender, the beginning of what can only terminate in a diluted doctrinal position, a morality stripped of conviction and definite orientation, a form of worship fallen victim to fadism.

Where does the truth lie? How is the changing demeanor of the contemporary Catholic Church to be evaluated? Such questions, whether spoken or left unformulated, trouble many a conscience in this world of ours already so filled with uncertainty. But, what is more perplexing, there is no definitive answer to any of them. We can do no more than carefully examine each phenomenon-of-belief which is undergoing change and endeavor to estimate the significance of the change, to anticipate where it might lead and what man might make of it, to judge it in accordance with the norms of past tradition and the needs of the future.

It seems, therefore, that the tendency of our times is to criticize everything, to submit every iota of doctrine or observance to reevaluation. The demon of change, or the angelic countenance of progress (depending on one's point of view), intrudes its presence everywhere. Not even the Bible itself has evaded the probing finger of the spirit of change. On the contrary, the new perspectives and methods of criticism introduced into the study of Sacred Scripture during the past century have had a great deal to do with changes being enacted or proposed in many other areas, such as sacramental theology, liturgy, the ecumenical movement, the orientation of morality, etc.

Because the changing approach to the Bible is so far-reaching in its effects, it is important that the believer have at least a basic comprehension of some of the things that have been done in the way of scientific treatment of the Old and New Testaments. The following chapters represent an attempt to aid the reader to attain this comprehension. It is hoped that those who are well versed in biblical study may find here one or two fresh ideas, and that those who are less familiar with the recent trends in criticism of the Scriptures may be aroused to further interest in this most timely subject.

Many questions are raised in this work. Few are answered. And nothing is really resolved or settled. A number of examples of the contemporary approach to involved biblical problems are presented; none of these is treated with any degree of completeness, and no conclusions of absolute value have been reached. It will be up to the reader to form his own opinion of the value of the "new" approach to the Bible. He will have to answer for himself the question: will this modern treatment of the Word of God undermine man's faith, or will it lead to a greater, purer, and more unreserved faith?

The Immutability of Truth
and the Changing Face of the Old and New Testaments

In years gone by people who found life worrisome and full of troubling vicissitudes, people who were confused or pulled this way and that by various philosophies of life or fads of thought throbbing about them in their atmosphere of time and space, could at least find consolation in sitting back, emitting a sigh of relief, and opening "The Book," the Word of God. Here at least they could be sure of enjoying the cleansing feeling of an immersion in the truth. In their Bible they could listen to the voice of truth itself, for through the words of Sacred Scripture it was God who was addressing them.

Within the last century, however, and particularly within the last fifty years, the picture has changed considerably. Actually, as early as the eighteenth century the public was presented with attacks against the "truth" contained in biblical teachings. Rationalists, such as Voltaire, brought to the fore what they considered to be the moral degeneracy sanctioned by the Old Testament, for example: the lies of the Patriarchs [1] or the barbaric cruelties of the Jewish conquest of Palestine.[2]

In the nineteenth century the Bible was challenged again, this time more seriously, by the world of science. From the time of Galileo this particular cloud had been banking up on the horizon. Finally, the sentiment that the Bible and science portray two contradictory worlds could no longer be suppressed. The six

---

1. Cf. Gen. 13:10 ff.; 20:2; 27:1-29.
2. Cf. Jos. 6:21; 8:2, 24-25; 10:20, 26. Cf. also A. Barucq and H. Cazelles. "Les Livres Inspirés." In *Introduction à la Bible,* edited by A. Robert and A. Feuillet, Desclée & Cie., Tournai, 2nd edition, 1959, Vol. 1, p. 62.

days of creation in Genesis, [3] the sun standing still for Joshua, [4] honey having a special aptness for brightening the eyes, [5] the hare being designated as an animal that chews the cud, [6] etc., were proposed as instances in which Scripture was in error, that is, "unscientific."

Toward the end of the nineteenth century, criticism began to focus more intently on the historical value of biblical data. As, through an accumulation of extra-biblical source material, gaps in our knowledge of the history of the ancient Near East were filled, contradictions began to appear between what was learned in this way and the information reported by the Bible. Questions like the following arose:

Why does the book of Daniel make Belshazzar the son of Nebuchadnezzar, [7] when his actual father was Nabonidus, the fourth in the line of succession from this king? Why does the book of Judith make Nebuchadnezzar a king of Assyria, [8] when in fact he was a ruler in the Neo-Babylonian empire and there is evidence to show that he never set foot in Nineveh, the capital city of Assyria? Moreover, if the biblical texts themselves are carefully compared with one another, it would appear quite difficult to reconcile some of them, for example, the accounts in Joshua of how the conquest of the land of Canaan was achieved seem to be in conflict.

Once the historical question had been posed, there was no holding back the floodgates of criticism. The Old Testament became in the minds of certain critics hardly more than a collection of Hebrew folklore, a glorified body of myths. The New Testament and the very person of Christ did not go unmolested. As careful study made it apparent that the Gospels cannot be accepted as firsthand, eyewitness accounts of the evangelists, Jesus Christ came to be viewed as a myth created by the original Christian

---

3. Cf. Gen. chaps. 1 and 2.
4. Cf. Jos. 10:12-14.
5. Cf. I Sam. 14:29.
6. Cf. Lev. 11:6; Dt. 14:7.
7. Cf. Dan. 5:2.
8. Cf. Jdt. 1:1.

community, an historical personage, but a person about whom the New Testament gives us very little factual information.

Hence, today even the public at large is confronted with the problem: is truth to be found in the Bible? If so, where? In what sense? Can Sacred Scripture still be regarded as the "Word of God," or is it merely the outcome of the contrivances of primitive religious men or communities?

A thorough attempt to answer this type of questioning would presuppose an analysis of the nature of truth, a consideration of the evolving meaning of history, a survey of the actual accomplishments of biblical scholarship, and evaluation of all these elements taken as a totality, and much more besides. The present work represents only an endeavor to sketch an outline of the implications of this involved issue, by pointing to some of the more significant facets of the nature of "truth," and by trying to envision what lies behind assertions such as "We know now that the account of Noah and the Ark is but a fable," or "We do not always know with certainty that Jesus actually said everything attributed to him in the Gospels."

Throughout the centuries, many philosophers and theologians of great renown have attempted to attach a precise definition to "truth." Thus, contemporary manuals often view truth as the very perfection or entity of a thing insofar as it is able to be an object of intellection; [9] or again, truth, whether in regard to things, concepts or words, always consists of a certain conformity between the intellect and the reality in question. [10] There is nothing astoundingly new about such definitions, of course; we not only find practically the same expressions in St. Thomas: truth can be said to be in the intellect insofar as it is in conformity with the reality understood; [11] truth consists in the "adequation" of the intellect and the thing in view; [12] but also in St. Augustine: "All things are true so far as they be; nor is there any falsehood,

---

9. *Sacrae Theologiae Summa*, B.A.C., Madrid, 1958, Vol. 2, p. 71.

10. Cf. *Summula Philosophiae Scholasticae*, J. S. Hickey, Dublin, 1953, Vol. 1, p. 151.

11. Cf. S.T., I., Q. 16, a. 1, c.

12. Cf. S.T., I., Q. 21, a. 2, c.

unless when that is thought to be, which is not"; [13] and even in Plato: "And he who says that which is, says the truth." [14] The point I wish to make is that a long tradition of thought assures us there is such a thing as truth and it has an absolute quality about it, for it is existing reality itself, insofar as it is known.

Although the preceding may seem rather abstruse, it may point to what lies behind the quandary of those people who are disconcerted by the "new" approach to the Bible. The continuing efforts of thinkers throughout history to delimit more and more precisely the nature of truth has had its effect on the common man, no matter how far removed he may be from the philosopher's tower. Every era has seen its own brand of preoccupation with the search for what is true and what are the norms of truth, and thus, while we are living in an age in which relativism and rationalizing have precipitated a mental fog as thick as soup, paradoxically the prerequisites which we of this day and time establish for truth are severe indeed. Conformity between mind and reality are scarcely satisfying to us; we question the mind, we question the reality, we question even the question. We refuse to acknowledge anything as true unless it practically imposes itself upon our intelligence with an evidence that cannot be denied. Unless a proposition carries such force, we find it easy to relegate it to the scrap heap of probabilities. In the pragmatic world of the twentieth century, unless something is immediately pertinent to our lives, that is, eminently practical, its truth becomes an academic question, and is readily dismissed as irrelevant or inaccessible to the mind.

While the philosophers of ages past have endeavored to specify the nature of truth and give it an exact definition, then, the common man of our times has adopted his own rigid attitude toward the true: unless he can be convinced that the latter is of great practical value to him, he is simply not interested; he is not the skeptic of earlier days who insisted "there is no truth,"

---

13. *The Confessions of St. Augustine*, translated by E. B. Pusey, The Modern Library, New York, 1949, p. 136.

14. "Euthydemus." From *The Dialogues of Plato*, translated by B. Jowett, *Great Books of the Western World*, William Benton, Vol. 7, p. 72.

he is the busy, busy man who has no time for the truth that is.

But how does Sacred Scripture fit into this menagerie of affirmations about truth? Until recently we could not say that it did. To the majority of Catholics, including the clergy, the Bible remained untouchable. [15] It was simply the Word of God, a book which gave us divine facts and meant literally what it said. Here was the truth, pure and simple, and it could not be questioned. To be sure, there were scholars digging away, turning up this dilemma and that, probing ever deeper into biblical literature, tearing it apart piece by piece. But fortunately, or unfortunately, such scholars seemed to converse only with other scholars and to be read only by still other scholars, their impact upon the public in general being, to say the least, slight.

Just as when a distant star explodes somewhere in the universe and the resultant light of the cataclysm is sooner or later recorded on earth, however, so the efforts of scriptural scholars could not go forever unnoticed. In Catholic circles, with the publication of Pius XII's encyclical *Divino Afflante Spiritu,* 1943, the work that had been going on for years began to surface. To the latter were added new endeavors to investigate the Bible thoroughly from every angle. Seminary professors, their students, clergy,

---

15. It should be noted that during the nineteenth century and well into the twentieth, Protestant biblical scholarship, though in many instances leaning too far in the direction of liberalism or rationalism, made many more positive contributions to an objective understanding of the Bible than did Catholic exegesis which was frustrated at every turn by being forced to adopt too conservative a policy. It has only been in the last few decades that a more objective and mature Catholic approach to the Bible has become fairly widespread. For a number of interesting treatments of the relationships between Protestant and Catholic approaches to Sacred Scripture cf. *Scripture and Ecumenism,* edited and with introduction by L. J. Swidler, Duquesne University Press, Pittsburgh, 1965; W. Kasper, "The Church under the Word of God," *The Church and Ecumenism (Concilium),* Paulist Press, New York, 1965, Vol. 4, pp. 87-93; G. Thils, "Le choix d'un critère," *La "Théologie Oecuménique,"* É. Warny, Louvain, 1960, pp. 35-41; *Christianity Divided,* edited by D. Callahan, H. A. Oberman and D. J. O'Hanlon, Sheed & Ward, New York, 1961; H. Cazelles, "Le Travail de la Critique," *op. cit.,* pp. 290-314; A. Feuillet and P. Grelot, "La critique littéraire du Nouveau Testament," *ibid.,* pp. 142-151.

and religious have gradually been made aware of the massive effort of scientific biblical criticism to reevaluate the Scriptures; little by little all of those whose prime goal in life is the conservation and promotion of Christian doctrine have taken note of the many serious implications which the modern approach to the Bible has with regard to the presentation of the faith. And in the last few years, the general public has begun to feel the impact of this movement which has dedicated itself to a more mature appreciation of the Bible.

This brings us to the crux of our problem. A public which has had a rather childlike understanding of the Bible and which has been virtually ignorant of the historical background in which the books of God's Word were composed, has been abruptly presented with the findings, theories, and speculations of a mature biblical scholarship. Is there any wonder that many individuals should be dumbfounded? A world of spiritual literature that for so long a time was familiar, consoling, and sure suddenly has become strange, foreign, rended by doubts. In an all too condensed span of years a great many people have been and are being made acutely conscious that even the Word of God is not immune to the confusion, so characteristic of our age, about what is true and what is not. We are unavoidably confronted with the discomforting thought that even the Bible cannot be accepted at face value; in a world in which it is so difficult to lay hold of the truth, it now seems that not even Sacred Scripture itself unequivocally offers the truth. The truth of the Word of God has to be submitted to the same harsh, critical standards by which the other realities of our world are judged. The revealed Word of God is, after all, not untouchable. The question has to be heard and answered: do we read the truth in Sacred Scripture? If so, of what does it consist? What is the nature of this truth?

The nucleus of the solution to this extremely complex problem is to be sought in the finite nature of human comprehension of truth, in the way truth, although absolute in itself, is conditioned by the times and peoples from which it emerges.

Truth is indeed the expression of reality through intelligence.

And reality itself is absolute, in the sense that it is what it is, when it is (for temporal being). For example, God is the reality of realities; he is what he is, absolutely, and this is not altered by the fact that he may be conceived of in as many ways as there are minds. But, the expression of a reality through an intelligence is always personal and thus in a sense unique; with respect to man, every expression of reality is in time, in situation, and is therefore qualified by the limitations of the historical moment. In a word, all truth is absolute, but the way it is apprehended and expressed by man is always relative, and subject to being perfected. The very word "truth" is an expression of a concept which can only be imperfectly grasped by the mind or conveyed through the attempt of language to define it. Hence, no two men have exactly the same appreciation of what truth is, and certainly two cultures could evaluate truth in widely divergent terms.

If, then, we wish to find the truth in Sacred Scripture, we must approach our project from the perspectives: what was truth for the ancients? How does their viewpoint compare with our own? And, since the problem necessarily revolves around the historical value of the texts, we must consider the Israelitic and then the Christian mode of reporting "history." As we proceed, a great deal of emphasis will be placed on the relativity of the significance of the biblical texts: for they are relative to the amount of knowledge we have of their background, and they are relative to the infinite expanse of the Mystery of God which even they cannot contain. (Some very interesting insights into the way a culture and its *Weltanschauung,* its way of viewing the world, can shape the presentation of such concepts as "truth," or "immutability," can be read in Leslie Dewart's provocative *The Future of Belief,* Burns & Oates, London, 1967; Herder & Herder, New York, 1966.)

Part 1

Truth and Religious Folklore in the Old Testament

What was antiquity's notion of truth? What precisely was the difference between the attitude of the peoples of the Bible toward truth and our own? We can attempt here only a general answer. The Semite was a man whose values were concrete. His thought and his vocabulary did not lend themselves readily to abstractions. Thus, he formulated his view of the true in terms of the basic relationships of his life with other men and with God.

When the Semite dealt with other men, truth meant conformity between what they said and what was fact. [1] In the Decalogue, sin against truth is conceived of in terms of false testimony given against one's neighbor. [2] That this concept of truth as governing relationships of the Hebrews with one another was highly esteemed is evident from declarations such as we meet in the prophet Hosea: the Lord condemned the sons of Israel because there was no truth ("faithfulness") in the land. [3] "Truth" could also refer to the justice of the sentence of a king or judge: "Loyalty and faithfulness preserve the king, and his throne is upheld by righteousness," that is, by just and truthful judgment. [4] Truth, therefore, was regarded by the chosen people as an element essential to the preservation of peace and justice in the community.

---

1. Cf. Dt. 13:15.
2. Cf. Ex. 20:16.
3. Hos. 4:1.
4. Pr. 20:28.

On the other hand, truth had a somewhat different connotation when it applied to man's relation with God. It often designated a person's faithfulness to God.[5] But it could also denote God's faithfulness to his promises.[6] Truth was also supposed to characterize the reign of the Messiah.[7] Finally, in the book of Daniel, divine truth is identified with divine revelation.[8]

From this brief survey, we have an indication that for the Hebrews the nature of truth was neither precisely defined nor intellectualized. It simply described the qualities of a certain number of interpersonal relationships among themselves, or between themselves and the Lord. Furthermore, even in this confined domain we see evidence of a marked evolution from a rather questionable attitude toward truth on the part of the Patriarchs, for example, Abram's lie about Sarai,[9] or Jacob's ruse,[10] to a more highly developed appreciation of its value, as witnessed by the prophets and by some of the psalmists. In brief, then, the Israelite approached truth quite concretely. In everyday business matters, he expected truth from his neighbor, and not deceit, exactly as we do. He trusted in the perfect truthfulness of God, being certain that Yahweh could be counted on to fulfill his promises. But when there was question of a more abstract type of truthfulness, as in the historical objectivity of a religious composition, this was quite another matter. Here it was basic realities which were of paramount importance, and not details. For instance, in the revelation of the Decalogue, the thing that was important was that the commandments are ultimately Yahweh's, and not the precise way in which historically they were communicated to man.

These considerations are of definite moment when we turn to the problem of contemporary biblical scholarship. When

---

5. Cf. II Kg. 20:3.
6. Cf. Ps. 33:4.
7. Cf. Ps. 45:4.
8. Cf. Dan. 8:12; 9:13.
9. Cf. Gen. 12:13.
10. Cf. Gen. 27:24.

any number of modern scriptural interpretations are proposed, for example, that which reduces the crossing of the reed (and not "Red") sea to practically a natural adventure; [11] or that which evaluates the manna in the desert as the symbolical figure of an haggadic midrash, [12] the immediate reaction often is "If this is the case, have not the authors deceived us?"

The question is not so much that of having been deceived as of having deceived ourselves. When an author sets something in writing, he has a personal intention of conveying some reality, and he chooses the *form* of literature which he deems to be the most suitable for his purposes. His writing must be presented in a mode which can be easily grasped by his readers. Once the literary form has been selected and the writer's thought has been committed to writing, however, the elements of situation and time take over. A literary form that at one time was familiar, can gradually become strange. An intention that at one time was clear, can gradually become obscure. This is the destiny awaiting every written word. Even the Word of God, inspired though it is, is not exempt from this limitation. For too long men have deceived themselves with the notion that they could page through their Bibles and root out the literal intention of the author simply by applying to the Divine Word the meager instrument of their own judgment framed in the concepts of their own times.

It could be concluded, then, that throughout centuries Sacred Scripture has been *misinterpreted.* Or is this term perhaps poorly chosen? Might it not be better to say that throughout the years of study and contemplation devoted to the Sacred Writings, they never have been anything but *partially interpreted,* they never have yielded the full richness of the truth they contain?

Is it not presumptuous to declaim that the reality of which God's Revelation is a sign, the economy of his creative-redemptive action, ever could be adequately measured by any human device, even by a divinely guided definition — as long as that definition

---

11. Cf. Ex. 14.
12. Cf. Ex. 16.

is subject to the limitations intrinsic to all human expression? The written word is finite not only because it must be couched in a specific literary form, not only because it is always a part of a situational framework, but above all because it is forever *human*.

At the same time, nonetheless, the scriptural Word is divine, totally divine. In an integral way it is the inspired work of God. Through human words, divine realities are transmitted. [13] In virtue of this supernatural relationship, the content, the depths of meaning to be found in God's revelation, and the significance of his Word for men of all times are inexhaustible.

How complex, therefore, is the operation of precisely delimiting the truth revealed in the Bible. Not only is there the difficulty of discovering the meaning originally intended by the human author, there is the added challenge of endeavoring to grasp as fully as possible the reality, and often the mystery, which God *is* revealing throughout time through the Writings he has inspired.

Thus a great deal is involved in discerning the ultimate meaning of revealed truth. To be sure, the inspired author was wholly dedicated to the pronouncement of absolute truth. But what was this truth? As we begin our search for the answer to this question, antiquity's conception of *history,* and particularly that of the children of Israel, the people of God, becomes most important. Quite often, when the truth of Scripture is called into doubt, it is because "revelation" is assaulted as being non-historical. At other times the criticism is posed in this way: what modern science has shown to be incontrovertibly true cannot be reconciled with some of the data of the Bible, and hence we can only conclude that the Bible gives us a false picture of the history and the historical situation of man.

This type of critique of Sacred Scripture or its historical value is almost inevitably traceable to a rather superficial examination of what the inspired writings are actually saying. When

---

13. For a thorough study of this theme, cf. J. Levie, S.J., *The Bible, Word of God in Words of Men,* translated by R. Capel; P. J. Kenedy & Sons, New York, 1961.

the sacred author presents some situation or event, we cannot always take his story at face value. We must always ask ourselves: is he talking about something that happened historically? Or is he creating a story to depict some mysterious element of man's situation in history? Or is he combining something of both approaches at the same time? Careful study of the text can frequently show that the historical value of particular events is of secondary importance to the author. He is concerned first of all with the intervention of God in history: this special presence of God is true, is historical, in the most absolute sense. The entire Old Testament witnesses to the fact that for the Israelite the very essence of God is to be *He Who Acts* for his people. The details which serve to ornament this action are sometimes a matter of history, sometimes more or less the product of fiction.

For the sacred authors was not history above all an economy? The economy of salvation? The salvific Will of God relentlessly and lovingly drawing mankind into its embrace?

CHAPTER ONE

THE MYTH OF THE FLOOD

Any number of passages could serve as excellent witnesses to the variety of approaches used by Old Testament authors in portraying religious truth. Very commonly these authors would borrow plots, themes, images, terms, mythological settings, etc., from pagan religious cultures with which Israel had enjoyed some contact, would purify them, and would use them under divine inspiration to transmit God's revelation. Even though for a number of decades now biblical scholars have generally acknowledged this kind of dependency, still, the suggestion that the writers of the Bible were not totally original and the admission to the presence of mythical elements in the Old Testament have disconcerted more than a few people.

Since it is particularly this reference to the mythological nature of parts of the Bible that is frequently found disturbing, an explanation of what is meant by "myth" in this context and a few samplings of biblical mythology might prove enlightening. First of all, what is meant by "myth" as applied to passages of Sacred Scripture?

For the ancients the main object of mythologizing was to describe in a symbolical way some world reality. [1] If one of

---

1. For a treatment of myth in relation to the Old Testament, cf. John L. McKenzie, S.J., *Myths and Realities*, Bruce Publishing Company, Milwaukee, 1963. For a more general background to mythology and religion, cf.

their accounts or traditions was "mythical," this did not necessarily exclude its "historicity." At times the formulation of the myth did preclude any historical preoccupation, but at other times it could have a certain basis in history. In any event, the myth represented an effort to transmit through concrete images and symbols realities which in themselves were transcendental.

In general, the religions of the ancient civilizations of the East abounded in myths devoid of historical perspective. Thus the gods and goddesses of the fertility cults were not actually taken to be historical personages, but were valued as symbols representing mysterious forces at work in the universe. The mythical wars between the gods giving rise to the emergence of creation were not interpreted literally, but were appreciated as a manner of portraying the enigmatic energies underlying the incessant conflicts rending the cosmos. The question of what the origin of these stories might have been, or of whether or not sometime in the past such events as those described in the myths really happened was usually of minor interest to these peoples. They were aware of forces functioning in the world, forces which implicated man and profoundly influenced him, but which he could neither comprehend nor master; the myth furnished an instrument through which the significance of these cosmic functions might be expressed.

With respect to the use of mythology, however, the religion of Israel separated itself radically from the other religions of

Étienne Drioton, Georges Contenau and Jacques Duchesne-Guillemin, *Religion of the Ancient East,* translated from French by M. B. Loraine, Hawthorn Books, New York, 1959; Sir James George Frazer, *The Golden Bough,* Vol. 1, abridged edition, The Macmillan Company, New York, 1960, (original copyright 1922); T. H. Gaster, *The Oldest Stories in the World,* Beacon Press, Boston, 1952. W. F. Albright, *From the Stone Age to Christianity,* Doubleday & Company, New York, 1957; M. Eliade, *Birth and Rebirth,* translated from French by W. R. Trask, Harper & Row, New York, 1958; M. Eliade, *The Sacred and the Profane,* translated from French by W. K. Trask, Harcourt, Brace and World, New York, 1959; M. Eliade, *Myths, Dreams and Mysteries,* Harper & Row, New York, 1960; H. and H. A. Frankfort, J. A. Wilson, T. Jacobsen, *Before Philosophy,* Penguin Books, Baltimore, 1946.

its locale and era by its inculcating of a perspective that was not only historical, but historical in a very special sense. The establishment of Israel as a people depended upon an actual intervention of God in history. The growth of Israel was determined by the continuing action of God through quite specific historical persons. This concern for history is naturally reflected in the Sacred Books relating the development of the alliance between God and the people he had chosen. [2]

This, nevertheless, does not imply that the Old Testament is a true history or the product of historians. Nor does it mean that when we talk about an historical aspect, we signify "history" in the modern sense of the term. Not infrequently in the Old Testament we find actual persons and events mingled with purely mythological data. Moreover, when myth does appear, it has much the same function that it had in the religions contemporary to the appearance of the Hebrew Faith, although with this distinction: myth in the Bible is always an effort to express in one way or another some facets of the historical relationship of God to his people. Hence, in Old Testament literature, history and myth are not mutually opposed but complement one another; at times a considerable distance separates the two; at times they approach very near indeed to the line purportedly differentiating them.

Among the many passages in the Old Testament which possess mythical overtones, the story of the flood as told in Genesis, chapters 6 to 8, provides a good example of a rather extreme type of biblical myth, one in which only a slight degree of historical perspective is involved. In its major features and most of its details, the account derives from a myth which was the common patrimony of the peoples of the ancient Near East. More or

---

2. Cf. R. A. F. MacKenzie, S.J., *Faith and History in the Old Testament,* University of Minnesota Press, Minneapolis, 1963; J. L. McKenzie, S.J., *The Two-Edged Sword,* Bruce Publishing Company, Milwaukee, 1955; Bruce Vawter, C.M., *The Conscience of Israel,* Sheed & Ward, New York, 1961; Ignatius Hunt, O.S.B., *Understanding the Bible,* Sheed & Ward, New York, 1961; B. W. Anderson, *Understanding the Old Testament,* Prentice-Hall, Englewood Cliffs, New Jersey, 1957.

less complete versions of the story have been found in the Akkadian, Hittite, and Egyptian languages, and fragments of the myth have shown up in the literature of still other peoples. It seems that the earliest form of the flood myth, appearing in a document known as the *Epic of Gilgamesh,* can be traced to the people of Sumeria, and probably dates from around the beginning of the second millennium. It is of interest to note, in passing, that the capital of the Sumerian people was located on the site of Ur, the city inhabited by the ancestors of Abraham.

For the sake of comparing it with the biblical account of the deluge, we shall devote a page here to a summary of Tablet XI of the *Epic of Gilgamesh.* This will provide us with a starting point from which we can draw out the significance of similarities between the accounts, and point out the differences in religious content.

The story begins with a mortal king, Gilgamesh, seeking from a god, Utnapishtim, the secret of immortality. Utnapishtim reveals to the former the tale of how he became a god. The following are pertinent excerpts from the text:

Shurippak ... which on Euphrates' [banks] is situate —
That city was ancient, (as were) the gods within it,
When their heart led the great gods to produce the flood ....
"Man of Shuruppak, son of Ubar-Tutu,
Tear down (this) house, build a ship!
Give up possessions, seek thou life ....
Aboard the ship take thou the seed of all living things.
The ship that thou shalt build,
Her dimensions shall be to measure ...."
On the fifth day I laid her framework.
One (whole) acre was her floor space,
Ten dozen cubits the height of each of her walls,
Ten dozen cubits each edge of the square deck ....
I provided her with six decks,
Dividing her (thus) into seven parts ....
Six "sar" (measures) of bitumen I poured into the furnace ....
Three sar of oil the basket bearers carried,

Aside from the one sar of oil which the calking consumed . . . .
Whatever I had of all the living beings I [laded] upon her.
All my family and kin I make go aboard the ship . . . .
I watched the appearance of the weather.
The weather was awesome to behold.
I boarded the ship and battened up the entrance.

With the first glow of dawn,
A black cloud rose up from the horizon.
Inside it Adad thunders,
While Shullate and Hanish go in front,
Moving as heralds over hill and plain . . . .
For one day the south-storm [blew],
Gathering speed as it blew, [submerging the mountains],
Overtaking the [people] like a battle . . . .
The gods were frightened by the deluge . . . .
The gods cowered like dogs crouched against the outer wall . . . .
The gods, all humbled, sit and weep . . . .
Six days and [six] nights
Blows the flood wind, as the south-storm sweeps the land.
When the seventh day arrived,
The flood (- carrying) south-storm subsided in the battle,
Which it had fought like an army.
The sea grew quiet, the tempest was still, the flood ceased.
I looked at the weather: stillness had set in,
And all of mankind had returned to clay . . . .
On Mount Nisir the ship came to a halt . . . .
When the seventh day arrived,
I sent forth and set free a dove . . . .
Since no resting-place for it was visible, she turned round.
Then I sent forth and set free a swallow . . . .
Then I sent forth and set free a raven.
The raven went forth and, seeing that the waters had diminished,
He eats, circles, caws, and turns not round.
Then I let out (all) to the four winds
                    And offered a sacrifice.

Ea opened his mouth to speak, saying to valiant Enlil:

"Thou wisest of gods, thou hero,
How couldst thou, unreasoning, bring on the deluge?
On the sinner impose his sin,
On the transgressor impose his transgression!
(Yet) be lenient, lest he be cut off,
Be patient, lest he be dis[lodged]!"
Thereupon Enlil went aboard the ship ...
He took my wife aboard and made (her) kneel by my side.
Standing between us, he touched our foreheads to bless us:
"Hitherto Utnapishtim has been but human.
Henceforth Utnapishtim and his wife shall be like unto us
gods." [3]

Having thus summarized the Akkadian version of the flood
myth, let us now turn our attention to a parallel résumé of the
biblical story of the flood:

The earth was corrupt in the sight of God, and it was filled with
violence.
And God said to Noah: "The end of all creatures of flesh is
in my mind;
The earth is full of violence because of them.
I shall destroy them with the earth.
Make an ark of resinwood;
Make it tight with fibre and cover it with pitch inside and out.
This is how you shall make it:
The length of the ark three hundred cubits,
Its width fifty cubits, and its height thirty cubits . . . .
But I shall establish my covenant with you;
You are to go into the ark,
You, your sons, your wife and your sons' wives with you.
Of every sort of living creature of all flesh you shall bring two
into the ark . . . .

After the seven days the waters of the flood came upon the
earth . . . .

3. *Ancient Near Eastern Texts*, edited by James B. Pritchard, Princeton
University Press, 2nd edition, Princeton, New Jersey, 1955, pp. 93-95.
When words are set off in brackets, this represents restoration of the text;
words in parentheses are explicatory.

The floodgates of the heavens were opened
And rain fell on the earth forty days and forty nights . . . .
And every living thing on the earth was wiped out . . . .
Then God remembered Noah . . .
And God sent a wind over the earth and the waters sub-
sided . . . .
The ark rested on the mountains of Ararat . . . .
Noah opened the window he had made in the ark and released
a raven.
It flew to and fro until the waters had dried off the earth.
Then he sent a dove . . . .
But the dove found no place to alight . . . .
He . . . again sent forth the dove from the ark.
The dove came back to him in the evening,
And there in her mouth was a green olive leaf! . . .

Then God said to Noah:
"Go out of the ark . . . ."
Noah went forth . . . .
Then Noah built an altar to the Lord . . . .
When the Lord smelled the sweet odor he said to himself:
"I shall never again curse the ground on account of man,
For the inclination of man's heart is evil from his youth;
I shall never again destroy every living creature as I have
done." [4]

Now, in comparing these two accounts of the flood, we find,
among others, these similarities:

Divine determination to destroy all living creatures, except
for one family.
A command to build a ship.
Directions on how to make the ship.
Species of all living things are taken aboard.
The family to be saved enters the ship.
The flood comes; the days of its duration are indicated.
The instrumentality of the wind.

4. Cf. Gen. 6-8.

All life is wiped out.
The flood subsides.
The ship comes to rest on a mountain.
Various species of birds are used to test for dry land.
Exit from the ship and offering of sacrifice.
The reason for the flood related to man's sinfulness.
Divine favor for the survivors.

Obviously, such consistent parallelism cannot be accidental. The biblical story is doubtlessly dependent upon this myth of a universal flood, a myth which was commonly known to the peoples of the area and time in which the biblical tradition emerged. But if the story of Noah and the flood is not original, does it have any historical value at all? If not, how can we maintain that this myth pertains to divinely inspired revelation?

Since the scriptural version of the deluge is more or less built upon the structure of the Sumerian myth, the flood which Noah survived could hardly have any more historical reality than the flood experienced by Utnapishtim. Moreover, the people of the ancient Near East did not conceive of Gilgamesh, Utnapishtim, Enlil, etc., as persons of history, and they did not look upon the myth as the recounting of an historical event. The characters and occurrences of the story were but symbols to them. How, then, could Noah be more than a symbol?

Still, can we deny all historical value to the myth, even to the Sumerian version? It would not seem so. For although the myth is construed of symbols, the symbol is used to express a reality present in history. In this particular story, the very vividness and preciseness of the description of the flood suggests an eyewitness account of a terribly devastating inundation (for example, the phrase: "and all of mankind had returned to clay"). Hence, there must be some historical basis underlying the various accounts of the flood. Werner Keller, in *The Bible as History*, mentions the following evidence to support this contention:

The great layer of mud, which covered every living thing like a shroud and leveled the ground until it was as "flat as a roof," must have been seen with his own eyes by someone who had had a marvelous escape. The exact description of the great storm argues for this assumption. Utnapishtim expressly mentions a southern gale, which corresponds closely with the geographical situation. The Persian Gulf, whose waters were flung over the flat country by the gale, lies south of the estuary of the Tigris and Euphrates. To the last detail the weather conditions that he describes are characteristic of an unusual atmospheric disturbance: the appearance of black clouds and a roaring noise — sudden darkness in broard daylight — the howling of the southern gale as it drives the water in front of it. Any meteorologist recognizes at once that in tropical regions coastal areas, islands, but above all alluvial river flats are subject to a spiral type of tidal wave which leaves devastation and destruction in its wake, and which is often caused by cyclones, accompanied by earthquakes and torrential rain. [5]

To these observations can be added the fact that archaeologists digging at Ur have discovered a stratum of clay about eight feet thick which is apparently the residue of a great flood which is thought to have taken place about 4000 B.C.. Traces of human settlement were found both above and below the clay deposit.

Using the foregoing evidence as a basis, we offer the following conjecture as to how the myth of the flood may have taken form: floods, possibly even very great floods, were a familiar phenomenon to the peoples of the period of history with which we are concerned; the power of water was something awesome to these primitives, and was frequently associated with their gods; it was natural enough for them to esteem that there must be some sort of divine power and reason behind such a destructive force. The flood waters were, then, a tool of the gods; the gods exercised a certain degree of command over the waters, and

5. W. Keller, *The Bible As History*, William Morrow and Company, New York, 1956, pp. 38-41. Although we quote from Keller because his presentation does have some merit in pointing to certain *possibilities* of historicity, it must be admitted that his views are, on the whole, outdated, exaggerated, and insufficiently critical.

one who could conquer the waters would be assimilated to the gods. The use of the flood story in the *Epic of Gilgamesh* could have its explanation in a thinking which more or less followed these lines. The creator of the myth made use of a familiar historical catastrophe, introducing well-known mythical personages into it, in order to transmit a message involving transcendental realities.

What were these realities? Exactly what was the purpose of the dramatization of the deluge? These questions can be treated more sensitively through a consideration of the ideas orienting the epic as a whole, for the flood story is but a small part of the latter. The essentially secular nature of the general theme of the epic has been well singled out by Pritchard:

> The poem deals with such earthy things as man and nature, love and adventure, friendship and combat — all masterfully blended into a background for the stark reality of death. The climactic struggle of the protagonist to change his eventual fate, by leading the secret of immortality from the hero of the Great Flood of long ago, ends in failure; but with the failure comes a sense of quiet resignation. [6]

In the *Epic of Gilgamesh,* then, we encounter a rather profane story whose purpose is to come to grips, in mythical terms, with the mystery of life and death. The historical nucleus can be reduced to the fact that men do live, love, hate, struggle and die; somehow this endlessly repeated process comes under the influence of powers that transcend man; finally, all the elements are dealt with in a symbolical way within the framework of a tale about a deluge which no doubt pertained to historical reality, but across the centuries assumed legendary proportions.

It was upon this foundation that the author, or authors, of the biblical tradition erected the account of Noah and his ark. To the problems which were posed by the myth (life, death, the destructive power of the forces of nature, etc.) but not really

---

6. *Op. cit.,* p. 72.

answered, the inspired writer now offered the solution: there is one God who is the creator of man; his one and only desire for man is to lead him to perfection, to save him; when man through his evil ways turns away from this God, he brings destruction upon himself; good men, however, enjoy the favor of God and receive his blessing; in conclusion, despite the wicked tendencies of mankind, the story ends on an optimistic note, as God seals his covenant with Noah and promises never again to destroy every living creature.

The myth is remarkably purified of a notable quantity of its extravagant elements: there is one God, not many gods; the flood is no longer explained as a more or less irrational or vengeful action of the gods, but is clearly intended to signify God's will for the purification of mankind; God is portrayed as being in complete command of what happens, no longer is there any question of gods "cowering like dogs" and "sitting and weeping." Through the flood God's great displeasure with man's sinful ways is manifested, and yet it seems that he compassionately acknowledges man's innate weakness and inclination to evil. Finally, through Noah God makes a new offer of friendship to the human race. The approaching covenant between Yahweh and Abraham and the initiation of the People of God is prefigured here.

Did Noah actually exist? Did he converse directly and personally with God? We might just as well ask: did Gilgamesh exist, did he in fact talk with the gods? An affirmative answer would seem rather presumptuous. It is not impossible, however, that there was a Noah, an individual situated somewhere among the forefathers of Abraham. Nor is it inconceivable that he was a man known for his virtue. Some such background could have provided the basis for the choice falling upon this representative of the lineage of Abraham to play the role of the hero in the myth of the ark and the flood.

It is interesting to note, nevertheless, that according to the popular etymology of the Hebrews, the word "Noah" signifies "rest," or "he who gives comfort"; this would seem to add weight to the opinion that Noah is a purely symbolical figure, that through this symbolism mankind should take consolation in the fact that God assures us his providential care.

In any event, we shall conclude our remarks on the flood account by saying that whether or not there was a flood, or an ark, or an historical personage by the name of Noah is, with respect to the study of the book of Genesis and its significance in divine revelation, of little consequence. As a general rule, when in our reading of the Bible we find a skeleton of history clothed in legendary ornamentation, it is rather useless to ask what is precisely historical and what is not, for the line between the historical and the mythical is often very difficult to distinguish.

Most likely the story of Noah is an instance of the transposition to prehistoric times of relationships between God and man which in the persons of Abraham and his successors begin to take on historical dimensions. The secular myth of the Sumerians, the Akkadians, the Babylonians, is given a specifically religious character, as man is made aware of the fact that the one God is incessantly attentive to his fate and is deeply and personally interested in his behavior.

CHAPTER TWO

THE HEROIC EXPLOITS OF JOSHUA

In examining the first eleven chapters of Genesis, we should not be surprised to find frequent introduction of mythical elements. These chapters deal with times and events antecedent to recorded history and are necessarily rooted in religious folklore. But with Abraham, we enter an era which can be justifiably called "historical." In the persons of the Patriarchs we are concerned with individuals upon whose real existence depends the very origin of the people of Israel. Unless a certain Semite, under the influence of quite an extraordinary experience, detached himself from his clan and went forth with his family in search of a promised heritage, the development of the Hebrew people, a people of covenant from its inception, is rendered very difficult to explain. One of the most salient points of Old Testament revelation is that God did indeed intervene in history to choose for himself and form a people, the people of Redemption.

We would be mistaken to conclude, however, that with the advent of Abraham, Isaac, and Jacob the Bible begins to obey the rigorous laws of the modern scientific method of writing history. Quite the contrary. The Old Testament consistently adorns its heroes with legendary traits. It is true that the sincerity of the sacred authors is reflected in their honesty about the shortcomings of some of the most idealized of characters: Jacob is a cheat and liar; Moses lacks confidence in himself and is even hesitant about God; David submits to adultery. Still, this does not prevent the biblical tradition from painting its dominant figures in glorious colors, and depicting their feats in terms that sometimes take on epical proportions.

An example which demonstrates this tendency is found in the exploits of Joshua, the successor of Moses. After taking over the leadership of Israel, he experienced an exceptionally propitious beginning, for, upon approaching the Promised Land, he received from Yahweh the assurance: "I shall deliver to you every place where you set foot" (Jos. 1:3).

Then came the miraculous crossing of the Jordan at flood stage and the stunning overthrow of Jericho. The conquest of the land of Canaan, however, suffered a brief delay: an expedition of three thousand men was repulsed at Hai; still, this defeat only set the stage for a new manifestation of Joshua's military prowess, as he totally destroyed the population of Hai by means of a cleverly laid ambush.

These successes of Joshua incited the five Amorrite kings of Jerusalem to form an alliance and to march against Gabaon which had tricked its way into a peaceful arrangement with the Israelites. As a countermeasure Joshua and his men launched a surprise attack, and in this engagement Joshua achieved perhaps his most astounding victory, for on this day: "the sun stood still and the moon stayed, while the nation took vengeance on its foes . . . . Never before or since was there a day like this, when the Lord obeyed the voice of a man; for the Lord fought for Israel" (Jos. 10:13-14).

The preceding, in brief, are some of the highlights of the initial victories of the Israelites in the conquest of the Promised Land under the generalship of Joshua. To what extent are we at this moment dealing with historical data? And to what extent are we immersed in legend? Here again it is difficult to draw a precise line of demarcation, but the following observations may throw some light on the subject.

From the historical point of view, several assertions can be validly made: in contradistinction to the case of Noah, there is no reason to challenge the existence of Joshua as a definite personage of history who did in fact lead the people of Israel into the land which was to become theirs. The chronology of the Bible indicates that this invasion took place around the thirteenth century B.C. There is some archaeological evidence to support this indication.

There is, for instance, the matter of the "walls of Jericho." North of the present village, Eriha, which has replaced Jericho, there remains a mound of ruins known as Tell es-Sultan. Excavations made between 1907 and 1909 unearthed on this site two concentric rings of fortifications formed by walls about ten to twelve feet apart. The inner wall was about twelve feet thick throughout; the outer wall was about six feet thick and twenty-five to thirty feet high. The discoverers of the walls estimated that the outer wall fell about 1200 B.C. and must, therefore, have been the one destroyed by Joshua. Professor John Garstang, however, who led another expedition to Tell es-Sultan in 1930, maintained that the inner wall was the more recent of the two and must have been the one leveled by the Israelites. It was his opinion that the wall was destroyed in about 1400 B.C. Another leading achaeologist, Hughes Vincent, after studying the evidence, has dated the destruction of the fortification between 1250 and 1200 B.C. All of these proposed dates compare reasonably well with biblical chronology.

Also reminiscent of the Bible story are other qualities of the ruins found at the site of ancient Jericho: Professor Garstang testified that the space between the two walls was filled with fragments and rubble. There were clear traces of an extraordinary fire, masses of blackened bricks, cracked stones, charred wood, and ashes. In the vicinity of the walls the houses were burned to the ground and their roofs had crashed down on top of them. Could this condition of the city be related to Joshua 6:24: "The city itself they burned with all that was in it . . . ."?

Further investigation showed that the stones of the outer wall had fallen outward, while the inner fortification had collapsed in the opposite direction, falling inwards. In addition, several sizeable cracks and fissures were discovered in the walls.

All of this led Garstang to conclude that the city must have been shattered by an earthquake. Physical geography informs us that Jericho does in fact lie within an earthquake zone. [1]

Unhappily, recent probes into the mound of Tell es-Sultan (that is, those of Kathleen Kenyon) seem to have discredited the claims of Garstang. The strata in the Jericho mound provide us with nothing but a blank for the period of the Israelite invasion (1500 to 1200 B.C.). Hence, archaeological study of this area neither confirms nor disproves the biblical account. No doubt the Hebrews took the city of Jericho, but hardly in the phenomenal fashion described in the sixth chapter of Joshua. [2]

After razing Jericho, the Israelites moved on to the conquest of Hai. And what does extra-biblical information have to say about Hai? First of all, it appears from archaeological investigation that the site of Hai was unoccupied from 2400 to 1000 B.C. How, then, could a battle have been fought over it? Various solutions have been proposed, none of them very conclusive. W. F. Albright has forwarded the hypothesis that Bethel, a town very close to Hai and in fact destroyed, probably by the Israelites, in the thirteenth century B.C., has been confused with Hai by popular tradition. On the other hand, the word "Hai" means "the ruin," and H. Vincent has maintained that the Canaanites, having formed a coalition against the Hebrews, made use of their ruins as a fortification in an effort to repulse the advance of the invader. All in all, nothing is certain about the historicity of the strategic coup on Joshua's part at Hai. [3]

But, what about the sun "halting in the midst of the sky" at Gabaon? Ignatius Hunt has observed that he is familiar with some twenty different attempts to explain this passage. Among these can be listed the theory of Van Hoonacker (the victory at Gabaon was made easier by some sort of storm which darkened the sky, i.e., instead of the sun "halting," it simply failed to give its light because of the cloud screen) and that of Daniel-Rops

---

1. Keller, *op. cit.,* pp. 154-56.
2. Hunt, *op. cit.,* p. 104.
3. Cf. J. Delorme, "Le Livre De Josué," *Introduction à la Bible,* Vol. 1, p. 396.

(the "miracle" refers to a heavy hail followed bv an abnormal light effect which prolonged twilight until the following dawn). Joseph de Vault [4] questions whether these "pseudo-scientific" endeavors are really necessary. His analysis of the text (Jos. 10:7-15) suggests a negative reply: "In explanation of the text, we should remark first of all, that we have here two views of the battle. The first is in prose (vv. 7-11) and records the fact of the great victory achieved with Yahweh's help in the form of a mighty hailstorm. The second is poetic (vv. 12-14) and gives Joshua's famous war cry apostrophizing the sun and the moon. This is followed by an editor's comment . . . ." Joshua hoped for time, for daylight, in which to vanquish the enemy totally. The enemy was crushed, so the time was granted, and this was expressed poetically in verse 13a, prosaically in verse 13b. We can sum these views up by saying that to be satisfying, a solution must take into account both the special providence of God over his people and the literary form of the text. This, de Vault seems to do.

What can we surmise, then, about the historical veracity of Joshua's triumphs in the conquest of Canaan? We can take our first clue from the fact that the Hebrews themselves did not list the book of Joshua among the "historical" books of the Old Testament. Rather, it is classified as the first among the "prophetical" books. This intimates that the book was primarily considered to embody a message of faith, to give significance to the religion of the Israelites, to portray the presence of the might of God in the community as he conducts it to success in its Holy War, and not to relay a precise account of a series of historical battles.

It remains a fact that Israel did occupy the land of Canaan, and unless the story of Joshua had some historical basis, this occupation remains inexplicable. Sabatino Moscati has these comments to make:

The Hebrew penetration of Palestine is related in the form of a series of campaigns, directed towards the center, the north

4. "The Book of Josue," *Paulist Pamphlet Bible Series,* p. 20.

and the south of that region. The mention of Israel on a stele set up by the Pharaoh Mer-ne-Ptah (1230 B.C.), and the archaeological evidence of the destruction of cities, though here there arise certain problems and obscurities, lead to the attribution of these events to the second half of the thirteenth century before Christ.

The Hebrew movement of penetration was not necessarily exclusively one of violent conquest, but may have been carried out in part by a peaceful process of infiltration. The nomadic newcomers assimilated themselves gradually to their new environment, passing from their old manner of life to a settled agricultural one. While they occupied certain cities, they established themselves principally in country regions, which included much hitherto unoccupied territory. [5]

The story of Joshua, thus, has the following significance for us: it is basically a type of epic, directed by religious intent. The account has an historical nucleus, but the description of events is extensively hyperbolized. The first author who undertook the work of narrating the conquest of central Palestine most likely built his story around various local traditions of diverse origin. These were put together into a continuous story of which Joshua was made the hero. His actual role in the conquest was doubtlessly much less than what is attributed to him by biblical tradition. This primitive account was fused with other traditions and later reedited by other authors who added new material. The purpose of the later redactor was to reaffirm that Yahweh had given this land to his people.

Taken literally, the book of Joshua contains many statements which are simply not true. Taken religiously, as the authors meant it to be taken, this sacred writing reveals a divine truth which contributes beautifully to the panorama of the economy of salvation. In the words of Hunt:

The book of Joshua is a deeply religious epic. It presents

---

5. S. Moscati, *Ancient Semitic Civilizations,* Capricorn Books, 1960, pp. 126-7.

the entire conquest as a holy war: the Canaanites, with all their pagan worship, are to be exterminated, and the land, as the abode of a theocratic people, is to become dedicated to God. The theme of the book might easily be stated in a phrase that occurs several times: "... Yahweh was fighting for his people!" [6]

J. Delorme adds:

The role attributed to Joshua manifests a constant divine activity. At each stage of sacred history, the design of God falls upon the shoulders of a man who seems to sum up all of his people in his own person. Joshua makes incarnate in a way the unity of Israel which God introduces into his heritage. He meets the requirements of the ideal of docility proposed to the people of God. His victories demonstrate the action of God on behalf of his chosen community. His very name is of special significance in biblical tradition (Num. 13:16 tells us that Moses changed Joshua's name from Hoshea, "Deliverance," to Yehoshua, "Yahweh = Deliverance"). It expresses his vocation and his participation in the great work of God, which the Bible continually defines as a Deliverance. With Joshua, God bestows a territory on his people in delivering it from its enemies. More liberations will follow, and the hope of this people will reach out towards still others, which will be more decisive, until the moment when God sends another Yehoshua, his Son, Jesus. [7]

---

6. Hunt, *op. cit.*, p. 102.
7. Delorme, *op. cit.*, p. 401.

CHAPTER THREE

THE WISDOM OF JUDITH

In treating of Noah and Joshua, we have been dealing with accounts whose formation was quite complex, requiring many centuries to receive their final edition. Thus, parts of the book of Genesis were put into written form possibly as early as 1200 to 1100 B.C. And yet, the text continued to be combined with other documents or revised until the sixth century before Christ. The history of the composition of the book of Joshua reflects the same complexity: some passages were most likely committed to writing during the Davidic period, although they had existed in oral form for a considerable time prior to this; nonetheless, the book did not receive its last revision until sometime after the discovery of Deuteronomy in 622.

In view of the involved character of these sections of Sacred Scripture, and in light of the religious preoccupations of the authors, it is quite understandable that the historical density of the Old Testament in these "early" books should be relatively slight. There is certainly more "historical truth" in the story of Joshua than in that of Noah, but even the former falls far short of meeting the demands of contemporary standards for history. It would seem, however, that as the Hebrew culture progressed and became more refined, a keener sensitivity for historical exactness would have emerged and been inculcated in the later books of the Old Testament, so that here at least we could be sure that the story is for the most part factual. To our consternation, this expectation is not always rewarded.

We might be justified in saying that in general as the books of the Old Testament approach closer to the time of Christ in date of composition their historical content increases. But even to the last, these remain books of faith and their orientation is principally religious. History keeps to the horizon, except for the central theme of Yahweh being very much a part of the history of his people. One of the most recent of the writings belonging to the ancient dispensation exemplifies this point very well. This is the book of Judith.

Although there is some uncertainty about the date of composition of Judith, some placing it in the third and others in the first century before Christ, there is no doubt that it is one of the last books to be added to the body of Old Testament literature.

On the surface, the story appears to be a history of a sweeping invasion on the part of the armies of the King of Assyria, Nebuchadnezzar, under the leadership of the general, Holofernes. City after city, nation after nation, fall before the relentless onslaught, until finally the army of Holofernes is put to rout by the faith, sanctity, and wisdom of the beautiful widow, Judith, at the gates of the city of the Israelites, Bethulia.

Numerous precise details serve to create an impression of historicity: the walls of Ecbatana, stronghold of Arphaxed, King of the Medes, were seventy cubits broad, the towers one hundred cubits high; it was in exactly the twelfth year of his reign that Nebuchadnezzar defeated Arphaxad; when Holofernes marched into the land of Gabaa, he remained there with his armies exactly thirty days; when the latter besieged Bethulia, he had under his command a hundred and twenty thousand footmen, and twenty-two thousand horsemen, etc.

Nonetheless, if we try to evaluate the book of Judith in terms of history, we immediately encounter a plurality of biographical and geographical errors. To mention a few: the actual Nebuchadnezzar (604-562) was king of the Neo-Babylonians empire and not of the Assyrians, whose empire collapsed in 610 B.C. Although Judith has him reigning in Nineveh (Judith 1:1), the latter no longer even existed when he came into power; furthermore, the book has many references to conditions and practices which were not a part of the Jewish life until after the Babylonian captivity, the way of life portrayed in the book is plainly post-exilic, and it is inferred that the Temple is in full operation: in point of fact, it was destroyed by the Nebuchadnezzar of history and was not rebuilt until the Persian period. The supposition that the story may have some connection with the time when the Persians were in the ascendancy (558-336 B.C.) finds support in the fact that the name Holofernes, applied to the purportedly Assyrian general, is actually Persian in origin.

What can be concluded from all this? Superficially the book of Judith is a detailed historical narrative. And yet, many of the details are contradicted by the facts as they come to us from other passages in the Bible itself, as well as from reliable extra-biblical sources of the history of the period. Could we say that the author wished to teach a spiritual lesson and simply utilized diverse names which were prominent in Hebrew tradition, without regard for historical accuracy? Such an opinion is partially sound, but no doubt is also oversimplified.

It would be quite difficult to believe that any learned Jew could be confused about the roles played by Assyria and by Nebuchadnezzar in the real history of Jerusalem. Nor would such a writer accidentally transfer to a pre-exilic period practices and customs which all of his readers would recognize as deriving from a later era of the people's history. This leads us to take the position that the historical "errors" found in the book of Judith were made designedly. The author knew that his audience would immediately detect his non-historical usage of names, events, and customs, and realize that his story was to be interpreted symbolically for its religious value, its "wisdom"; all historical content was not necessarily excluded, but was secondary to the writer's theological preoccupations.

In the book of Judith, therefore, we encounter a type of literary form known as "wisdom literature." The purpose of the story as adapted by the author, whether originally it had any basis in fact or not, seems to be to teach a lesson and not to recount history. Nebuchadnezzar is a symbol of the enemies of Jerusalem; he is a figure of the pagan whose pride must be humbled. The episode of Judith unfolds as a drama in which a simple, but wise and holy woman, brings about the downfall of the armies of this haughty king who dared even to think of himself as a god. The virtues of Judith sparkle with a magnificent splendor in contrast with the vileness of the invader: her cleverness and courage, her prudence, calmness, and steadiness in a critical situation make the conquest of the proud general, Holofernes, seem almost child's play. The woman Judith is described by the author as beautiful, and indeed her beauty is reflected in the quality of her actions and in the tone of her discourses. She is, in effect, a wonderful symbol of the wisdom of the unquestioning faithfulness to Yahweh.

If we evaluate the story of Judith from a spiritual viewpoint, we find it rich in content and cannot help but sense the inspiration in its message. If the intent of the author was to produce a didactic and religious piece of literature, he has succeeded very well. It would be tragic to lose sight of the real value of this dramatic moment in the pages of Sacred Scripture, only because we insist on debating about apparent historical inaccuracies which have a very good chance of being part of the writer's literary design.

Thus in Judith, one of the last books of the Old Testament, as well as in Genesis, one of the first, we find a lack of concern for profane history. At the same time we discover a profound consciousness of the sacred history conducting to salvation, in which Yahweh chooses a people, guides his people, and assures them protection against all obstacles, if only they will serve him faithfully. But in order to make this discovery it is necessary that we probe beneath the surface, that we sift through appearances and maintain an alertness against prejudices which come to us from "traditional" interpretations and which can so subtly influence our evaluations of biblical texts. Unless we take into account the complexity of delving into writings composed from thirty-five hundred to two thousand years ago, unless we constantly keep in mind that we are engaged in a task of trying to decipher the intentions of authors who wrote in a situation vastly different from our own and for people far removed from us in time, customs, and mentality, we are in danger of missing by a wide margin the point of the revelation which it was the will of God to convey through the instrumentality of human beings, of a community, of an era.

CHAPTER FOUR

THE VALUE OF THE NEW APPROACH
TO THE OLD TESTAMENT

The Dangers Exemplified in some Approaches

We now arrive at the point of having to attempt a formulation of some sort of conclusion to our hasty perusal of several sections of the Old Testament, made in light of the outlook of contemporary exegesis.

In our Introduction we maintained that change is an ambiguous element in our lives. It may be either constructive or dissolutive. Frequently it is extremely difficult for the mind, which is at the center of the whirlpool of alteration, to discern with certitude the precise direction of the flow of change. Unquestionably, then, every possible effort must be made to criticize as objectively as the extent of our knowledge allows all new ideas, ways of thinking, approaches, methods, etc. All advantages and eventual dangers must be anticipated as realistically as can be done.

How does this apply to biblical scholarship? First of all, we must emphasize that the "new" approach employed in the examination of Sacred Scripture throughout our century has yielded results the positive value of which is beyond challenge. The meaningfulness of the Word has thereby been increased manifold. We have been brought so much closer to an accurate realization of the truth which God has willed to reveal. Moreover, this approach, at least in its most fundamental features, has been in use for a sufficiently long time now that the contributions it has made can be judged to be permanent acquisitions, and not just the ravings of so many twentieth century self-styled charismatics. The reason for this is that the conclusions offered by our modern students of the Bible are based on diligent scientific research as well as probing faith, and not merely on overly subjective, critically unjustifiable interpretations of what the Word of God is thought to say.

There are, nevertheless, certain perils inherent in the new approach. An excess of which biblical scholarship can very easily be guilty is the tendency to overgeneralize its conclusions. For example, once research has shown that some passages of the Bible unquestionably have been influenced by extra-biblical literature or traditions, there immediately arises the temptation to minimize the originality of the Scriptures, making them everywhere dependent on foreign sources. When this happens, the proper perspective of the study of the Bible is falsified and our appreciation of the uniqueness of revelation is jeopardized.

A brief examination of some of the facets of the system evolved by the well-known Julius Wellhausen will point out several of the misconceptions to which a biased scientific approach to Sacred Scripture can lead. This biblical scholar of the late nineteenth century theorized that a number of written "documents" lies behind the composition of many of the books of the Bible; while there is much to be said in favor of his theory, and it contributed significantly to the advance of biblical studies, his system suffers from deficiencies which are capable of seriously marring our grasp of the real meaning of revelation. An initial failing of the system was to reduce to almost nothing or to reject completely the part played by the supernatural in the emergence of the Word of God. Wellhausen leaves us with the impression that the pages of Scripture tell us only about man himself and his development, and have little to do with an actual intervention of God in history.

Wellhausen's system can be criticized, secondly, for having

overextended itself; that is, it drew conclusions about the evolution of Israel which could not be justified merely by the *literary* principles upon which it based itself. To illustrate: pursuing the indications of his documentary theory, Wellhausen esteemed that the Law, as represented by the text of Deuteronomy found under the reign of Josiah in 622, had to be a production of an origin posterior to the time of the prophets. This was scarcely more than a conjecture of his made on the basis of literary evidence alone. Since his time, however, much has been learned about the ancient East through archaeological and epigraphical discoveries which have indisputably established the fact that the Law was in existence prior to the prophetical movement. [1]

The system of Wellhausen can also be found wanting in a third respect. It is the latter's contention that the various documents which make up the Pentateuch received their final edition at a comparatively recent date. These texts, therefore, only appeared centuries after the actual events, and it is only with much hesitation that historical value can be accorded to texts so far removed in time from the occurrences they describe. For the school of Wellhausen, then, many of the biblical accounts are no more than legends, man-made creations. All of the texts of the Pentateuch are to a degree rendered suspect.

Yet, contemporary research has shown that Wellhausen's dating of the documents in question is inaccurate, that they can be traced to an earlier origin than he supposed, that their historicity is more dense than he speculated. Thus, a more thorough scientific approach to the study of the Old Testament, abetted by diverse findings which have been added to our knowledge of the world in which the Bible was formed, has pointed to the inadequacy of the theories of Wellhausen on several fronts. In spite of this, his views have been widely influential in biblical circles and continue to influence some scholars today. The fact is, there is a good deal of truth in what Wellhausen has to say; it is unfortunate, however, that he and his followers have over-

---

1. H. Cazelles, *op. cit.*, p. 305.

estimated the potentialities of his system to give us the *full* truth about the Bible.

* * *

A second example of an exegete's going beyond the limits imposed upon him by his sources and method is presented to us in the way the Norwegian Sigmund Mowinckel has reasoned to the observance among the Hebrews of an annual feast of the "Enthronement of Yahweh." Most commentators on the psalms are in agreement that some kind of liturgical context provided the background for the composition of a certain number of the psalms. Thus, Psalm 24 furnishes an example of a psalm composed for the use of pilgrims going up to the Temple: "Who will ascend the mountain of Yahweh, and who will stand in his Holy Place?" (v. 3).

There exists a group of psalms categorized as "Psalms of Enthronement." Many details characteristic of the coronation of the kings of Israel appear in these songs treating of the royalty of Yahweh (cf. Ps. 92, 93, 95-100). We see in these psalms numerous reflections of court life: there is a solemn entrance into the Temple; Yahweh then takes his place on the throne, he is draped in regal vestments, the trumpets sound, and the court, the army, and the various officials express their obeisance.

Mowinckel concluded from this data that there must have existed an annual celebration of the enthronement of Yahweh. In order to fill out his theory and describe the rites which took place on this occasion, Mowinckel borrowed from an analogous Babylonian feast, the feast of Marduk.

This hypothesis of Mowinckel suffers from two major difficulties: there is not the least evidence in Sacred Scripture of a particular feast in honor of the kingship of Yahweh; hence, he was forced to reconstruct the feast from non-Hebraic sources. Secondly, the content of the Psalms of Enthronement can be satisfactorily explained without recurring to the supposition of a special feast. There is certainly some connection between the psalms in question and the worship of Israel, but considering the facts that are known at present, we can only evaluate Mowinckel's deductions as insupportable. [2]

These criticisms of Wellhausen and Mowinckel are simply intended to illustrate the way in which we can easily become overly enthusiastic in applying a certain type of "logic" to the Bible, and thereby produce conclusions which are unwarranted by objective evidence. Such instances of excess should serve to alert us to the jeopardy in which we place ourselves when we plunge too unreservedly into any particular "new" approach. Wellhausen's loss of the sense of the supernatural in the history of Israel and his minimizing of historicity were indeed serious misfortunes; his failure was one of lack of caution and of faith: he presumed too quickly that his theories were justifiable, not pausing to inspect carefully the ground upon which he trod; his confidence in the powers of the instruments of human research was also too narrowly defined, as he forgot that the Sacred Books are in effect a history, but a very special kind of history, a history of faith and salvation.

It may seem that the previous discussion has amounted to little more than a raking over the bones of a remote and rather obscure history which should be left dead and buried. But are we not to learn from the mistakes of the past? The case of Wellhausen above all signals the snares in which it is so easy for the biblical scholar to become entangled. The Bible is a book written by God as well as by men. It is a writing that is unique as to the history of its composition, the truth it contains, and the forces which were at work in effecting it. Always it must be approached as a mystery, as well as scientifically. Still, the temptation is ever present to treat it all too humanly, to dissect it and never put it together again.

It is this pitfall which we, each of us, must avoid at all costs. For the ordinary Bible reader as well as the scholar can commit

---

2. Cf. P. Drijvers, *Les Psaumes*, Les Editions du Cerf, Paris, 1958, p. 154.

the sin of humanizing the Word of God. There are, for instance, those who having learned that some of the "miracles" of the Old Testament were more or less literary creations rather than historical accomplishments, impulsively conclude to the non-existence of the miraculous. Then there are others who have detected the presence of folklore in the Hebrew writings and immediately are ready to discount the whole of revelation as so much pious legend. There are still others who experience no qualms in lifting a scriptural passage out of its context and bending its meaning to fit their own personal needs, so that they can feel justified by "God's Word" in what they do.

There are many ways of approaching the Bible, and many of them are wrong. Whatever approach we use, whatever method we employ, we must seek first of all to find God's truth, and not merely interject our own personalities and prejudices into the revelation which is ultimately of divine origin.

The Personal Benefit Derived from a Religious-Scientific Reading of the Bible

One occasionally hears the objection "If I approach the Bible with a religious, scientific spirit, how will this benefit me? The discoveries of modern research seem to me to be rather sterile, academic, devoid of spiritual relevance. It makes little difference to me whether or not there was a Noah and an ark; nor does it matter to me how Joshua and the Twelve Tribes got into Palestine; I fail to see the bearing on my life of the question of the existence of Holofernes and the heroics of Judith! Scholars may spend their time disputing about these things if they wish, but how can their discussions make me a more religious person? Isn't it valid for me simply to open my Bible, read it, and interpret it the way I feel will do me the most good?"

One aspect of the response to this challenge has been treated succinctly but very competently by John L. McKenzie, S.J. [3] He

---

3. John L. McKenzie, S.J., *The Two-Edged Sword*, Bruce Publishing Company, Milwaukee, 1956, pp. 17-21.

phrases the problem in this way: Many of our contemporaries approach the Old Testament as the Word of God, and they seek in it an increase of faith, hope, and charity:

> They find no such thing in the analysis of the sources of which the five books of Moses are composed, in comparisons between the laws of Moses and the laws of Hammurabi of Babylon, or between the Babylonian flood story and the story of Noah . . . . Many Catholic writers have been concerned with defending biblical inerrancy, the validity of Old Testament history or of Old Testament predictions of the Redeemer. Necessary as these arguments may be, not a few critics allege that they are of no meaning or value to the Catholic faithful, who are not interested in these disputes, and whose supernatural life will not grow by acquaintance with the discussions of the biblical schools.

McKenzie answers by first of all asserting that it would be paradoxical, to say the least, if the more we know about the Old Testament the less it means to us. Yet this is what the above complaints infer. Moreover, it is true that learning does not of itself constitute spiritual progress, and possibly contemporary biblical science has been remiss in directing its research in such a way as to produce spiritual fruit as well as mere knowledge.

The solution, however, does not lie in going backward, for example, to the "spiritual" or "allegorical" interpretations of Scripture so popular among the Fathers of the Church. Nothing can be gained from receding to the past; we cannot rest content with the exegetical methods of previous generations, for we now realize that they fail to give us an accurate picture of the true meaning of Sacred Scripture. But it is this meaning which we are obliged to seek; not to do so would be to betray the Word of God by attempting to build our spirituality on some kind of human substitute.

There is no intention of suggesting here that the Christian writers and biblical commentators of the past have not made contributions to the understanding of revelation and the deepening of spirituality whose beauty and validity is of a permanent quality which can enrich the faithful of all ages. But it must be remembered that these men were human, and their methods and personal insights were also human, so that the results of their genius are forever subject to being perfected by later ages.

If there is an answer to the vexing problem of the practical value of a religious-scientific approach to the Bible, it must lie in a better appreciation, by scholars themselves as well as by laymen, of what modern biblical study can contribute to the maturing of spirituality in today's world. The world in which we live is a critical world which revolves around science. Only a critical and scientific approach to the Bible can render it an influential force in such a world. Furthermore, if this work is properly conducted, in the "spirit of wonder" which the Word of God merits, it can only lead to a deepening awareness of the supernatural energy which had to direct the evolution of the people of God, from its primitive beginnings in the persons of the Patriarchs to its consummation in the eruption of the New Israel.

As regards the Old Testament in particular, it is the story of the will of God to save mankind, as this will focuses for a moment on one race. If the research of scholars can help us to understand this people better — their literature and the world in which they lived — it cannot help but sharpen our perception of the relationship between God and ourselves. But we have to give it that chance.

The Particular Problem of the Interpretation of the Fact of Original Sin

There is still another way in which modern biblical criticism can profoundly affect Christian spirituality. While it may be true that the historicity of the deluge or of the conquests of Joshua is of scant concern today, it is equally true that the background from which these accounts emerged is the same background that has produced other accounts around which the entire development of the Christian vision of the world has been structured.

The same book which contains the story of Noah's ark relates the episode of our first parents and original sin. The first three

chapters of Genesis, at least as interpreted by tradition, seem to
state that all mankind has descended from a primordial couple, and
because of the sin of the first man, the entire human race has come
under the yoke of sin and stands in need of redemption.

Taking Genesis quite literally, St. Paul has assured us that
through one man sin has entered the world, and through sin
death; on account of the offense of one person, all have been
condemned. [4] It is on these texts of Genesis and Romans that
Christian theology, for the most part, has based its notion of
original sin.

Now, more than a few of the fundamental dogmas of the
Church have been developed in dependence upon the ancient
conception of original sin. As Boyer has put it "The Incarnation
of the Word, or at least his coming in humiliation and suffering,
the institution of the sacraments, the present situation of mankind
in regard to its salvation, the economy of grace . . . follow as a
consequence of the sin of Adam." [5] It is evident, then, that
any revision in the way we conceive of the origin of man and
his fall from grace must perforce have wide-reaching effects upon
our comprehension of God's plan for man and his salvation.

In recent years, anthropologically, theologically, and biblically, the traditional explanation given for the origin of man and
his "fall" has been subjected to intensive criticism. The defensive
statement of Pius XII, incorporated in his encyclical *Humani
Generis* in 1950, gives ample proof of the seriousness of the
challenge. The pope insisted:

> Christians cannot lend their support to a theory which involves
> the existence, after Adam's time, of some earthly race of
> men, truly so called, who were not descended ultimately from
> him, or else supposes that Adam was the name given to some
> group of our primordial ancestors. *It does not appear* (em-
> phasis mine) how such views can be reconciled with the
> doctrine of original sin, as this is guaranteed to us by Scrip-

4. Cf. Rom. 5:12-19.
5. C. Boyer, "Le Péché Originel," *Théologie du Péché*, Desclée & Cie.,
Tournai, 1960, p. 243.

ture and tradition, and proposed to us by the Church. Original sin is the result of a sin committed, in actual historical fact, by an individual man named Adam, and it is a quality native to all of us, only because it has been handed down by descent from him. [6]

What are some of the difficulties which undermine confidence in the traditional presentation of man's origins? To begin with, anthropologists often emphatically protest that while man is a very singular species and his appearance on earth was most likely the result of a monophyletic process with a certain uniqueness about it, to suppose that the entire human race emerged from a single couple would seem rather presumptuous. That is, it seems probable that all men have descended from one primitive stock, but this stock was composed of a group of humans brought into being by the same evolutionary phenomenon at the same time, and was not the family of an original pair.

Edward Boné has summarized in able fashion the actual orientation of the thought of scientists in relation to the numerical density of the original human stock: first of all, the expanse of time and the fragility of the human phylum in its beginnings have made it impossible for paleontology to verify or exclude empirically the notion of monogenism, that is, the theory that all men have descended from one pair. In the actual state of our genetic and evolutionary knowledge, however, science conceives the process of hominization as *spread out* over a zone whose bridging requires a plurality of generations; methodologically, science has to think of the appearance of man in terms of a population limited in numbers, but hardly reducible to a single individual or couple. This position is directly inspired by observations and theories on the level of animal species subject to experimentation.

Boné points out, nevertheless, that modern anthropology has strongly emphasized the biological originality of man, and this might justify some reserve in extrapolating to man processes which have been noted in the remainder of the organic world. He admits

6. English edition, published by the Catholic Truth Society, London, 1957, p. 22.

that such a reservation will probably not find a place in scientific methodology, but speculates that the current which has sensitized the savant to the exceptional newness of man could possibly move him to be less unreceptive to the notion of man's being capable of benefitting by a transexperimental source of knowledge. [7]

Although science, therefore, cannot demonstrate that the human race has descended from an original "population" rather than from one couple, almost all of the evidence it has at its disposal at the present time inclines it to accept this position. This means that anyone imbued with the scientific spirit will find it difficult to accept a doctrine based on the claim that mankind had only a single set of parents. This would seem to presuppose a special, miraculous intervention, not in harmony with an obviously pre-established order; and why would the designer of such an order have to intervene to compensate for a deficiency in his own plan?

But the anthropological objection is not the only one posed against the traditional view of the origins of man. Theologically and biblically also the traditional view leads to an impasse. From the viewpoint of theology, it makes no difference exactly how man appeared on earth, as long as it is maintained that his emergence was ultimately the effect of the creative activity of God. Once the thesis is granted, however, that one man and one woman are at the origin of the human race and in the sin of this one man, Adam, all have fallen, theologians have problems to face. How could all men be condemned to suffering and death on account of the failure of one individual, in whose decision they had no part whatsoever to play? How could the infinitely perfect justice of God permit one man's choice, and from the evolutionary perspective a very primitive man at that, to direct the entire development of mankind and indeed to condition the very laws of the universe? Furthermore, supposing that an "original sin" was committed and has subjected all men, even the unformed infant, to condemnation, how is this condition transmitted?

---

7. E. Boné, "Un siècle d'Anthropologie préhistorique," *Nouvelle Revue Théologique,* July-Aug., 1962, pp. 709-34.

In *Humani Generis* Pius XII stated that original sin is a quality which we all inherit because it has been handed down "by descent" from Adam. This would appear to fall in line with the common Catholic opinion that Adam's sin is transmitted through generation. Still, the question remains how is original sin transmitted through generation? Through generation of the body? Through generation of the soul? Catholic tradition has for centuries taught the "immediate" creation of each soul by God at the instant it is "infused" into the body. This would mean that we have received by generation from Adam only our bodies. But since sin is strictly a spiritual condition, how can it be transmitted by purely corporal generation? This difficulty so disconcerted St. Augustine that he wrote to St. Jerome that if it was not opposed to faith to postulate a certain kind of generation of souls, then this opinion would be acceptable to him. [8]

St. Thomas attacks the problem from a different angle. Original sin is a sin of nature; it follows that if the nature is transmitted, the sin is transmitted. The parents communicate the nature by disposing living matter to the point that it becomes capable of receiving a spiritual soul. At the moment of union of the soul with the body the nature becomes complete. Assuredly, the inherited sin is in the soul, but through the mediation of the nature. [9]

As ingenious as the explanation offered by St. Thomas may be, is it satisfactory? Exactly what is signified by a "sin of nature"? The result of sin is a state of enmity with God due to the absence of his grace which alone unites us with him in friendship on the supernatural plane. How can the mere transmission of the physical component of a nature account for the absence in the spiritual principle of man of a totally spiritual force, the divine life?

If man is conceived in a state of enmity with God and from the first moment of his existence is deprived of sanctifying grace, this must be attributable to the fact that God withholds his grace,

---

8. Cf. *Epistola* 166, n. 25, as quoted by Boyer, *op. cit.*, p. 280.
9. *Quaestiones disputatae de Potentia,* q. 3, a. 9, ad. 4.

that in creating the soul he causes it to come into existence in a body in such a way that it possesses neither a participation in the divine life nor the power to submit completely its own faculties and those of the body to the requirements of the divine law.

The difficulty with this approach, of course, is that it seems to make God the cause of original sin, for it makes it appear that he creates us as his enemies. But is this not perfectly in accord with the logic of the ordinary doctrine on original sin? Does not the Church teach that God individually creates every human soul, and every human soul comes into being deprived of grace, in a state of weakness and enmity with God?

Some will respond, the reason God creates the soul in such a condition is that Adam fell, and in so doing he lost for all his descendants grace and the original integrity that was human nature's. The divine life is essentially a gift, a gift which God desired to bestow upon mankind, but which he made dependent upon the choice of Adam whom he selected to represent the race that would arise from his loins. Because the first man sinned, all of those who have inherited from him his nature have also fallen heir to his weakness and to his deprivation of grace.

If this is true, then the state of original sin, which is above all the absence of grace, is not primarily transmitted by generation; the procreative act of the parents produces the corporeal principle in man, and the creative act of God brings about the soul; the human person is conceived in a state of weakness of nature and lack of grace because God has withheld strength and grace on account of the rebellion of the father of the race.

Supposing this analysis to be correct, not only can it help render the transmission of original sin less an enigma, it may also open the way to the solution of another aspect of the problem. If we insist that original sin must be passed on through generation to the descendants of Adam, we naturally have to maintain that there was only one "first man" and from him and his female counterpart all humans have descended. Otherwise, how could those not born of the line of Adam come under the affliction of original sin and stand in need of redemption by Christ?

On the other hand, if we agree that original sin is a condition of frailty and deprivation of grace permitted by God to persist in human nature because of the failure of the representative of that nature, we are left free to suggest two lines of thought:

1. Since it is human nature as such that suffers from the result of original sin, it suffices that all men share one and the same nature in order to be affected by the sin; it is irrelevant whether they descend from the same ancestor or not, as long as they are truly human beings and share the condition of human nature common to all men.

2. Since Adam is representative of the human race, this intimates the possibility of looking upon him as symbolical of mankind; thus, "Adam" could be either a group of the first humans, whose newly acquired consciousness and freedom and the way they used these powers set the pattern for all of their progeny, or he could be the entirety of humanity in the very finiteness of its intelligence and freedom immersed in a finite world and reaching out toward an integrity lying somewhere in the future. This viewpoint, to be sure, raises problems of its own, but, *Humani Generis* notwithstanding, freedom should be left to investigate all of its possibilities.

Ultimately, however, it is not to anthropology nor to theology that we must turn for the solution to this multi-faced problem; the answer for the believer has to lie in the Bible itself and in its interpretation. In this regard, the more one contemplates the history of the development of the Catholic theology of original sin, the more it begins to appear that our theologians of the past have forced the texts of Genesis, in particular, but also those of St. Paul, to say more than they were ever intended to say. Perhaps this opinion can be substantiated by outlining precisely what the key passages have to tell us, and then looking briefly at the context and literary form of the texts.

The first man is called "Adam," which is the Hebrew word for "man"; the term is used in a general sense throughout the first three chapters of Genesis; in 4:25 it is used as a proper name for the first time. Thus in Gen. 2:16-17 "the man" is told that he is not to eat of the tree of knowledge of good and evil. He is assured that the penalty for disobedience will be death. A serpent deceiving the man's wife, both the woman and man are led to disregard the divine imperative. They immediately become conscious of a disorder in their passions, and in shame try to conceal themselves from their creator. God, nevertheless, finds them, curses the serpent, promises the woman travail, and forecasts suffering and death for the man. The Lord then drives "the man" out of paradise, and to the east of the garden of Eden places the cherubim with a flaming sword to guard the way to the tree of life.

In the fifth chapter of the epistle to the Romans, St. Paul makes the lesson of Genesis more explicit: Sin has come into the world through one man, and death has come through sin; many have died on account of one man's sin. By one man's disobedience many have been made sinners; one man's offense has precipitated condemnation for all. In I Cor. 15:22 Paul adds, "For as in Adam all die, so also in Christ shall all be made to live." (Cf. Eph. 2:3 also.)

This constitutes, in substance, the biblical background for the doctrine of original sin. The texts at our disposal are not extensive and the form they take does not make them subject to quick and facile interpretation; the consistent use of vivid imagery and symbolism throughout the Genesis account and the antithetical procedure employed by Paul do not make it easy for us to extract what God is revealing about the condition of man. One thing is certain: neither in Genesis nor in Paul should we expect to find data that pertains to the *scientific* aspects of man's appearance on earth; in both cases the authors are solely interested in treating of the religious situation of mankind *as a whole* in its relationship to God.

In looking more deeply into the all-important matter of the authors' intentions, we see that the first eleven chapters of the book of Genesis are very much preoccupied with the problem of good and evil. It is emphatically stated that all that God created was good. And yet, there appears a serpent, which God has also made and which is evil and cunning enough to tempt woman to sin. But it is the sin of "the man" that is vital; sin enters the world not through God but through man's abuse of his power. After Adam's sin there follow one upon another the sin of Cain, the cruelty of Lamech, the corruption of men at the time of Noah, the offense of Ham, the pride of the people of Babel.

The theme of the abundance of evil in the world pervades these chapters. Everywhere there is suffering and death, violence, and inability to control passion. How can such evil be explained? It cannot be attributed to God, for he is good and all that comes from him must be good. If there is evil in the world it must be because of man himself; it has to be his responsibility.

Is not this essentially the message of the story of the fall of Adam and Eve? Man has somehow, mysteriously, in a way that the author makes no real attempt to explain but simply portrays through symbols, brought the thorn of unharnessed desire, the painfulness of a life of suffering, the tragedy of the rending separation of death, upon himself. This is not to say that passion, suffering, and death are not natural to man and except for sin would not have been part of man's life, but rather that the extent to which man is able to control himself, the manner in which he accepts suffering or tries to alleviate it, the attitude with which he faces death or respects life, depend upon his use or abuse of his intelligence and freedom.

Is there actually anything in the text of Genesis to justify our going beyond the conclusion that Adam and Eve are representative of mankind's responsibility for the condition that afflicts it? Is there anything that we can say with certitude points specifically to *how* mankind became responsible? The serpent is obviously a symbol. The garden, the tree of life, the tree of knowledge of good and evil, are obviously symbols. Throughout the first eleven chapters of Genesis we are dealing constantly with symbols: the murder of Abel by Cain; Noah and the Ark; the tower of Babel. Why in the case of Adam and Eve alone should we become so literal in our interpretation as to insist that the author is undoubtedly speaking of a personal sin committed by the first of all men from whom every man has descended? What exegetical basis do we have for declaring that this one sin is at the root of all the evil in the world, that all men inherit the effects of this sin because there is biological continuity between them and Adam?

We are already familiar with the way in which a popular myth influenced the composition of the story of Noah. But there also exist outside of the Bible other stories of man's creation, and myths concerned with a fall of the ancestors of man or with the origin of death. Can we say without hesitancy that the account of the creation of Adam and Eve and their loss of paradise is not in reality a divinely inspired adaptation of a popular myth, used by the author to demonstrate man's responsibility for evil?

A final criticism of the traditional interpretation of the fall of Adam seems to be in order here. The greatest evil brought upon man by original sin is said to be the loss of sanctifying grace. The latter is supposedly signified by the loss of paradise and deprivation of the intimacy of God. But this thesis too has its difficulties. It is clear enough that the author of the third chapter of Genesis has *physical* death in view as the punishment of Adam's sin. Loss of paradise means that access to the "tree of life," purely human life, is cut off. Loss of the intimate friendship of God signifies separation from his protective influence. There is no question of the loss of a share in the life of God, of spiritual death.

It might be objected, however, that Genesis must be re-read in light of the commentary on it furnished by St. Paul. Let us, therefore, reflect for a moment on the texts adduced from the epistles to the Romans and to the Corinthians. We note at once that Paul is not concerned with providing an exegesis of Genesis. He is citing the story of Adam as it was interpreted in the Judaeo-Christian thought of his time. And why should any of the Christians of that era think and speak of Adam in any other way than as one individual? The common understanding of the role of "Adam" in the communities to which Paul wrote furnished him excellent material for the deployment of one of his favorite teaching devices, the antithesis. When he wished to tell the disciples in these communities about the abundance of grace poured out upon mankind in the person of Jesus Christ, what better way to do it than by contrasting the redemptive activity of the Lord with the vain rebellion of the one man, Adam? Christ is one. For the sake of antithesis, Adam had to be one.

Since Paul is utilizing the Genesis account in a very literal and fundamental manner, ignoring its symbolical overtones; since he is interested in emphasizing the solidarity of mankind in sin in order to contrast this race-fallen-through-Adam with the race-redeemed-by-Christ; since he is hardly concerned with making an anthropological statement about the origins of humanity, can theology be treading on very firm ground when it uses Paul to find in Genesis a justification for the extremely narrow traditional exposition of original sin?

The texts of Paul certainly clarify the doctrine of the oneness of all men in sinfulness and the condemnation they deserve. They also reveal that physical death is not the worst evil to be effected by sin, but that this universal destiny of man is only the symptom of a far more serious punishment, that of a spiritual death which renders us the enemies of God and necessitates rebirth through baptism. But to ask Paul to tell us more about the actual way in which the human race originated and lost the favor of God is demanding too much of him.

To what point are we brought by these reflections? The objections which have been mentioned, and which derive from disciplines as varied as anthropology, theology, and exegesis, at the very least justify a thorough rethinking of the traditional doctrine of original sin, together with its implications about the descendancy of mankind. The difficulties proposed will have to be resolved in a more satisfactory way than in the past if the Church's fashion of presenting the enigma of "original sin" throughout the last twenty centuries is to be kept in force.

On the other hand, are we not overly concerned with *defending* a set of conceptions which we have inherited from the past, conceptions which are human and not only can, but *must,* evolve if they are to live? Would it not be wiser to turn our eyes more

attentively to the possibilities invested in a new approach? If we
accept the proposition that the Bible tells us very little about the
origins of man, except that he is ultimately God's creature, that
God created nothing in man but goodness, that somehow man
on his own initiative has chosen to alienate himself from God
and thus has come to bear the responsibility for the evil that
flows from sin, where does this leaves us?

A position along these lines does not threaten the dogma of
original sin. Rather, it makes it more intelligible. It does not
question the belief that all men share in a sinful condition and
from the depths of their being cry out for redemption. But it does
admit that we do not know exactly how man came to be in this
condition, nor can we say precisely what aspects of the human
condition are the effect of sin as distinguished from those qualities
which pertain naturally to man.

If this more flexible perspective is adopted, then, we see at
once that it is not essential to insist that original sin was the
sin of one man, or even of one group; nor is it necessary to
maintain that all men have descended from this one man and that
because of him mankind literally lost immortality, and suffering
became a part of earthly existence. These things should not
be regarded as impossibilities, of course, but it must be recognized
that they belong to the order of theological speculation and not
to that of the divine revelation upon which faith reposes.

Are we not free, therefore, to pursue other speculations which
eventually might prove more fruitful for the Church than those
she has particularly honored in the past? To be sure, the reason-
ings of the Fathers, of the doctors of the Church, of the councils,
should not be scorned as if they were valueless or erroneous.
They should be taken for what they are: partial insights into the
meaning of man's sinful condition, based upon the principles
of biblical exegesis available at the time, but in no sense definitive
elaborations of the reality which God has revealed and which
we have called "original sin."

What might the above-mentioned speculations be? Their
content depends upon the result of the research and rethinking

of traditional positions being done at present by scholars in various fields. A paragraph from Pierre Teilhard de Chardin's *The Phenomenon of Man* furnishes a interesting starting point for one line of thought:

> Suffering and failure, tears and blood: so many by-products (often precious, moreover, and reutilizable) begotten by the noosphere on its way. This in final analysis, is what the spectacle of the world in movement reveals to our observation and reflection at the first stage. But is that really all? Is there nothing else to see? In other words, is it really sure that, for an eye trained and sensitized by light other than that of pure science, the quantity and the malice of evil *hic et nunc,* spread throughout the world, does not betray a certain *excess,* inexplicable to our reason, if to *the normal effect of evolution* is not added the *extraordinary effect* of some catastrophe or primordial deviation? [10]

Chardin seems to be saying here that while a certain amount of evil (suffering-death-sin) would seem to fit in very naturally with the universe and the pre-established laws governing its finite elements, when one begins to reflect on the totality of Evil in the world, moral evil in particular, he has to ask himself, how could *this* result merely from an evolutionary process? When a person is a believer in God the Creator, this question becomes all the more acute. As Cardinal Newman has so well expressed it,

> And so I argue about the world: if there be a God, since there is a God, the human race is implicated in some terrible aboriginal calamity. It is no longer in accord with the idea of its Creator. This is a fact, a fact just as real as its existence; and thus the doctrine of what in theology is called original sin becomes almost as certain to me as the existence of the world and the existence of God. [11]

If we admit to the existence of some sort of "primordial

---

10. P. Teilhard de Chardin, *The Phenomenon of Man,* Harper & Row (Torch Books), New York, 1961, p. 311.
11. Newman, *Apologia,* Chap. 5.

deviation" or "aboriginal calamity" in the history of the emergence of man — but we do not accept the Genesis account of man's origin and fall, at least in its conventional interpretation — then how can we explain the reality signified by the terminology "original sin"? If a single pair was not at the origin of the human race, if it is not the sin of this pair which we have inherited, how can we speak of "original" sin? The source of our difficulty here is twofold, lying partly in the analysis of the reality itself of the human condition, and partly in the terminology used to express the reality.

As for the reality itself of the "fallen" state of man, various opinions have been proposed. Schoonenberg writes:

Is it perhaps permissible to connect the situation induced by original sin, not with the sin of one single individual, not with the first man in the chronological sense, but with the sin of the whole world? In such a case it might perhaps be of no importance exactly when and where sin entered the picture, and as a consequence, we could say that Revelation tells us nothing about the degree of self-consciousness and freedom of the first human generation. [12]

Dubarle declares in a similar vein:

We see original sin now as a truly tragic and actual situation: no longer merely the loss of wonderful gifts at a great remove from our day and condition, but the moral and religious perversion in which every man finds himself inevitably plunged by reason of his birth into a perverted environment: ignorance of God, or idolatry and a more or less profound corruption.

Mankind is oppressed by a countless mass of sins: it is impossible accurately to pinpoint the individual responsibility for this. In each generation the harmfulness of this distinct downfall is reactivated by new sins. [13]

---

12. P. Schoonenberg, S.J., *God's World in the Making*, Duquesne University Press, Pittsburgh, 1964, p. 83.
13. A. M. Dubarle, O.P., *The Biblical Doctrine of Original Sin*, Herder and Herder, New York, 1964, p. 244.

Views such as those of Schoonenberg and Dubarle seem to have this in common: they imply that the evil in human nature as we know it is not traceable to one sin which all have inherited, but is a factor which derives from the very finiteness of this human nature, a factor in which all of us share some responsibility. Or to put it more simply, man possesses a limited and imperfect freedom in a limited and imperfect world; from the time that the process of evolution, guided by the laws and energy of divine providence, first produced conscious and free beings, these "human beings" were able to use their power of freedom to choose moral good in accordance with their nature; but because of the very fact that they were human, and indeed human at a very primitive level, these first representatives of our race were also capable of failure, capable of using their freedom against the exigencies of their nature.

We might think of the appearance of sin as part of human behavior in terms of *divergence,* a fundamental principle of the evolutionary process. Science has shown that when a significant threshold is crossed, when a truly new form of being emerges from lower forms of being, this new entity immediately begins to experiment, to try out new combinations, and thus to diversify itself, to spread out in various directions; some experiments are more successful than others, tending to become a stable aspect of the species; if the characteristic established is a strong one, it helps to perpetuate the existence of this type of being; if the characteristic is one of weakness, it contributes to the disappearance of the species. (We are not concerned here with summarizing an adequate or precise biological exposition of the evolutionary process, but with simply drawing an analogy between human development and a trend which some men of science see present in evolution. For treatment of several controversial aspects of the issue, cf. J. Rostand, *Ce Que Je Crois,* Grasset, Paris, 1953; J. B. Murray, S.J., "Teilhard and Orthogenetic Evolution," *Harvard Theological Review,* vol. 60, 1967, pp. 281-295.)

If man is truly a product of evolution, if human existence is really in continuity with the rest of the created universe, then man too, on the moral level, must be subject to the principle of divergence. This means that when the threshold of human freedom was crossed, man was destined to experiment with his freedom, to use it and to misuse it, to love and to hate, to do good and to do evil. With the emergence of human freedom, sin inevitably appeared, for this freedom was necessarily imperfect, not the complete master of itself, although itself truly responsible.

Such theorizing, however, raises its own problems. If we accept this picture of man's origins, can we speak of a "primordial deviation" of such great proportions that it has profoundly altered the world of man from what God wanted it to be? If we cannot show the reality of such a moral, "aboriginal calamity," provoked by some extraordinary abuse of freedom on the part of the fathers of the human race, then does it not appear that God himself, the designer, is ultimately responsible for the evil in the world, since it has infallibly resulted from human freedom as he created it? In such a case, what becomes of the infinite justice, mercy, and wisdom of the creator? How could an all-good and providential God fashion a freedom that would inevitably produce the evil and chaos that the history of man has witnessed?

Although these problems are unquestionably quite real and complex, this does not mean they are insuperable. Let us consider first of all the issue of the aboriginal deviation, the "fall." Suppose we accept the following propositions to be true:

1. When human life emerged, it was shared by a small populace of free and conscious beings, and not merely by one couple. This we posit as being scientifically more probable than the theory of monogenism.

2. These individuals possessed the grace of God, the possibility of obtaining salvation. This we postulate as revealed truth. Genesis points symbolically to a very special friendship between God and mankind prior to sin, and the whole of Scripture shows that God has created man to share eternal life with him; the first humans must have been capable of reaching this goal, thus they must have enjoyed the grace which is a prerequisite for

entrance into eternal life. (In speaking of "grace" we mean essentially man's participation in God's own life. In passing, we observe that along with the doctrine of original sin, our entire approach to "grace," that is, the relation of the "natural" to the "supernatural," must be rethought. Do we have here two distinct spheres? Or simply the divine energy drawing nature itself to full actualization of its potential — in intimate union with the Creator and Lord who at a specific moment in time united divinity and humanity in one Person?)

3. Sin did not yet exist in the world, it could not exist until man failed to use his freedom morally. Since we must assume that the first men were extremely primitive, we must infer that the intelligence they possessed and their moral capability of distinguishing between right and wrong was of a very low degree.

Using these propositions as a starting point, can we arrive at a feasible explanation of the "fall" of the human race? When man emerged, he would have been very much a savage, more animal than rational. His actions would have been directed predominantly by passion and instinct, and only secondarily by the light of reason. Only gradually would the power of intelligence and its capacity for making moral distinctions make their presence felt, only little by little would man begin to exercise his power of free choice, of self-determination. He possessed "grace," yes, but most likely this was grace on a primitive level corresponding to the stage of his development. This man could murder, could steal, could hate, could behave sexually quite like an animal, and feel little or no guilt, for it would appear to him that he was doing only what was necessary to preserve his existence.

Gradually, however, man's superior faculties began to enjoy a degree of control. With self-awareness came consciousness of dignity. With the exercise of free choice came a sense of responsibility. Man knew good and evil as such. But again, the importance of doing right or wrong must not have been very clear to early man; his sense of guilt would have been minimal, his awareness of responsibility slight; he must have been like a child entering the "age of reason."

Eventually, though, as man's consciousness of his powers of thought and of decision evolved, his choices took on more serious moral implications. In various ways he began to realize that he was the master of his actions, that he could love, that he ought to love, and that a failure to love was of grave significance. His notion of love, no doubt, was rudimentary — perhaps a feeling of duty towards family, a sense of dedication to the welfare of the tribe. In any event, the human race found itself in a situation in which it was capable of making and had to make truly moral decisions.

Where does the "fall" come into the picture? It is disputable whether we should even speak of a "fall." The word suggests the loss of a superior state of being. Could we not just as well speak of a failure to progress, to achieve conscious-free evolution, a failure of man to bring to realization much of the potential of his intelligence and freedom? The tragedy that struck primitive man would not be that he was cast down by sin from an ideal existence, then, but that as he became conscious of his special powers and responsibilities he failed to utilize morally the former and to fulfill adequately the latter.

Try to visualize the situation as it affected the clusters of primitive human beings whose behavior has conditioned the physiological and psychological fiber of human nature as it has been inherited by their progeny, and has created the moral atmosphere for all to breathe. From the first, each and every man passed through a life which included a series of moral crises. In the beginning the decisions were less significant, less conscious, less moral. But even the slightest truly responsible choices, because they were contributing to a pattern, had to have some effect on the formation or deformation of the moral integrity of mankind. As men's decisions become more fully human, as they revolved about vital matters such as life and death, love and hatred, their constructive or destructive influence intensified. Over a period of many thousands of years, the more or less pliable nature possessed by man at the moment of his emergence imperceptibly solidified into the raw material with which men would henceforth commence their earthly existence.

If we see certain weaknesses deeply rooted in man, an inclination to evil so difficult to eradicate, a universal tendency to turn to the base, the material, indeed the savage, an omnipresent egotism everywhere raising its head to strike out at love, can we not trace this frailty in man to those primitive millennia, and in fact to every sinful act that has helped to aggravate the wound? Is not this the "fall"? Is not this the "death" man has undergone, the death of failing to become what God has given him the possibility of becoming?

But can this type of explanation of man's loss of his original innocence be reconciled with the goodness of God? Does it not appear to say that given the universe the way God has ordained it to be, "original sin" and the totality of evil that obtains in the world necessarily result from the creator's design and thus are ultimately attributable to him?

Christianity has always confessed that the existence of evil and the relationship of freedom and grace in man are aspects of the *mystery* of the plan of redemption; by reason of the very fact that they participate in this mystery, the problems they raise cannot be fully answered. So it is with the question just posed. It does indeed seem that the appearance of sin is inevitably the concomitant of the emergence of a finite, human freedom capable of making authentic choices. This does not imply, however, that any particular choice is ever determined, that any particular sin ever had to be committed. Basing our judgment on faith, we can state that God has never refused any person the grace essential for him to use his freedom morally, the grace necessary and sufficient to help him overcome his inclination to sin; and yet, using our reason to evaluate human freedom for what it is in itself, we can affirm with certitude that sin had to be, that man would assuredly at some time or another reject grace and abuse his liberty.

We can assert, therefore, that in his decision to provide for the emergence of free will in man, God thereby allowed the introduction of moral evil into his universe. [14] How can we

---

14. We prescind here from the special problem of the existence and influence of Satan and the other fallen angels.

justify this action on God's part? Can we not refer ourselves to the classic adage: God has permitted a certain amount of evil, in order that a greater good might be achieved? As for the quantity and intensity of evil in the world, it would be most rash and ill-advised to try to trace this to God. It is at this point that man must look only to himself. Cardinal Newman is quite right when he observes that the world we know is not the world the way God has desired it to be. This is evident not only from what man has been in the distant past, but above all from what he is in the present. How much of the abundance of the evil in the world today can be traced to man's failure to embrace the teachings of *Christ* and his grace? Primitive man is not the only man who has fallen. The fall of modern man, his obstinacy toward the graces of redemption, his deafness to the call of the Lord, is much more knowledgeable and willful than the pride and disobedience of the first men. The tragedy of "original sin" has been constantly renewed throughout the history of man. And its effects have ever been the same: the sins of humanity prevent the world from becoming what God wants it to be. The *totality* of evil in the world, then, is not of God's making, is not the inevitable result of the creation of human freedom; it is the consequence of an accumulative, disastrous rebellion of a creature toward his loving creator. This attests not to the least weakness or imperfection in God, but only to the fact that he has loved enough to create a power so great that it could be used against him and thus in a sense escape even his control.

If it is granted that the negative side of our human condition, our "fallen" state, has originated somewhat in the way that has been described, then perhaps we should cease to speak of "original" sin. [15] The latter terminology has little significance for modern man. It necessarily evokes the traditional, mythical image of Adam: the perfect man, created in an absolutely ideal state, from which he fell by committing the first of all sins, a sin which would

---

15. Except when treating the significance of the terminology in the history of the Christian theology of original sin, of course.

be passed on by generation to all of his offspring. Would it not be better to speak of the weakened or infected condition of man's nature, a condition which he inherits because every sin leaves its mark on the one human nature which all men share in common? Thus the *reality* signified when we talk of original sin is preserved and made more intelligible, as we grasp more lucidly the profundity of man's frailty, the desperation of his plight, the depth of his need to be saved.

To sum up, the view we have suggested would not require an original couple and a first sin as prerequisites for explaining the universality of sin and need for redemption; nor would infused knowledge be presupposed; suffering, concupiscence, and physical death would not literally have been brought into the world through original sin. But these need not have taken on their actual tragic proportions. It is in this sense we maintain that the world we know is not the world as God would have wished it to be. The human race has sinned, and its sins have accumulated one upon another. They have produced a condition that has become part of human nature perhaps in a manner parallel to the functioning of "mutations" in the mechanism of evolution on the biological level. It is for this reason that all men who are born come into the world with "darkened intellects," "weakened wills," inclinations to evil, opaqueness toward grace, in brief, with the condition that tradition has termed "original sin."

There is a final implication of this appraisal, one which is of maximum importance to the Christian vision of the world. When we hear the traditional description of original sin and its effects, we cannot help but form the conclusion that the coming of Christ was something of an accident. It was only because Adam was so foolish as to eat the forbidden fruit that we have been fortunate enough to benefit by the Incarnation. O happy fault!

Our speculation about the true significance of man's wounded nature leads to quite another appreciation of why God became man. We would say that the Incarnation, understood in all of its implications — as the Son becomes man, and through man becomes all in all as he totally unites his universe to himself —

was foremost in God's mind when he created. He determined to create an evolutionary process from which man would emerge because he had determined to become one with his creation. The coming of Christ was primary, was central in the thought of God, and was not merely a kind of fringe benefit of man's sin. It is true that the *way* Christ came and the means by which he chose to redeem us were doubtlessly conditioned by the manner in which mankind has exercised its freedom, but this does not alter the fact that intimate communion with the being he has brought into existence is God's fundamental purpose in creation and in the Incarnation. Salvation *from sin* is an essential aspect of the divine plan, but a secondary aspect.

This concludes our treatment of some of the major contemporary trends in the interpretation of the Old Testament. It is hoped that through what has been said, particularly with regard to the matter of original sin, the reader may be aided to some extent to perceive more clearly the possibilities and the values inherent in the new approach to the Old Testament. The latter must be tested by time and by thorough reflection, and not too hastily or enthusiastically embraced, of course. Nonetheless, the findings of modern scriptural research have posed a serious challenge to a number of conceptions and traditional rationalizations which our theology has for centuries taken more or less for granted. The question has been raised and must be faced: Does much of the common teaching of the Church which has been based on an extremely literal interpretation of the Bible need to be rethought and restated?

If the evaluation of original sin presented here appears to constitute a rather radical departure from ordinary Catholic theology, the opinions expressed are not totally lacking in support. Noteworthy theologians and exegetes such as Dubarle, Smulders, Lyonnet, Schoonenberg, Rahner, and de Lubac have, in their turn, suggested various original interpretations of the fallen status of mankind. [16]

---

16. Besides the works of Dubarle and Schoonenberg already cited, cf. P. Smulders, *La Vision de Teilhard de Chardin, Essai de réflexion théologique,* 1964; P. Schoonenberg, "Erbsunde und 'Sunde der Welt.' "

We cannot help feeling that the study of the significance of original sin, as well as the analysis of many other features of revelation, could be greatly facilitated and could yield much richer fruits if only there might be more honestly allowed the freedom of procedure reflected by St. Augustine who, when perplexed about trying to explain the transmission of original sin, wrote to the Bishop Optatus: "When something which is by nature obscure surpasses our limited capacity for understanding, and its mystery is not laid open to us by Sacred Scripture, then it is rash for us through mere human conjecture to define anything with respect to it."

Orienterung, XXVI, 1962, pp. 65-69; K. Rahner, *Das Problem der hominization;* H. de Lubac, *La Pensée religieuse de Teilhard;* additional sources and insights into this topic can be found in Paulette Martin's review of Dubarle's work, *National Catholic Reporter,* September 15, 1965, p. 9, and in Robert T. Francoeur's review of *The Evolution of Man* by B. Ryan, *National Catholic Reporter,* November 10, 1965, p. 9; cf. also Jean de Fraine, *Adam and the Family of Man,* Alba House, Staten Island, N.Y., 1965, and P. Schoonenberg, S.J., *Man and Sin,* University of Notre Dame Press, Notre Dame, Ind., 1965.

APPENDIX TO THE DISCUSSION OF THE
DOCTRINE OF ORIGINAL SIN

In the months since the foregoing chapter was finished, theologians have continued to study intensely the problem of reconciling the dogma of original sin with the theory of evolution. Of special interest are the articles published by Maurizio Flick and Zoltan Alszeghy. [1] Moreover, new material was added to the controversy in an address by Paul VI to a symposium of theologians assembled to discuss the problem, July 11, 1966. [2] To complement the observations we have already made, therefore, we shall summarize the article of M. Flick published in *La Civiltà Cattolica,* July 1966, and comment on it in light of the remarks made by Pope Paul.

Flick's article is in essence a résumé of the present *status quaestionis,* with a few critical comments and a number of positive suggestions directed toward a solution of the dilemma. The professor observes first of all the tension existing between those who value the findings of science and regard evolution as the best explanation of the facts that science has discovered about the origin of the world of man, and those who look upon evolution as merely a fragile hypothesis which the science of faith should hardly take seriously.

---

1. Cf. our Systematic Bibliography.
2. Cf. *La Civiltà Cattolica,* "Sul domma del peccato originale," August, 6-20, 1966, pp. 322-25.

He then notes that the *facts* ascertained by science *suggest* that the first men were quite similar to irrational animals and only gradually developed their powers to think intelligently and to make morally responsible choices. Furthermore, the evolutionistic conception of the origin of life is more favorable to polygenism than to monogenism. All things being considered, then, theologians have no choice but to examine the implications of the evolutionary origin of mankind, in reference to the interpretation of the doctrine of original sin.

The author goes on to point out that, even if eventually science should abandon evolution as a means of explaining the origin of life, it would represent an appreciable gain in our understanding of the faith if it could be admitted that the dogma of original sin is reconcilable with that theory, regardless of the theory's intrinsic merits.

He also notes that the principal elements of the doctrine, at least with respect to the primary level of revelation, are 1) the necessity of being reborn in Christ in order to be saved; 2) the origin of the misery of our human condition from sin. And these two elements, he asserts, are not related to evolution.

The reservation is added, nevertheless, that theology, even though admitting as possible the evolutionistic explanation of human origins, cannot interpret the Paradise account as if it were merely a myth. On the other hand, the opposite extreme of excessive literalism must be avoided.

In a second section of his article, Flick traces the development of two theological currents concerned with the relation between the account of Adam and evolution. Those who represent the first tendency minimize the opposition between science's vision of man's origin and the drama of the Garden of Eden. The latter, they say, is built around a conception of history, then almost universally accepted, which believed that a being was more perfect the closer it was to its origin; but this perspective is certainly not a matter of Catholic doctrine. Hence, such items deduced from it as the corporal perfection of Adam, his universal knowledge, etc., are not necessarily to be received as part of man's original condition. At the same time, such theologians are willing to admit, besides the possession of grace, certain "preternatural" gifts of Adam: immortality and integrity.

For these scholars the "paradise period" was quite brief, thus leaving no traces discoverable by science; then, with the fall, humanity suffered a profound spiritual-corporal decline. Research of prehistoric man, therefore, has found and will find vestiges of fallen man alone, and will never be able to show that at one time a more perfect state was not enjoyed by the original man.

But recently there has emerged a second and more radical current of thought. Those who share in this tendency, according to Flick, do not underestimate the value of the opinion expressed above, but they do find it rather artificial in that it continues to recur frequently to the intervention of divine omnipotence and treats evolution merely as a particular scientific theory applying to the origin of life, rather than as the general law of becoming in all material being — as universal as the divine activity which creates and conserves the entire visible universe. Those who maintain the second viewpoint offer the criticism that the creator would seem to contradict himself if, having chosen to bring about the perfection of the created universe (the "total Christ") gradually, he intervened almost from the beginning, as if to correct his own law of evolution.

These theologians ask, therefore, if it is not possible to express the "history" of Adam in terms more meaningful to a world so imbued with the perspective of evolution? They point out that a similar "transposition" has taken place with regard to the doctrine of creation, which was revealed in a world-vision proper to the Semitic people of antiquity, but which is applied today by the faithful to an image of the world completely different from that of the sacred author.

One possible transposition, they propose, would be to express the evil leading to our needs of a Redeemer not as a *fall* from a state of perfection possessed in the past, but as a *distance* from a goal of perfection not yet attained by evolution.

Flick notes, nevertheless, that serious objections have been raised against this interpretation. An "evil" of the sort described would be inevitable, and would be imputable only to the author of the system of evolution. Original sin would thus be reduced to the necessary condition of man as a creature essentially moving toward total perfection. But how could such a conception of original sin be reconciled with the Genesis account which clearly intends to teach that man's misery should be imputed to man and not to God? At the same time, this objection does not exclude the possibility of conceiving of original sin as a *failure* to reach the degree of evolution which man should have achieved, due to a refusal on man's part which closed the way to evolution, or at least put it on a false route.

In line with the latter view is the theory which locates "original" sin not in an act of mankind's first parent, but in the collectivity of all the sins of humanity, a burden which must be carried by every human born into the world. Because of the very ambient in which he is conceived, every infant is destined to live with a certain insensitivity to the call of love, resisting the divine salvific will and opposing the current of evolution animating the universe. The child ineluctably enters a deformed society, a society which has truly made of itself an enemy of God.

While conceding the truth contained in the above theory, Flick cautions that it should not be regarded as a complete explanation of original sin, for it seems to overlook what revelation apparently says about the special effect of a sin committed *at the beginning* of man's history. For the theology professor of the Gregorian University, then, the possibility of conceiving of original sin from an evolutionary perspective depends upon the possibility of attributing a decisive importance to "the disobedience of a single man" (Rom. 5:19) in the deviation or in the retard of evolution.

Flick feels that a hypothesis can be formulated which satisfies this demand. He proposes that the evolution of the human species might be comparable to the development of the individual. At a certain moment, mankind achieves the possibility of choosing between good and evil. Here evolution must cross a new threshold which is specifically different from all those which have preceded it in the course of evolution, for at this point man was destined by God to become a creature vivified by grace, a perfection which would divinize him and hence totally exceed the created order. Not only would this transformation lie beyond the power of natural evolution itself to produce, it would also require free acceptance on the part of man — and not merely result inevitably from the unrelenting drive of evolution.

Because of the particular nature of the crossing of this threshold, it becomes apparent that for the first time in the history of the world, evolution could be thwarted. Mankind could and did place itself in opposition to the creative will of God, and sin spread throughout the world. Henceforward, even though the world continued to develop, the type of perfection it achieved was quite different from what it would have been if the offer of the original form of supernatural life had been accepted: man's personal development together with that of the world as a whole would have been much more perfect, as he would have learned to eliminate suffering and to pass from his earthly to heavenly existence without the tragic "rupture" constituted by death as we know it.

Although evolution has been frustrated, nonetheless, God's plan of elevating man to supernatural participation in his life — in conjunction with the process of evolution — is not rendered vain. Evolution will achieve its goal, but in virtue now of the merits of the Incarnate Word who enters the world, dies, and rises from the dead. In this new order man is still able to arrive at total perfection, but only in the eschatological stage of existence, since on earth everyone is born in a condition different from that in which he would be if evolution had progressed in the way originally intended by God. Even when he receives grace, he still must overcome the lethargy of nature he inherits, and must endure suffering and the tragedy of death.

It is Flick's contention that the hypothesis summarized above effectively unites what has been revealed about the beginning of the history of salvation with what is suggested by an evolutionistic vision of the world, without diluting the dogma of original sin. It is true that from this viewpoint the blessed state of "original justice" is only offered and is not really possessed — still, some of the early scholastics were permitted to hold freely opinions analogous to the one stated.

In relation to polygenism, it should not be imagined that the "collectivity" of sins described earlier refer to *a collective* sin committed by all men living at the beginning of history. Nor is it conceivable that God would deprive of grace men already possessing it, simply because some other individual had sinned.

Theologians have offered various solutions to this thorny aspect of the problem. It has been proposed that in the state of "original evolutive justice" there existed a number of individuals who had not yet arrived at a full development of their moral personality. The first to arrive at "full psychical maturity" committed a sin, with the result that the internal-instinctual drive in the others toward ulterior supernatural evolution was blocked off, so that the way could be opened only through the saving grace of Christ.

Secondly, though men may not have descended from a common father, from an evolutionary viewpoint this would not render them autonomous among themselves. All come under the one process of "hominization." This fact together with the biblical concept of "corporate personality" can help us to grasp more easily how he who was not physically its father, could exercise an influence on the entire race. In the latter case, the whole community is envisioned as quasi-incarnate in some specific person. (The patriarchs and kings, for example, enjoyed this position with respect to all the "sons of Israel." Why shouldn't an analogically similar role have been played by the first sinner of the human race, whether or not the other members of the race were his descendants?) This notion would seem to agree quite well with the special vocation of mankind, not only as individuals but *as a whole*: the vocation of bringing to full reality the people of God.

Flick observes finally, "presupposing this collective vocation, and recalling that, in our hypothesis, the first sinner is the only person who, at the decisive moment, was able to accept or reject the divine call, we can comprehend all the more easily that his response was in effect the response of all mankind, through which not merely the physical person of the sinner, but the totality of humanity as a corporate person, determined its situation before God." [3]

In light of the preceding, Flick declares, the impossibility of reconciling the dogma of original sin with the theory of polygenesis does not seem nearly so evident as it did at the time of *Humani Generis.*

Now it is very interesting (and perhaps significant) that only nine days after the publication of Flick's article, in an address to a small symposium of carefully selected theologians and scientists gathered to discuss the mystery of original sin (among whom were included E. Dhanis, C. Moeller, R. MacKenzie, P. Benoit, E. Boné, Z. Alszeghy, M. Flick, C. Rahner, and M. Labourdette), Pope Paul VI made the following observations:

1. Although Vatican II never expressly treated the subject of original sin, in the schema *De Deposito Fidei Pure Custodiendo* there was included an eighth chapter: *De peccato originali in filiis Adae.* The Council was unable to take up this chapter, but it did reaffirm the Catholic doctrine of original sin. In the dogmatic constitution *Lumen Gentium,* in full consonance with divine revelation and the decisions of the magisterium in the councils of Carthage, Orange, and Trent, there is clearly taught, according to Paul VI, "the fact and the universality of original sin, as well as the intimate nature of the state from which mankind has fallen through the offense of Adam" (cf. *Lumen Gentium,* c. I, n. 2).

Pope Paul also affirmed that the constitution *Gaudium et Spes* (the Church in the Modern World) makes even more extensive reference to the dogma of original sin. He noted that in speaking of the condition of man in the contemporary world, the document recalls the tragic consequences of original sin, in strong and effective terms — although the Council does not present original sin as the unique source of evil among men. It speaks of the

---

3. M. Flick, "Peccato originale ed evoluzionismo. Alla ricerca di una soluzione." *La Civiltà Cattolica,* July 2, 1966, p. 25 (translation mine).

lack of balance under which the modern world struggles as being connected with the more fundamental disequilibrium rooted in the heart of man (Introd., n. 10), and finds in the sin of the first man the principal font of moral disorder existing in humanity: "Although he was made by God in a state of holiness, from the very dawn of history man abused his liberty, at the urging of personified Evil. Man set himself against God and sought to find fulfillment apart from God" (chap. 1, no. 13).

Hence, Paul concludes, Vatican II did not intend to deepen and complete the Catholic doctrine on original sin, already sufficiently stated and defined in the councils of Carthage, Orange, and Trent; it only wished to confirm and apply it insofar as required by its primarily pastoral aims.

2. After reviewing the position taken by Vatican II, the Holy Father noted that the task of those assembled for the symposium was quite different from that of the Council, and expressed his desire that the fruit of their inquiry of the meaning of the doctrine of original sin in light of the contemporary findings of the sciences of anthropology and paleontology would be a definition and presentation of original sin which would be more modern, that is, more capable of satisfying the exigencies of faith and of reason as pertaining to man in our epoch.

Paul then praised the object of the symposium, remarking that the bishops and priests of today's Church cannot worthily fulfill their mission of enlightening and saving the modern world, if they are not equipped to present, defend, and illustrate the truth of divine faith with concepts and terms which are more comprehensible to minds formed by our contemporary philosophical and scientific culture, and cited the words of John XXIII inaugurating Vatican II: "The substance of the ancient doctrine of the deposit of faith is one thing, and the way in which it is presented is another" (A.A.S., LIV [1962], 92).

3. The Pope adds that exegetes and Catholic theologians are conceded all the freedom of research and judgment required by the scientific character of their studies and by the pastoral aim of the salvation of souls, within the limits, of course, assigned by

the magisterium — which is the proximate norm of truth for all the faithful. Thus, the assuming of excessive liberty in interpreting the dogmas of the Christian religion is explicitly reproved.

4. After the preceding observations, which appear to be little more than introductory, Paul VI arrived at the real focal point of his discourse. He regards as revealed by God the doctrine of original sin, as to its existence and universality, as to its quality as a true sin in the descendants of Adam and its unhappy consequences for the soul and for the body. He cautions the participants in the symposium in their task of seeking a more profound and precise sense in the biblical texts to be most careful to keep in mind the perennial norms reflected in the *analogy of faith,* the declarations and definitions of the councils, and the documents issuing from the Apostolic See.

Paul, therefore, sees as *apparently* irreconcilable with authentic Catholic doctrine the explanation of original sin given by certain modern authors who, taking as their starting point the presupposition — which has not been demonstrated — of polygenism, deny, more or less clearly, that the sin, whence is derived so much of the evil afflicting mankind, was above all the disobedience of Adam the "first man," and the figure of the future Adam, committed at the beginning of the history of man. (Cf. *Gaudium et Spes,* nos. 22, and 13.)

This type of interpretation does not, Paul insists, agree with the teaching of Sacred Scripture, of sacred tradition, and of the magisterium, according to which the sin of the first man was transmitted to all his descendants not by way of imitation, but by propagation, a sin which effects the "death of the soul" of every man, and constitutes, from the moment a child is born, a privation and not merely a lack of sanctity and of justice.

The Pope, in conclusion, notes that the theory of *evolution* would also seem inadmissible to the degree that it should fail to accept resolutely the immediate creation of each and every soul by God, and to maintain as decisive the importance which the disobedience of Adam, the universal "protoparent," had for the fate of mankind. Nor should this disobedience be conceived as if it did not result in Adam's loss of the sanctity and justice in which originally he had been established.

* * *

What is to be thought of the hypothetical explanation of original sin proffered by M. Flick, particularly in light of the address of Paul VI? And how is the position we have outlined earlier in the chapter affected by these recent comments on the mystery of original sin? An analysis of Paul's remarks would seem in order first of all.

Let us emphasize from the outset, it is not an easy task to evaluate accurately the full import of the Holy Father's words, or to discern with certainty the scope of his intentions. One might too hastily isolate certain of the Pope's conservative statements, and prematurely conclude that he intended to block the way completely to some of the more recent attempts to explain original sin. *All* of what Paul VI said must be taken into consideration.

It should be remembered that he did not consider it impossible to arrive at a more profound and modern understanding of the mystery of original sin. Nor did he deny that a rather broad freedom is left to exegetes and theologians in their research. If these statements of the Holy Father are to be taken seriously, then they provide some basis for hope for great progress in the endeavor of reconciling the scriptural account of man's origins and fall with the data of modern science.

On the other hand, we cannot deny that the general tenor of the address was extremely cautious. The Pope was especially concerned that any new theories proposed by exegetes or theologians respect the *continuity* between Sacred Scripture, the Church's dogmatic tradition, and the present teaching of the magisterium. Every original interpretation must account for the various essential elements we have received through revelation and which have been preserved throughout the history of the Church.

To reinforce the position he adopts, Paul recurs to specific documents of Vatican II. But a careful examination of his use of the Council texts leaves some question in the reader's mind. One has the impression that perhaps the Pope has slightly strained the words of the Council fathers, in order to bring them more into line with what he wishes to say. In any event, as Paul himself concedes, the Council manifested no intention of resolving the problems raised by modern efforts at interpreting the significance of "Adam" and his "disobedience," as well as by the question of how the sin is transmitted — although there is no doubt about the reaffirmation of the existence and universality of the state of original sin.

The difficulty posed by Paul VI's affirmations becomes still more acute when he discusses the critical question of the elements contained in Scripture, tradition, and the magisterium. For this is *the* question: what are these elements and how are they to be delimited?

The Holy Father's remarks in this regard must be weighed carefully, for various statements seem to carry diverse force. Thus, the Pope affirms in an absolute tone that there can be no doubt about the existence and universality of original sin; he includes in his categorical statement the assertion that the councils also define the "intimate nature of the state from which mankind has fallen through the offense of Adam." He does not, however, make precise the conditions of the state of original justice to which he refers.

Later in his address, when he treats the more controversial issue of the possibility of reconciling polygenism and the dogma of original sin, Pope Paul becomes somewhat more guarded in his tone. Thus he says *it would seem* that the position of those who accept the theory of polygenism and more or less deny that original sin — whence have proceeded so many evils afflicting mankind — is above all constituted by the disobedience of Adam, the "first man," is not reconcilable with authentic Catholic doctrine. We might note that the Pope does not dismiss polygenism itself as unacceptable, but simply describes it as non-demonstrated. But he does seem to look upon polygenism as a theory based on fragile grounds, and in the same context emphasizes that Adam was the "first man," that his sin is transmitted through *propagation,* and that the sin results not merely in a "lack" of sanctity and justice, but in a definite *privation*.

Again, Pope Paul declares that the theory of evolution *would seem* inadmissible if it does not allow for the immediate creation of every human soul and the decisive importance of Adam's disobedience which resulted in the loss of his original innocence and justice.

In summary, therefore, the position taken by the Holy Father embraces the following points:

Polygenism is a presupposition which has not been proved true. "Adam" should be interpreted as referring to the first man, the father of the entire race.

Original sin is rooted in the disobedience of this individual. This sin is transmitted through propagation.

The sin is the basic source of evil in the world.

Adam *de facto* enjoyed a condition of original justice which was lost through sin, a justice of which his descendants are deprived.

Human beings, in their total natural composition, are not products of the process of evolution, for God *immediately* creates *each* human soul.

Paul VI does not, however, seem indisputably to align all of these aspects related to original sin as pertaining absolutely to the dogma itself. Rather, his fundamental intention may well have been to remind his audience of exegetes and theologians that these are details normally *associated* with the dogma, and that any interpretation must weigh them most delicately, while at the same time accounting for the doctrinal significance attached to them in the Church's tradition.

To be sure, the overall effect of the Pope's talk was definitely disappointing, its more conservative elements forcing into the background the several positive and hopeful remarks. One might say that, at the very least, the address was premature in its evaluation of the modern attempts to reconcile science and theology in relation to man's origins. Nevertheless, neither the conservative tone nor the ultimate significance of Paul VI's discourse should be exaggerated. The address was more or less informal in nature, and, as has been indicated, it was basically aimed at emphasizing the essential necessity of respect for the traditional teaching of the Church when striving to arrive at a deeper understanding of the mysteries entrusted to us through revelation, and not at definitively settling certain details of the presentation of the dogma of original sin.

Possibly the address is most open to criticism, however, not so much in its details as in the basic attitude toward the *real development* of dogma which it betrays. One can only conclude from the Pope's words that he understands the development of dogma merely as the process of achieving deeper comprehension of the sacred mysteries by finding newer and more modern *terms* for expressing eternal truths. In other words, there is no *substantial* progress in our grasp of the truth itself, only our terminology evolves.

It would seem to us that there is a vital distinction to be made which can both preserve continuity between tradition and the "new theology" and allow for real development of dogma, but a distinction which the magisterium has slighted. We are in full agreement that as it is objectively present in the divine nature "eternal truth" is immutable. But this same truth *as it is KNOWN* (and not merely "formulated") by us can and must change. Otherwise any but a most superficial development of our understanding of the mysteries of salvation is inexorably excluded!

By way of illustration, Catholic tradition of the past has unquestionably regarded "Adam" literally as one individual and the father of the entire race. This was doubtlessly the conception of Adam in Paul's mind when he wrote Romans. Yet, if today we admit the theory of polygenism, then obviously it cannot be true that Adam was the original parent of all men, and propagation cannot be the medium of transmission of original sin. This would mean that Catholic tradition has presented an erroneous picture of the history of the origins of mankind.

However, in the last analysis, is this an adequate approach

to the problematic? Must we not look first to the *substance* of
the eternal truth with which the Church is ultimately concerned?
What real difference does it make to the economy of salvation
whether or not "Adam" was one man or a multitude? What
difference does it make whether the means of "transmission" of
original sin was generation, or simply possession of human *nature*
in *this* world? As Flick has pointed out, the essential implications
of the dogma of original sin are that the *entire* human race is
subject to the necessity of being reborn in Christ in order to be
saved, and that the misery of the human condition is the fault
of man himself and not the result of the primary intention of God.

Now, can we not admit that the authors of tradition, and
indeed the very creators of the Scriptures, were not adequate
to the task of perfectly and definitively communicating the
mystery they were commissioned to transmit? If this be granted,
then not only would their verbal expression of immutable truths
be found wanting in reference to modern terminology, but *the
very truths themselves* would be only *partially* grasped and communicated. (We might suggest as an analogy the different vision
a person receives of the same piece of skin tissue observed first
by the eyes alone, and then under a high-powered microscope.
Both visions are "true," and yet the latter is so much more
accurate and penetrating.) Hence, the fundamental truth of
man's universal sinfulness and need for salvation remains indeed
immutable, but the attempts to portray the details of the origin
of this situation all share in the finitude of human intelligence
and are subject to real change and development. We would not,
therefore, say that Catholic tradition was teaching an untruth
in affirming "Adam" to be one individual; we would assert
rather that this was an attempt to explain the mystery of original
sin which at one time was the best expression of the truth available, but an explanation which with the passage of time and
progress of science at least shows signs of no longer being sufficiently accurate or satisfying.

Pope Paul's brief discourse, however, to all appearances does
not take into consideration the possibility of making the distinction
discussed above. Hence, the openness of our contemporary

magisterium to the potentialities lying within an acute and solidly based comprehension of the sense of the development of dogma remains a large question mark.

Prescinding from this issue for a moment, let us turn to a comparison between the propositions of Flick and the cautions set forth by Paul VI. There is little doubt that Flick has made a concerted effort to bring into line with Catholic tradition his suggestions for a new interpretation of original sin, but does his effort comply with the standards of Paul VI?

Flick insists that the misery of the human condition originates in original sin, and is not related to evolution. He tries to depict original sin as the offense of one man, at the beginning of human history, the first man to become capable of mature exercise of his psychic faculties. He emphasizes the absolute necessity of the grace of Christ for the salvation of every human being. And he deciphers many of the weak points in some of the other new theories on the matter. To this extent his thought seems to be quite in agreement with that of the Pope.

On the other hand, he allows for the possibility of polygenism, and the transmission of original sin in a way other than by generation. His position regarding the immediate and individual creation of each human soul is not clearly defined. "Original justice" is envisioned as a condition offered but never actually possessed.

Now, even though Flick's reasons for the perspective sketched in the preceding paragraph are founded on firm theological, exegetical, and scientific principles, and constitute no attack on the essence of the doctrine of original sin, his viewpoint can hardly be reconciled with the tenor of Paul VI's address. This is precisely because the points he makes reflect a substantial development of dogma, a kind of progress which the Pope's restrictions seem to preclude.

Approaching Flick's article from another tack, however, even if his type of reasoning and hypothetical probing does go beyond the limits Paul has counseled, even then does he actually succeed in reconciling the religious concept of man's origins with the vision suggested by evolutionistic science? To a certain degree, yes, but his exposition leaves itself open to several objections.

In insisting that man's misery originates in original sin, he makes it clear that this unhappy condition is not related to evolution. Is this not an overstatement? It would seem that from the evolutionary perspective a certain amount of suffering and even moral degeneration is necessarily implied in man's development. A natural relationship between an evolving universe, an evolving rational-volitive creature, and moral and physical evil would appear to be ineluctable. We simply cannot evade the conclusion that if God willed an evolving universe, he foresaw in his volition the inevitable appearance of *some* degree of evil, physical and moral. The problem of original sin would bear, then, not on the existence of evil in the world, but on the *intensity* (and perhaps on a kind of threshold-in-reverse) of evil and its consequences.

Secondly, Flick's endeavor to allow for polygenism and, nonetheless, retain the uniqueness of the influence of Adam, appears a bit forced. He proposes that "Adam" would be the first *individual* to achieve mature use of his mind and will. Again, this hypothesis is hardly consonant with the normal course of evolution. Once man appeared, there would be groups of men living on a very elementary intellectual and moral level, but they would progress toward a higher level more or less *together*. On what basis can we assume that one of them would far outdistance the others, so that God would allow that man's immoral decision to determine the course to be followed by the evolution of the race? Moreover, at this stage what is meant by "mature" psychic development? From the viewpoint of evolution such an individual's moral sense could, at best, be no more than relatively primitive. And if several groups of humans, evolving independently, existed in different localities on earth and had no inter-relations, how could the decision of this hypothetical Adam influence the immediate decisions and evolution of the latter? This phase of the professor's argumentation, therefore, is not altogether satisfying.

Yet, if "original sin" is not the act of one individual, and if it is not one sin committed by the collectivity of humans alive at the beginning of history, or if the offense of a single individual cannot even be said to be of "decisive importance" in the matter, then what is this sin? It can only be — as we have described in the previous section of the present chapter — the *condition* of mankind resulting from a gradual, more or less universal and definite trend of the human race contrary to the creative design of God. It is this condition which has persisted throughout man's history, which even today not only exists but continues to develop (through the personal sins of modern man) and to afflict the race of its originators and victims, and which determined the mode assumed by the concrete aspects of the Incarnational-Redemptive earthly events in the life of the Son of God.

It is especially in light of the most profound and ultimate meaning of the Incarnation and Redemption that the doctrine of original sin, which is subsidiary to these greater mysteries, must be framed. As a matter of fact, the entire discussion of the problem of eliminating contradiction between the theological and evolutionary visions of man's origins leads us to believe that the basic orientation of the debate is commanded by one's Christology and theology of grace. The universal concern seems to be that if our doctrine of original sin is altered, then we run the risk of making God guilty of the evil in the world, of denying his original gift of divine life, of destroying the basis for the need of redemption by Christ.

Logically we must conclude, then, that progress in the understanding of the mystery of original sin will be stymied without a thorough rethinking of traditional Christology and the related doctrine of grace. Some authors of the past for instance, have assumed the existence of two distinct and independent economies of grace. They postulate the divine life originally possessed by humanity without reference to Christ, and then signal a second offer of the divine life, coming after the fall and depending completely on the redemptive merits of Christ.

As was observed earlier, this dichotomy is open to question and does not respond very well to the exigencies of the type of evolutionistic thought proposed by a Teilhard de Chardin. If in creating an evolving universe, God thought first and foremost of the Incarnate Word, if all was to be ordained from the beginning toward the "Total Christ," then there could not be two economies of grace; that is, *all* divine life communicated to man is in strict dependency on the ontological and existential reality of the Son of God become man.

Could it not be that our understanding of the nature of sanctifying grace and its loss has been grossly over-simplified? Have we not, in effect, reduced our concept of the divine life to something like a ticket of admittance to heaven? With the sin of Adam, all tickets were destroyed, and mankind was obliged to wait until a new block of tickets was purchased by Christ. Such imagery is certainly not very flattering to our theology and reflects something of an over-simplification itself; yet, is it not fundamentally accurate?

Now, if we envision the total economy of grace as *one* continuous creative and salvific effort of God, existing from the beginning, never broken off, and in ultimate dependence on the merits of our Lord, then possibly the significance of the loss of the divine life in relation to original sin will become more intelligible. From this viewpoint sanctifying grace would not be a reality totally present to mankind at one moment and totally absent the next, until the death and resurrection of Christ instantaneously restored it, something after the fashion of a water faucet being turned off and on. Quite the contrary, sanctifying grace would be the uncreated yet creative and transforming divine energy present in mankind from the beginning, tending toward his supernaturalization, an energy never completely snuffed out. (Would not the presence of such a force both help us to explain and at the same time be confirmed by the existence in the world of truly saintly people prior to the time of Christ? Think for example of such personages as Abraham, Isaiah, the Jewish martyrs in the persecution inflicted by Antiochus Epiphaneus, or Moses and Elijah appearing in glory with Christ at the transfiguration.) In any event, the matter of the actuating presence in the world of sanctifying grace between the "fall" and the coming of Christ could certainly bear with further study.

In what sense, then, would the divine life be "lost" through "original" sin? As we said previously, we should be wary of the use of the word "original" which in itself may prejudice and obscure our understanding of the issue at stake. The expression "lost" is subject to the same criticism. From the evolutionary perspective we are concerned not with one act of one individual, but with an indefinite multitude of acts of an indefinite number of individuals, through which is established a state of opposition to the creative and evolutive will of God and thus an opaqueness to his divinizing energy. We can validly presume that there were individuals who constituted exceptions, who progressed toward moral integrity through right use of their freedom, who grew in the power of love, and accepted grace on their own level. But the general trend of humanity was in the opposite direction, away from original innocence. The overall effect of this trend at the beginning of man's history was indeed an intensification of evil, moral and physical, in a world which God had willed and given the possibility to be fundamentally good and relatively free from evil's domination. An atmosphere was established — by man — which placed (and continues to place) obstacle after obstacle in the way of the design by which God desires to draw the entire world to perfection through the inter-operation of natural-evolutive energy and supernatural-divinizing life.

If grace has always been in the world, however, then what contribution has been made by the life, death, and resurrection of Jesus Christ? First of all, as we have already insisted, the divine life was offered to man *originally* only in virtue of the eternally planned Incarnation. Secondly, the merciless crucifixion of our Lord resulting from rejection by his own people constitutes tragic testimony to the perennial obduracy of humanity toward God's offers of love. In other words, if it had not been for the loveless climate created by the human race's sinfulness, the specific mode, circumstances, culmination, and efficacy of Christ's coming might have been thoroughly different. Finally, the Lord came not simply to die, not simply to purchase us with his blood, but to establish his Church as the ultimate means of rendering the divine grace effective in the world, of gradually overcoming the situation produced through human iniquity, and of bringing to fulfillment the original goal of the creator: the Total Christ.

To conclude our remarks on the subject of original sin, therefore, let us briefly sum up our position. A tremendous amount of study and reflection remains to be done on the mystery before us. The dialogue and exchange among exegetes, theologians, and scientists must be allowed to continue with utmost freedom. At this time authoritative pronouncements on the subject could only be unfortunately premature. It is good to recall the data of tradition and the declarations of the councils. Yet, such recurrence to interpretations of previous centuries must be circumspect. It should never for a moment be forgotten that the fathers of the councils of Carthage, Orange, and Trent were not speaking in light of modern thought categories, such as those used by evolutionists. Nor did they grasp the scriptural nuances made available through contemporary exegesis' sense of literary form. Every precaution must be taken lest we *deify* our own *human* codifications or comprehension of mysteries that are divine in dimension.

Part 2

Modern Biblical Criticism and
the New Testament

CHAPTER ONE

JESUS OF HISTORY AND THE CHRIST OF FAITH IN THE NINETEENTH CENTURY

As we have observed, "historical truth" was treated by the writers of the Old Testament in a variety of ways. Some of the persons or events described were historical in the strict sense of the word, while others were more or less legendary. Thus, each of the passages revolving around the story of the ancient alliance has to be examined carefully, scientifically, before any conclusion can be reached about its historical value. The manner through which the inspired author desired to transmit the Word God entrusted to him has to be ascertained; that is, the literary form which he used must be determined as precisely as possible; we must do all we can to sift out his intention in writing.

But what about the New Testament? Do we not enter a new situation at this juncture, one in which there is a keener sense of the importance of exactitude in the transmission of testimony, a situation in which a premium is placed upon historical accuracy? We answer in the affirmative, but a qualified affirmative.

Throughout the Old Testament the major preoccupation was one of testifying to the intervention of Yahweh in history to choose his people and to manifest continually his predilection for this people. This *fact* of the action of God among his elect was for the authors who have given us the first volume of Sacred Scripture the focal point around which everything else converged. In the New Testament the identical fact assumes startlingly new proportions: God effects the greatest conceivable manifestation of his love for his people by becoming one of them and thus uniting himself in the most personal way possible to his universe. A divine person becomes incarnate, and on the foundation of this central historical fact the edifice of the New Testament is constructed.

The New Testament, like the Old, is the product of the faith of a community. It expresses the belief of primitive Christianity in its Savior. This faith presupposes, however, the existence of the person who constitutes its principal object. Unless Jesus Christ lived and spoke, suffered and died, rose and continued to live in his Church in approximately the manner described for us in the literature of the New Testament, then the *fact* of Christianity's appearance becomes inexplicable and its survival unintelligible.

The authors of the New Testament were committed to record the truth, the historical truth, about Jesus. They were witnesses of what he said and did, witnesses to the way in which his teachings and achievements were experienced, accepted, and remembered in the original community. But above all, they were witnesses to the kerygma, the preaching of the mystery of Jesus. They were not interested in narrating a life of Jesus, but in proclaiming the coming of God among men in the person of Jesus Christ for the redemption of all mankind. The kerygmatic perspective which runs throughout the New Testament is more than a little significant; its presence carries with it the implications that the epistles, and even the gospels, are much more than records of words and actions; they are the first statements of the Christian theology of the Word Incarnate. The second volume of Sacred Scripture, then, portrays for us not only the Christ of history, but also the Christ of faith. It is the Catholic Church's constant doctrine that the two are inseparable, that the Christ of faith is but the real Christ of history as fully appreciated by the Christian community which abandoned itself to him.

Certain commentators on the New Testament, however, working independently of the framework defined by the Catholic position, have challenged the doctrine which insists upon the identity of the Christ of history with the Christ of faith. Because their arguments have had such a marked influence on the contemporary study of the New Testament, it is essential that we review them here, as we strive to come to a more thorough grasp of the truth of the revelation of the New Alliance.

Let us turn back the pages of the history of biblical criticism to Germany in the nineteenth century and the Protestant exegetes who, under the impact of Hegelian philosophy, adopted a rationalistic attitude toward interpretation of the Bible as well as toward religion in general. Theirs was the position that religion and philosophy have the same content, the former, however, treating it through images, the latter through ideas. It was also their pretention that the supernatural and the miraculous exist only as states of mind peculiar to certain groups of individuals, and not as actual phenomena of the real world.

From this milieu in 1835 a youthful German scholar, David Strauss (1808-1874) who had just completed a study of Hegelian philosophy, authored a life of Jesus *Das Leben Jesu,* which constituted a turning point in the critical study of the life of Christ. He declared that "it is time to substitute a new fashion of considering the story of Jesus for the idea of a supernatural intervention or a natural explanation . . . . The new terrain should be that of mythology." While he maintained that historical events were at the origin of the gospel accounts, he insisted that the believing community had transformed them, embellished them, or added to them its own creations. The gospels, then, are basically myths which were unconsciously created by the emerging Churches. By "myths" he meant stories enveloping philosophical and theological ideas.

Following the same line of thought and almost equally arbitrary in its method and assumptions was the "school of Tübingen" of the mid-nineteenth century. The early Church was esteemed to be the synthesis of two opposite tendencies, Judaeo-Christianity and Pagano-Christianity. The gospels reflect the evolution which preceded the appearance of the synthesis. According to the founder of the school, F. C. Baur, the origin of the gospels can be reconstituted in this way: Matthew was written about 130 A.D.;

it is a tendentious deformation of a document supposedly going back to Peter; the latter writing was Judaeo-Christian in tone. Luke, which is anti-Petrine in tone, resulted from the rearrangement of the Pauline gospel of Marcion between 140 and 180. Mark, was a synthesis designed to neutralize the tendencies of the first two gospels.

This system simply ignored the data of tradition on the dates of composition of the gospels and their authors. Furthermore, instead of applying the method of literary criticism to the gospels, the exegetes of this school were content to try to fit the work of the evangelists into their own philosophical prejudices. Hence, Baur could say: "The essence of Christianity is not the person of Jesus, it is an abstract idea, elaborated at length throughout the centuries which have preceded our era. The role of Jesus was to represent a moment of capital importance in the evolutionary progress of this idea; he vivified it by injecting it into the Jewish world of messianism. But this was simply a stage along the way of progress." [1]

In France, Ernest Renan gave great popularity to the exegetical theories of the Germans through his *Vie de Jesus* which appeared in 1863. His philosophical position was one which called everything into doubt; for him, history is but a "conjectural science"; the life of Jesus is the "fruit of a fantasy which could not be more difficult to lay hold of," in which history and legend are mingled in an inextricable manner. His portrait of Christ was one of a gentle Galilean dreamer, a man who has given us a beautiful code for the perfect life.

Concomitantly to the efforts of the rationalists, there was emerging among the Protestants another approach to the New Testament, that which extensively employed "literary criticism." This method consisted fundamentally in analyzing the text itself, with the purpose of discovering how it was put together. The scholars of this school were particularly intent upon detecting the sources upon which the gospels are based. In 1838, C. H. Weisse, drawing upon his personal research, issued this conclusion: there

---

1. F. C. Baur, *Histoire de l'Eglise pendant les trois premiers siècles,* 1853.

are two documents at the base of the evangelical tradition, Mark and a collection of saying (*logia*), which offer a solid terrain upon which the history of Jesus can be constructed. The majority of studies produced in the second half of the nineteenth century took as their starting point this theory of the "two sources."

Under the impetus of this trend, in 1901 W. Wrede published a systematic study which, in its turn, also greatly influenced subsequent research. He tried to show that the gospel of Mark is not a writing which has recorded the memories of an eye-witness, but is a theological work elaborating the theory of the "messianic secret." Since Mark was regarded as the prime source of the gospel tradition, and since according to the view-point of Wrede Mark's gospel is theology, not history, the historical value of the gospels in what they tell us about Jesus was once again brought into question.

During this period which witnessed a veritable revolution not only in the methodology employed in studying the New Testament, but also in the attitude of scholars toward the gospels in par-ticular, Catholic exegesis remained at a mistrustful and con-servative distance. Outside of a few exceptions, Catholic scholars made little contribution to the development of biblical study at this time. In 1890, however, under the direction of the renowned Père Lagrange, a Dominican school for biblical study was established in Jerusalem; this school was characterized by its enthusiasm for considering the problems raised by higher bib-lical criticism; also to its credit was the publishing of the *Revue biblique,* an extremely important organ in the promotion of a scientific and respectable Catholic exegesis.

But aside from the endeavors of a few like Father Lagrange, Catholic commentators persisted in jealously defending the tra-ditional approach to the New Testament. Possibly this extreme cautiousness, along with the influence of the writings of such men as Strauss, Baur, and Wrede, had something to do with Alfred Loisy's [2] issuing his thesis which formed an important

---

2. Loisy was a Roman Catholic priest and a professor at the Catholic Institute in Paris, 1881-1893.

part of the biblical sector of the "modernist" movement. Loisy's position reflected the predominant themes of the more radical forms of German exegesis. He accepted the theory of the "two sources" and drew from it conclusions which if upheld would be disastrous for the Faith. Like Strauss, Loisy dissociated the Christ of faith from the Jesus of history. The Christ of faith is the creation of the early Christian community; we are separated by the barrier of this community from the actual events of the life of Jesus.

Thus a distinction was introduced between the Christ of history who, according to Loisy, did not want to found a church, but simply to invite to repentance as preparation for the Parousia, and the Christ of faith, who is God. Although the errors of Loisy, together with the ensemble of the religious system of modernism, were condemned by Pius X, the question of the relationship between the historical Jesus Christ and Christ as seen through the faith of the first Christians continued to rise again and again in twentieth-century biblical research. [3]

---

3. Cf. Dom Charles Poulet, *Histoire de l'Eglise*, Beauchesne, Paris, 1960, pp. 414-421; X. Leon-Dufour, "Brève Histoire de l'Interprétation," *Introduction à la Bible, op. cit.*, pp. 147-55.

CHAPTER TWO

JESUS OF HISTORY AND THE CHRIST OF
FAITH IN THE TWENTIETH CENTURY

The more radical tenets of the German school of exegesis and of writers of the genre of Renan and Loisy were not only disapproved by the Catholic Church, they were also, for the most part, abandoned by Protestant scriptural scholars of the early twentieth century. The groundwork had been laid, however, for serious consideration of the proposition that the Christ who is presented to us in the gospels is extremely different from the Jesus who lived, preached, labored, and died in Palestine two thousand years ago. Also transmitted to the present generation of exegetes is the tendency to approach the New Testament with a prejudice gleaned from the perspective of some philosophy or other.

These qualities are especially characteristic of the work done by the German scholar, Rudolph Bultmann, whose studies have had a tremendous impact upon contemporary exegesis. One Catholic author has even been moved to write, "It is unfortunate that in the last two years much of the creative energy of Catholic New Testament scholarship has been consumed in defending its own orthodoxy against the implication that Catholic exegesis has gone Bultmannian." [1] Because of their great importance, there-

---

1. Raymond E. Brown, "After Bultmann, What?" *Catholic Biblical Quarterly,* January 1964, p. 1.

fore, we shall review two of the areas in which the contributions of Bultmann have been significant: the method of Form Criticism (*Formgeschichte*), and the notion of Myth in the New Testament.

One of the major acquisitions of nineteenth-century biblical research was the realization that behind the evangelical tradition there lies a number of sources. Perhaps the greatest weakness of the scholarship of this period was that it attempted to search out and evaluate these sources in too "a priori" a fashion; that is, the exegetes of this time were too quick to impose upon the texts of Sacred Scripture their own philosophical predispositions without making a sufficient effort to locate in the milieu from which they had emerged the texts which they were examining. The German scholars of our century, becoming somewhat cognizant of this deficiency, resorted to a revised methodology: literary criticism which proceeded merely by comparing documents among themselves and trying to determine what their sources might have been was judged to be unsatisfactory. With the assistance of information gathered from modern sociological studies, the new school of thought purported to recount the history of the formation of the gospel prior to its having been put into writing. It was in this context that the approach of form criticism first began to be used. Its two most important originators were Martin Dibelius [2] and Bultmann. [3]

An interesting summary of the position of the form critics has been provided by Miles Bourke in his article "The Historicity of the Gospels," [4] and we shall refer to it here. Form criticism points out, first of all, that the indications of place and time in the synoptics are almost entirely artificial. These three gospels, furthermore, are not the compositions of three individuals who can be designated as "authors" in the way that we presently use this term; rather, they are "compilations of little units which were originally independent, which had originated in and circulated in the oral tradition of the Christian community and had

---

2. M. Dibelius, *Die Formgeschichte des Evangeliums*, 1919.

3. R. Bultmann, *Die Geschichte der synoptischen Tradition*, 1921.

4. Myles Bourke, "The Historicity of the Gospels," *Thought*, Spring 1964, pp. 42-46.

developed according to the laws of popular literature." [5] Form criticism sets for itself the goal of sectioning off and classifying these brief units, in an effort to ascertain what factors in the primitive Christian community accounted for their existence.

To the extent that the observations of the form critics are valid, our customary way of thinking of the historical Jesus and the gospels must be reshaped. For if the chronology of the Synoptics is more or less religious or symbolical rather than historical, if the gospels are not the eyewitness and homogeneous compositions of the evangelists, if the needs of the early Christian community dictated the choice and method of presentation of the gospel material, we must seriously ask ourselves whether the picture we have been given of Jesus is not artificial rather than real. Thus we are forced to probe more deeply into the assertions of the form critics, as we endeavor to evaluate them in light of the effect they might have on the historical value of the sayings and deeds of Jesus Christ.

According to scholars such as Dibelius and Bultmann, the two types of gospel material easiest to classify — the attempt to reconstruct the origins of the gospels having begun — are deemed to be the "sayings" of Jesus and the "narratives" about him; the former accent one of his memorable statements and the latter tend to concentrate on one of his miracles. Beyond these two categories, the remaining content of the gospels is found difficult to classify. Dibelius designates the majority of it as "legend." It should be noted, however, that for him "legendary" is by no means synonymous with "fictitious": "The legend form as such furnishes no decisive argument against the historicity of the hero or of an event — nor, on the other hand, does it give any guarantee that the account corresponds to reality." [6] For example, it is Dibelius' view that the passion account is a type of legend assembled by the early Christian cult for the purpose of presenting the condemnation and execution of Jesus in such a way that the hearer or reader would see in

5. *Ibid.*, p. 42.
6. *Die Formgeschichte . . .* p. 106.

these events the expression of God's will. In this case the "legend" would contain a good deal of historical truth. On the other hand, there is the legend of the "Christ myth" which makes Jesus the divine Son of God coming into the world from heaven, which is plainly discernible in the accounts of the baptism, temptations, and transfiguration of Jesus, and which for Dibelius has little to do with reality.

Bultmann designates the narrative material which is distinct from the miracle stories as "legend and historical narrative." He regards the separation of legend from historical narrative to be impossible, for ". . . . historical narrative is so completely dominated by legend that it can only be treated together with the treatment of legend." [7] Although the legend may have a historical basis, it is not particularly concerned with the historical as such; its character is religious and edifying rather than historical. Bultmann also observes that the gospels, in their final form, show the marked influence exercised by the "Christ myth."

In general, then, the method of the twentieth-century form critics has been to look upon the gospels as composed of small units and to strive to decipher these units, to classify them, and to explain their origin. It is admitted that occasionally within these fragments put together by the Christian community we catch a glimpse of the real person of Jesus, but more frequently it seems that we are simply witnessing the expression of the faith of the first Christians.

The form critics, to be sure, have deployed their principles in such a fashion as to come up with conclusions which Catholic exegesis must disavow as excessive, unjustified, and indeed destructive of faith in the historical value of the gospels. The school of form criticism has, nonetheless, made a number of positive contributions to the study of the evangelical material: it has drawn attention to the fact that the chronological indications in the gospels are so inconsistent that they can hardly be used to reconstruct a life of Jesus; it has pointed out instances of the same event's being related in very different ways in several

---

7. *Die Geschichte* . . . p. 261.

gospels — how are these differences, some of which are quite significant, to be reconciled? The *Formgeschichte* approach has been especially effective in helping to determine the literary form of the many brief units within the gospels, and in situating each passage in its proper milieu of life, its *Sitz im Leben.* Hence, the form critics unquestionably have a great deal to tell us about the formation of the gospels, in spite of some of their unacceptable presuppositions and deductions which tend to detach Christ from the Church and to call into doubt the supernatural itself.

Out of Bultmann's application of the principles of form criticism to the New Testament has grown his insistent demand that the gospels be *demythologized.* Since Bultmann's observations about the presence of myth in the New Testament are rather typical of those twentieth-century scholars who estrange the real person of Jesus from the gospel data, and have exerted a profound influence on contemporary exegesis, it seems imperative at this point to summarize his theories about the extent to which Christianity has created a mythical Jesus. We shall refer frequently here to the compendium *Kerygma and Myth.* [8]

A few preliminary remarks about the terminology used by Bultmann might prove helpful. Some of the key words he employs are rather unfamiliar and require explanation; other terms may seem to be familiar, but are manipulated in a special, technical sense; and at times there seems to be some equivocation in the manner in which certain words are handled.

Doubtlessly the most vitally significant word in Bultmann's treatment of *Kerygma and Myth* is "myth" or "mythological." The professor is careful to indicate that he does not speak of myth in that modern sense in which it is used practically as the equivalently of "ideology." Friedrich Schumann contends that by "mythology" Bultmann is designating "an attempt to furnish a 'secular proof' of the eschatological significance of an event of past history by the use of objective imagery." [9] In Bultmann's

---

8. R. Bultmann and Five Critics, *Kerygma and Myth,* ed. H. W. Bartsch, Harper & Row (Torchbooks), New York, 1961.

9. *Kerygma and Myth,* p. 182.

own words, myth is "the use of imagery to express the other-worldly in terms of this world and the divine in terms of human life, the other side in terms of this side." "The real purpose of myth is not to present an objective picture of the world as it is, but to express man's understanding of himself in the world in which he lives." "It is an expression of man's conviction that the origin and purpose of the world in which he lives are to be sought not within it but beyond it . . . ." [10] In certain passages Bultmann leaves the impression that the "mythology" of the New Testament has consecrated a false view of the world and must be eliminated, while at other times it would appear that the myth is but a form of expression which needs to be interpreted.

A term which is correlative to "myth" and of almost equal importance is "kerygma." The kerygma sums up the essential elements of the good news of salvation as it was first preached. For Bultmann it is "the proclamation of the decisive act of God in Christ." [11] Demythologizing aims at saving the kerygma by rescuing it from myth, that is, by piercing the mythical frame-work in which the gospel is set, stripping away the apparently objective imagery, and laying hold of the truth which the New Testament is actually trying to convey.

In discussing myth in reference to the events of the life of Jesus, Bultmann draws a somewhat subtle distinction between the "historical" and "historic." By the former, he means events which actually took place and which can be substantiated by the application of historical criticism to the past; on the other hand, the adjective "historic" is used to qualify something which occurred in past history, but which has a vital existential reference to our life today. In this case, it is the relevancy of the "historic" event *here and now* that is important, and not what historical criticism may have to say about what in reality happened. Thus an event described in the gospels, such as the resurrection, could be "historic," but not in the least "historical."

When Bultmann talks about something being *existential,* he is concerned with the aspect under which it affects human

---

10. *Ibid.,* p. 10.
11. *Ibid.,* p. 13.

existence as it really is in the present, and not as it might theoretically be. This usage is to be differentiated from *existentialistic* interpretations, which offer human consciousness a better understanding of what human existence is really all about. We shall see that such an interpretation of the New Testament is esteemed to be the only one that can save the kerygma from the undesirable effects of the mythologizing of the first Christians.

The attitude of the Christian today toward the kerygma must be one of *faith* in what has been achieved for the world by God's action through Christ. By faith we open ourselves freely to the future; we offer obedience to God by turning our backs on self and by abandoning every form of security (especially that of trying to "prove" the validity of the kerygma); faith involves a radical self-commitment to God in the expectation that we shall receive all from him. It leads to complete detachment from the world; the decision of faith, however, is never final, it constantly stands in need of being renewed in every fresh situation. [12]

Another concept of Bultmann's which we shall encounter, a concept which possibly represents the climactic point of his analysis of kerygma and myth, is that of *eschatological existence.* This is the type of human existence which "the decisive act of God in Christ" has made possible for the man who believes, enabling him to be a "new creature." [13] For the believer the age of salvation has already dawned and the life of the future has become a present reality.

Having thus hastily perused a portion of Bultmann's basic vocabulary, let us now examine more thoroughly his statement of the problem. The subject of the preaching of the New Testament, according to our author, is *the event* of Redemption. Bultmann insists that this proclamation is set forth in a framework which presupposes a mythical view of the world, and he begins his critique with an attack on this type of *Weltanschauung.* [14]

The cosmology of the New Testament is essentially mythical

---

12. *Ibid.,* p. 21.
13. *Ibid.,* cf. p. 20.
14. *Weltanschauung* is used here in the sense of being a particular way of envisioning the world.

in character. The world is viewed as a three-storied structure, with earth in the center, the heaven above, and the underworld beneath. Heaven is the abode of God and of celestial beings — the angels. The underworld is hell, the place of torment. Even the earth is more than the scene of natural, everyday events, of the trivial round and common task. It is the scene of the supernatural activity of God and his angels on the one hand, and of Satan and his demons on the other. These supernatural forces intervene in the course of nature and in all that men think and will and do. Miracles are by no means rare. Man is not in control of his own life. Evil spirits may take possession of him. Satan may inspire him with evil thoughts. Alternatively, God may inspire his thought and guide his purposes. He may grant him heavenly visions. He may allow him to hear his word of succor or demand. He may give him the supernatural power of his Spirit. History does not follow a smooth unbroken course; it is set in motion and controlled by these supernatural powers. This aeon is held in bondage by Satan, sin, and death (for "powers" is precisely what they are), and hastens towards its end. That end will come very soon, and will take the form of a cosmic catastrophe. It will be inaugurated by the "woes" of the last time. Then the Judge will come from heaven, the dead will rise, the last judgment will take place, and men will enter into eternal salvation or damnation. [15]

The above is the language of mythology and the origin of the various themes can be traced to the mythology of the Jewish apocalyptical literature contemporary to the New Testament epoch and to the redemption myths of Gnosticism, Bultmann maintains. Because of this and because there is nothing specifically Christian about the mythical view of the world as such (it being simply the cosmology of the pre-scientific age), the kerygma has been rendered incredible to modern man, for he is convinced that the mythical view of the world is obsolete. [16] Man's knowledge and

---

15. *Kerygma and Myth,* pp. 1-2.
16. *Ibid.,* p. 3.

mastery of the world have advanced to such an extent through science and technology that it is no longer possible for anyone to take the New Testament world view seriously.

It follows that the miracles of the New Testament can no longer be accepted. The mythical eschatology, that is, the imminent coming of Christ upon the clouds of heaven, is untenable for the reason that the Parousia of Christ never took place as the New Testament writers had expected: history did not come to an end . . . .[17] Similarly modern man finds what the New Testament has to say about the "Spirit" and the sacraments utterly strange and incomprehensible. [18]

There is only one approach to criticism of the New Testament which will be theologically relevant, and that is one which inculcates an interpretation which arises necessarily out of the situation of modern man. The gospel message must be reconciled with the world as man today knows it. Death, for example, cannot be evaluated as a punishment for sin. Modern man recognizes it simply as a necessary process of nature. Nor can the traditional doctrine of atonement be accepted: for how can the guilt of one man be expiated by the death of another who is sinless? [19] The resurrection poses just as difficult a problem. And as for the pre-existence of Christ, taken literally it is irrational and quite meaningless. [20]

In order to restore the relevancy of the New Testament, then, Bultmann turns his attention to the task of demythologization, in an effort to purify the kerygma of the mythical elements which cause it to be rejected by modern scientific man. On the one hand he notes that the kerygma cannot be saved by retaining some of the mythical features which characterize it and by dismissing others; that is, the mythical view of the world must be accepted or refused in its entirety. [21] On the other hand, criticism must be exercised in such a way not to *eliminate* the

---

17. *Ibid.,* p. 5.
18. *Ibid.,* p. 6.
19. *Ibid.,* p. 7.
20. *Ibid.,* p. 8.
21. *Ibid.,* p. 9.

mythology of the New Testament, but to *interpret* it.[22] We must realize that the importance of New Testament mythology lies not in its imagery (which only *appears* to be objective, that is, to deal with historical occurrences), but in the understanding of existence which it enshrines.[23] Bultmann's goal is to recover the truth of the kerygma for men who do not think in mythological terms, yet without forfeiting its character as kerygma.[24] For the New Testament the person of Jesus is the decisive *event* of redemption. The kerygma should not be altogether rejected simply because it speaks of this person in mythological terms.[25]

Bultmann concludes from this sketch of the problem that a solution lies uniquely in an existentialistic interpretation of New Testament mythology. This species of interpretation alone can get at the truth of the kerygma underlying the mythological form and render it relevant to the situation of modern man here and now. The vital message of the New Testament is to be found in its understanding of human existence, and only an existentialistic approach adequately reveals the nature of this understanding.[26]

What would be the content of an existentialistic, nonmythological interpretation of the Christian understanding of human existence? St. Paul shows us that the life of the man who is entangled in the affairs of this world is filled with anxieties.[27] Such a man, placing his trust in transitory earthly things, loses himself in the vain pursuit of security. He ends by becoming the slave of this world which is in revolt against God. In contrast to this, according to Bultmann, the New Testament sees the authentic life as a "life based on unseen, intangible realities. Such a life means the abandonment of all self-contrived security. This is what the New Testament means by 'life after the Spirit' or 'life in faith.' "[28]

---

22. *Ibid.,* p. 12.
23. *Ibid.,* p. 11.
24. *Ibid.,* p. 15.
25. *Ibid.,* p. 14.
26. *Ibid.,* pp. 15-16.
27. I Cor. 7:32.
28. *Kerygma and Myth,* p. 19.

Authentic human existence, therefore, must be a life of faith, faith which frees us from the world and gives us to God, here and now, in an eschatological existence. This new existence is presented in terms of an "indicative" and an "imperative." The indicative: having become one with Christ through faith, you *are* in the spirit, you are a new creature, etc; the imperative: accordingly, you *must* walk in the Spirit — through personal commitment, detachment from the world (self) — and thereby you are made capable of fellowship in community. [29]

It is evident enough that for the New Testament composers authentic existence without faith is unthinkable. But from the New Testament viewpoint, faith becomes possible only at a definite moment in history, in consequence of an event — the event of Christ. By "faith" the New Testament always means faith in Christ. Still, Bultmann asks, could it be possible to arrive at a Christian understanding of human existence *without Christ*? Should demythologizing be carried this far?

At this juncture, the German scholar endeavors to show that certain existentialist philosophers writing apart from the context of faith in Christ, Martin Heidegger and Wilhelm Kamlah in particular, have managed to achieve an understanding of human existence which parallels the Christian vision in several respects. He remarks that "Heidegger's existentialist analysis of the ontological structure of being would seem to be no more that a secularized, philosophical version of the New Testament views of human life." [30] Man's existence is characterized by anxiety and by tension between the past and the future. Either he must immerse himself in the concrete world of nature, and thus lose his individuality, or he must abandon all security and commit himself unreservedly to the future, and in this way alone achieve his authentic being. To Bultmann's way of thinking, philosophy thus expressed is saying the same thing as the New Testament and doing so quite independently.

Philosophy also agrees with the New Testament that man is

---

29. *Ibid.*, p. 22.
30. *Ibid.*, p. 24.

a "fallen" being, he has "gone astray." For Heidegger this means that man has lost his individuality and needs to recover true selfhood. For Kamlah man's natural inclination to commit himself has to be emancipated and enabled to become what it was meant to be. [31] But how is this recovery to be made? How is this emancipation to be effected?

Thinkers like Heidegger and Kamlah are convinced that all man needs in order to realize his "nature" is to achieve a true understanding of what human existence really is. No revelation is required. Philosophy by itself is quite adequate to the task. As Kamlah insists, "since it is the true understanding of Being, philosophy emancipates that self-commitment which is proper to man and enables it to attain to its full stature." [32]

Bultmann notes that this view is diametrically opposed to the position taken by the New Testament. The latter emphatically states that man is totally incapable of freeing himself from his fallen condition. He can be delivered only through an act of God. Every impulse of man is an impulse of a fallen being. Self-commitment cannot be achieved, it must be *received* as a gift from God, it had to be made possible through the event of redemption which was wrought in Christ .

Can the New Testament prove its case against the philosophers? No, for "proof" is excluded by the very nature of what faith is. The New Testament does not try to demonstrate its position (at least apologetics is not of the essence of its message, for where mythologizing comes into the picture there is some question of an attempt to give proof), it simply addresses man as a fallen creature, a self-assertive rebel, a sinner, and faith is required as a remedy for this "self-glorying," this "self-asserting." The believer does not submit himself to the kerygma as he would to a proof, he makes a free decision, he autonomously determines to commit himself to the event of redemption.

In this context, forgiveness of sins does not mean that punishment due for sin is remitted. This is too juridical and static

---

31. *Ibid.*, pp. 26-27.
32. *Ibid.*, p. 27.

an interpretation. Rather it means that man is freed so that he might be enabled to obey: man is delivered from himself, made capable of love. Such freedom has been made available to man because God has acted through Christ — eschatological existence (detachment from the world, openness to the future) has become possible. In brief, the event of Jesus Christ is the revelation of the love of God: this demands on our part *faith* in the love of God revealed in Christ. [33]

It would seem, therefore, that for Bultmann demythologization cannot go so far as to predicate a Christian view of existence apart from Christ, since Christian faith is essentially faith in Christ. This does not mean, however, that the event of Jesus Christ as it is presented by the New Testament escapes the need of being demythologized. And in this respect, an existential type of exegesis is mandatory.

The New Testament portrays for us a unique combination of myth and history. It claims that the Jesus of history is at the same time the pre-existent Son of God; side by side with the historical event of the crucifixion it sets the "definitely non-historical event of the Resurrection." [34] But is not all this mythical language (which speaks in terms of pre-existence, a virgin birth, miracles, a resurrection, and ascension) simply an attempt to express the *meaning* of the historical figure of Jesus and the events of his life? [35]

The attention of Bultmann is next directed to proposing certain guidelines for liberating the event of the Cross-Resurrection from the mythical perspective which tends to obscure its true significance. The Cross itself enjoys a mythical setting: we see the pre-existent Son of God being crucified in atonement for our sins. Here we have a mingling of sacrificial and juridical analogies which are untenable for us today. The traditional acceptance of this mythology does not do justice to the New Testament which is actually saying that the Cross not only releases man from guilt, but also from the very power of sin. The

---

33. *Ibid.,* pp. 30-32.
34. *Ibid.,* p. 34.
35. *Ibid.,* p. 35.

historical event of the Cross thus acquires cosmic dimensions as "we see in it the judgment of the world and the defeat of the rulers of this world . . . the cross becomes the judgment of ourselves as fallen creatures enslaved to the powers of the world.' " [36]

Bultmann goes on to say that "in its redemptive aspect the cross of Christ is no mere mythical event, but an historic fact originating in the historical event which is the crucifixion of Jesus . . . . In the last resort, mythological language is only a medium for conveying the significance of the historical event. The historical event of the cross, in the significance peculiar to it, created a new historic situation. The preaching of the cross as the event of redemption challenges all who hear it to appropriate this significance for themselves, to be willing to be crucified with Christ." [37]

But the event of the Cross cannot be understood apart from the event of the resurrection. It is Bultmann's contention that the resurrection is not an event of past history, nor is it a mythical event purely and simply. It would seem to be a mythical way of expressing for all men of all times the significance of the death of Christ. In any case, the resurrection cannot be a miraculous proof capable of demonstration and sufficient to convince the skeptic that the Cross really has the cosmic and eschatological meaning attributed to it. "An historical fact which involves a resurrection from the dead is utterly inconceivable!" [38]

On the contrary, the New Testament is interested in the resurrection of Christ because it is the eschatological event par excellence. The resurrection reveals to us that Christ in death has abolished death and brought life and immortality to light. *"Faith in the resurrection is really the same thing as faith in the saving efficacy of the cross."* We believe in the saving efficacy of the cross because we believe in its proclamation as a *triumph,*

---

36. *Ibid.,* p. 36.
37. *Ibid.,* p. 37.
38. *Ibid.,* p. 39.

and thus it is always presented in conjunction with the resurrection. [39]

The resurrection, Bultmann concludes, is not itself an event of past history. Historical criticism can only establish the fact that the first disciples came to believe in the resurrection, it cannot demonstrate that the latter ever actually took place. We cannot hope to strengthen our own faith in the resurrection by falling back upon that of the first disciples and in this way evade the element of risk which faith in the Cross and the Resurrection always involves. [40] Thus has the German exegete launched his effort to emancipate faith from the "objective" order, that is, from a world view which tries objectively to *prove* the truth of what the Christian supposedly accepts on faith. [41]

* * *

What are we to think of Bultmann's theories about demythologization? Although much of what Bultmann has to say is unacceptable (not only to Catholics but also to Protestant Scripture scholars, both liberal and the more orthodox — for different reasons), certain of the insights into the New Testament which he has offered are worthy of reflection. His desire to make the gospel relevant to modern man is in itself most praiseworthy. His point that faith is necessarily a risk, that it transcends proof, that historical research cannot measure the riches of the redemptive event of Christ is well taken. The emphasis he places upon eschatological existence, detachment from the world, and total self-commitment to Christ in faith, is profoundly Christian.

Bultmann, furthermore, is not easy to understand, and as Raymond Brown has very well observed, any criticism of Bultmann must be careful to avoid the following pitfalls: (a) To say that something cannot be proved by historical methods is not the same as saying that it never happened. (b) When it is asserted

---

39. *Ibid.,* pp. 40, 41; cf. II Tim. 1:10.
40. *Ibid.,* p. 42.
41. *Ibid.,* p. 210.

that a redemptive event in the life of Jesus is not historical (*historish*), Bultmann is often emphasizing the word *redemptive;* he is saying that redemption is accepted through faith and is not observable through the historical-critical method. (c) "Myth" does not mean a "fairy story," as it often does in everyday speech. Nor does "demythologizing" mean the expurgation of myth; it means the interpretation of myth in existential terms. [42]

Even with these factors being taken into account, however, there remains a number of Bultmann's assertions with which we cannot but disagree. A consideration of several of the points upon which Catholic belief and the Bultmannian viewpoint are sharply divergent would seem apropos at this moment.

In general, the latter unjustifiably attributes far too creative a role to the early Christian community. A believing community may indeed give a particular form to the expression of the object of its faith, but it does not create the substance of its belief, it presupposes it.

The existentialistic approach of Bultmann, moreover, gives the impression of being extremely naturalistic. With the divinity of Christ, his miracles and resurrection being eliminated through interpretation as myth, we are left to wonder if there is anything at all that was supernatural about Christ: just how did God act through Christ, in what respect were his life and death really different from those of other religious oracles?

In challenging traditional doctrine on these points, nonetheless, Bultmann has forced us to consider the extent to which the primitive community may have exercised a creative influence on the teaching of Christ, on the meaning of who he was and what he did. We shall return to this matter later, when we take up our study of the way in which the gospels were formed.

In the past the Catholic Church has been criticized for being too inflexible to take a serious look at the work being done by men such as Dibelius and Bultmann. Unquestionably it has studied their works, but only in order to equip itself better to reject

---

42. R. Brown, *loc. cit.,* p. 2.

them, not to learn from them. Thus, a Protestant, Ernst Lohmeyer has written:

> It is the hallmark of Protestant theology and Protestant faith that it never entrenches itself in a province of its own where it can enjoy its own content untouched by outside movements and upheavals. Its weakness is that it has too often surrendered to the spirit of the age. Yet that weakness is also its strength, for despite its association with the world, it has managed to preserve the unbounded freedom of its own faith and its location by God in the here and now.... That is why Protestant theology cannot, as Catholic theology could and does, ignore the challenge of demythologizing. It is therefore the special vocation of Protestant theology to associate itself with all the developments in science, and to reap the fruits from all the trees of secular knowledge. It cannot therefore ignore the challenge of demythologizing and, since that problem has a legitimate place in scientific theology, it becomes its own problem too.[43]

Now, in light of recent trends in Catholic exegesis and the whole atmosphere created by Vatican Council II, it is doubtful that intimations such as those made above would be repeated today. The contemporary Catholic Church is making an effort to demonstrate to the world that she has no intention of "entrenching herself in a province of her own," of divorcing herself from the fruits produced by secular science, of ignoring the challenge of demythologization. In a sense, in this respect the Church owes a debt of gratitude to scholars such as Bultmann who have compelled her to take a second look at her traditions, to deepen her grasp of the Scriptures, to insure her relevancy to the contemporary world.

Possibly there has been an excessive amount of material produced by Catholic exegetes in defense of their position against the trend of demythologization, but at the same time not a few

---

43. *Kerygma and Myth*, p. 136; the remark is part of an article based on a lecture given by Lohmeyer at Breslau in 1944.

excellent Catholic biblical scholars have recognized the strong points as well as the dangers in the challenge hurled by a Bultmann, and have indeed approached seriously the problem of myth and kerygma in the New Testament.

To return to our criticism of Bultmann's weak points, however, it would seem that his premises open the way to emptying the person of Jesus Christ of all real significance for anyone except the individual who happens to share his own special existentialistic perspective. Bultmann undoubtedly proceeds with good faith but perhaps, too much like the secular world to which he desires to make the gospel believable, he proceeds with too little faith.

Our author appears to deduce a great deal from the "pre-scientific," "three-storied" cosmology of the New Testament. To it he relates intimately belief in the miraculous and in the preexistence of Christ. Since for modern man this type of view of the world has become childish, unless the miracles of Christ and his "divinity" are reinterpreted, they too become absurd. The upshot is that there were no actual miracles, and Christ was simply a human being through whom God acted.

This theorizing fails to satisfy on several fronts: for one thing, it is not certain to what extent the New Testament writers themselves took literally the three-storied (heaven-earth-hell) vision of the world. Some would suggest that their use of these concepts is symbolical of dimensions of existence, and even the Old Testament sees this neat little universe as being transcended by God. But more important, on what basis does any branch of secular science have the right to pronounce for or against the possibility of the miraculous or of the Incarnation of the Son of God? If historical observation cannot perceive the "redemptive" quality of the actions of Christ, how can scientific, modern man declaim that such an intervention of God in nature is inconceivable?

Bultmann contends that the doctrines of the pre-existence of Christ as the divine Son of God and of the resurrection can be traced to themes of Gnostic mythology; the first Christians merely assumed these themes as ways of saying that the event of Christ transcends time(because the significance of his existence is able to evoke in us a change in human consciousness producing a deeper understanding of human life and liberating us for self-commitment to God). He does not seem to consider seriously the possibility of there being an eternal Son of God who did in fact hypostatically unite himself to a complete human nature.

Resurrection from the dead is *a priori* esteemed impossible. Miracles are not only declared impossible because contradictory to nature, they are condemned as destructive of true faith. Bultmann seems to be asserting that the divinity of Christ, his miracles, and his resurrection are myths which were useful and meaningful to Christians of another era, whose faith was pre-scientific and rather childlike. Today, belief in miracles must be eliminated. Miracles dishonor faith, for they merely represent an attempt to replace the risk inherent in true belief by substitution of supernatural "proofs." The "pre-existence" of Christ and his "resurrection" can be retained if properly interpreted: they are not part of the historical reality of Jesus but are modes of expressing the invisible activity of God who operates through Christ.

This position has the appearance of being fundamentally gratuitous. It is not based on a scientific examination of the New Testament texts themselves, but is an interpretation of the gospel flowing out of an exaggerated conception of the influence of Gnosticism on the first Christians, and the supposition that the miraculous is untenable for modern man.

More or less recent New Testament research has shown that the gospels are much more primitive and authentic in composition than Bultmann has suggested. Rather than the New Testament writers being influenced by the Gnostics, the dependency could very well be in the inverse sense. In any event, the pre-existence of Christ and his resurrection are clearly attested by the New Testament as *factual*. There is no hint that the first Christians considered these to be "modes of expression" rather than reality. The New Testament asserts without qualification that Jesus is the eternal Son of God, that, in effect, he rose from the dead. This is the Jesus of history and this is the Christ of faith. They are one and the same. There are, to be sure, myths about Jesus in the New Testament, but Bultmann has far from proven that the divinity of Christ or his resurrection are mythological.

At the same time, nevertheless, because the latter are presented as objects of faith, these aspects of the mystery of Christ escape verification. No method of criticism, biblical or historical, can now touch the preexistence of Christ or his resurrection. The first Christians believed that God became man, that the Word died and rose from the dead, and that he will come to judge the living and the dead. This is the Christian faith; it cannot be proved, disproved, or "interpreted." This is the faith that is a matter of decision.

The question, then, is: how great is our faith? How close to man has God willed to come? How much has he desired to do for our salvation? What *essentially* was the original Christian belief about these matters? For this too should be our belief.

It is paradoxical that in his ambition to rescue faith from inauthenticity, Bultmann has unwarrantedly limited its scope and the commitment it demands. When it is proposed to us today that a certain human being was also a divine person, that this person worked numerous miracles, and that ultimately he even rose from the dead, none of this makes faith any easier nor decreases its risk. All of these things, as aspects of Christ, form part of the object of faith and demand more of a "risk" on our part. If modern man chooses to say that they are "utterly inconceivable," this does not make them any the less conceivable or possible; it simply means that modern man chooses not to believe what Christianity has always proclaimed as revealed truth. This is no condemnation of the New Testament, but a sad reflection on the shallowness of "scientific," modern man who has lost his sense of the supernatural and his realization of just how much God has loved him.

Even though the picture of Christ which Bultmann draws for us is in certain respects only a faint sketch of the real Christ, he does cause us to focus our attention on a vitally important point: Jesus is indeed a person who transcends time, whose being is thoroughly eschatological. The words, concepts, and traditions of any specific era are by their nature incapable of ever capturing the whole of Christ. Bultmann is quite correct, therefore, in maintaining that (at least in certain instances) the New Testament notion of atonement is too juridical and static. We receive the idea from the Scriptures that when we sin we place ourselves in debt to God and that Christ sacrificed himself to pay our debt. But is the New Testament *interpretation* of the meaning of Christ's redemptive activity necessarily definitive?

In other words, is the juridical explanation of salvation the best possible explanation, or is it simply a mode of exposition which was satisfactory for early Christians, but one upon which we can greatly improve? We might ask: were we "redeemed" by the death and resurrection of Christ, or were these events, in conjunction with the entire life of Jesus, God's way of proclaiming to us that he had forgiven us and reconciled us to himself?

This may appear to be a fine distinction, but it significantly affects the orientation of our appreciation of the economy of salvation. By sin man is guilty of much more than creating a debt. Reduction of God to a creditor does not today seem to be a very theologically satisfying insight into the nature of God and the evil of sin. Sin disrupts a personal relationship, it alienates man from God. When God forgives man, he takes the initiative to reestablish the bond that has been shattered. When Christ sacrificed himself for us, therefore, it was not only to *pay* our debt or to *earn* our reconciliation, as to *communicate* to us the forgiveness freely granted by God, to *manifest* to us that it was God's will to forgive us.

Our role is that of participating in Christ's action through our faith in the efficacy of the testimony of his life, and of offering our own witness by sharing his cross. This interpretation of the redemptive significance of Jesus Christ is perhaps something of a demythologization (with respect to the excessively juridical outlook of the early Christians), but it is intended to complement the New Testament perspective and not to reject it.

When all is said and done, it might be admitted that the Lord is a myth, but "myth" here is applied analogically. We have been speaking of mythology in terms of ways of thinking, of manners of expression. Why not speak of a mythical mode of *being?* For Bultmann, mythology is "use of imagery to express the other worldly in terms of this world and the divine in terms of human life." Is not Jesus Christ *the* expression of the otherworldly, the divine, through a human nature and a human life?

The invisible cannot make itself visible. The divine cannot make itself human. But is there any more emphatic expression of love conceivable through which God, on this side of eternity, could reveal himself to man than by becoming Incarnate? If the Lord, in this special sense, then, is myth, is it surprising that his life should be described in "mythological" terms? No other portrayal of his existence would be authentic. Thus, in some instances not demythologization but understanding of the myth is called for, and in others we can only stand in faith and wonder at the depth and beauty of the myth which surpasses all understanding.

In *Kerygma and Myth* Helmut Thielick concludes a critical analysis of Bultmann's efforts to demythologize with the observation:

> In examining Bultmann's thesis and his personal orthodoxy care should be maintained to avoid anything like a heresy hunt. This is pioneer work, and there are bound to be casualities on the way. The Church should rather keep in view Bultmann's ultimate objective, which is to secure a firm basis for her own proclamation . . . . How far can the theologian go without incurring the penalty of excommunication for unorthodoxy? The criterion is never, or very rarely, whether we are travelling on the same road, but whether, as we travel along our different roads, we all look towards the same goal. It is not the road which determines our communion with the Church, but our direction, not the steps we tread, but the end on which our eyes are fixed. [44]

44. *Ibid.,* p. 174.

Catholic orthodoxy, of course, does not permit us to accept this statement without qualification, for we must insist that if Christ himself has laid out the road, and if he has entrusted his Church with the authority to point out that road, it does make a difference whether we are on that particular road or not. Christianity is the way, and it is the way God has fashioned, not a road that man is free to construct for himself. Nevertheless, we should not be too anxious to narrow that way excessively.

It should be possible for many different individuals with many divergent views to travel along the same way to the same goal. When someone's convictions differ widely from our own, our initial instinct should be to look for the value in what he has to say and not to begin to speculate immediately about the dangers to which his ideas may expose us. In this regard, therefore, Rudolf Bultmann should be appreciated for his endeavors to make our reading of the New Testament a more personal and meaningful encounter with the Word of God.[45]

* * *

Earlier in our study, we noted that the liberal, rationalistic exegesis of the late nineteenth century virtually rejected the gospels as historical accounts of the words and actions of Jesus. Although Bultmann also introduces an apparent dichotomy between the Jesus of history and the Christ of faith, he explicitly declares his opposition to the above liberalism, for it discards not only mythology but the kerygma itself. In a sense, Bultmann's attempt to save the kerygma constitutes an attempt to save something of the historical Jesus with whom the kerygma has to have some contact if it is to be deemed of any value. Brown points out that Bultmann has written many pages about the historical Jesus and his words;[46] he quotes R. H. Fuller to the effect that "there would seem to be some lines therefore in Bultmann's

45. Cf. P. Joseph Cahill, "Miscellanea Biblica — Rudolf Bultmann's Concept of Revelation," *Catholic Biblical Quarterly*, July 1962, pp. 297-306.

46. Brown, *loc. cit.*, p. 6.

thought which suggest that concern with the historical Jesus is both legitimate and possible." [47]

This concern has become that of the post-Bultmannians and has been concretized in a "new quest" for the historical Jesus. The trend to establish greater contact with the Jesus of history is discernible in the writings of such exegetes of the Bultmannian school as Ernst Käsemann, Günther Bornkamm, Hans Conzelmann, and James M. Robinson. [48]

The new quest considers the sources of the gospel as kerygma which announces to us how the primitive Christian community believed and preached Jesus as the Lord. This approach also embodies a special concept of history. Evangelical history is no longer treated as a pure science. "This history treats of facts and causes and of the externals of events, but it is even more interested in what Collingwood [49] calls the 'inside' of events. Here the historian thinks himself into the action to discern the thought of the agent. Not a clinical observation of what happened but an existential relation between the historian and the event is called for." [50]

While Bultmann endeavored to "save" the kerygma, his followers go still further. They are interested in showing that the portrait of Jesus which we receive in the kerygma faithfully represents the historical Jesus. These scholars seek to discover not only how the primitive Church understood Jesus, but how he understood himself. It is the contention of the new quest that the kerygma as presented by the Church in the gospels faithfully continues Jesus' self-understanding. This does not imply an attempt to reconstruct an ordinary biography of Jesus, but to "encounter the whole person of Jesus through the individual

---

47. R. H. Fuller, *The New Testament in Current Study*, Charles Scribner's Sons, New York, 1962, p. 32.

48. Brown, *loc. cit.*, pp. 6-7; Also P. Joseph Cahill, "Rudolf Bultmann and Post-Bultmann Tendencies," *Catholic Biblical Quarterly*, April 1964, pp. 153-78.

49. R. G. Collingwood, *The Idea of History*, Oxford, 1946.

50. Brown, *loc. cit.*, p. 7.

sayings and actions in which Jesus' intention and selfhood are latent." [51]

Although the methodology employed in this research considerably limits what can be accepted with "certitude" as authentically pertaining to the Jesus of history, it remains nonetheless encouraging to observe this concern for what Jesus really was. Brown notes, however, that while in 1959 Robinson introduced the new quest with optimism, [52] some of the post-Bultmannians have manifested misgivings about the new quest and Robinson has written: "... the foundation of the Bultmannian system which gave its great strength in post-war Germany — its grounding in *avant garde* critical New Testament scholarship and in the latest philosophical trends in German culture — had already by 1961 lost their solidity." [53]

Recent developments in the philosophical thought of Heidegger have also had their influence on the current approach of at least some of the post-Bultmannians to scriptural research. Their new tendency has its roots in a fresh and profound insight into the complex problem of "hermeneutic." In this context hermeneutic is related to language: "to being's expression of itself and to man's understanding of that expression." [54] When hermeneutic is directed toward the Bible, the entire process of God's speaking to us is involved: God's Word itself, the way it is expressed in Scripture, its interpretation across the ages, the way it is preached today. This trend would seem to promise to have definite repercussions on the fate of demythologization.

For Bultmann, the text of the New Testament to the degree it is mythical is unintelligible to modern man and must be "interpreted"; untenable mythical elements must be eliminated. In light of modern man's understanding of himself the New Testament's understanding of Christ is revised. In the post-Bultmannian

---

51. *Ibid.*, p. 9.
52. James M. Robinson, *A New Quest of the Historical Jesus*, S. C. M. Press, London, 1959.
53. As cited by Brown, *loc. cit.*, p. 13.
54. *Ibid.*, p. 18.

hermeneutic the process is to a degree reversed: the self-understanding offered by the New Testament presents us with a criterion for criticism of our understanding of ourselves. The language used by the first Christians, then, is accorded deeper respect. "The problem seems to be less of demythologizing language so that Scripture is *brought up* to modern man and more of criticizing modern man with his distorted relationship to himself so that he is *brought back* to Scripture." [55]

For a number of pages now we have been sampling some of the challenges thrown up against the traditional manner of interpreting the New Testament. We detected in our summary of a few currents of nineteenth-century thought a growing awareness that New Testament exegesis in the past had been far too naive. This brought about an opposite reaction of extreme liberalism in the treatment of the historical value of the gospels. In the twentieth century we have seen Protestant biblical criticism make valuable contributions to the study of the New Testament. Although the results of the "new quest" have been unfortunately slight, the post-Bultmannian trend gives reason to hope that a still greater appreciation of the Jesus of history will be forthcoming.

The new emphasis on hermeneutic and the fact that God expresses to man his Being through his Word in Scripture may prove especially fruitful. And this brings up the inevitable question: what is the position of Catholic biblical criticism in face of all the issues that have been raised? A thorough answer to this question is not within the scope of the present work, but the majority of the subsequent pages will be devoted to several samples of what contemporary Catholic biblical scholarship is doing. A brief consideration of the Pontifical Biblical Commission's *Instruction on the Historical Truth of the Gospels* will furnish a preamble for this study.

---

55. Brown citing E. Fuchs, *loc. cit.*, p. 19.

CHAPTER THREE

THE INSTRUCTION OF THE BIBLICAL COMMISSION ON THE HISTORICAL TRUTH OF THE GOSPELS AND GOSPEL HISTORICITY

In the past, for the most part Catholic exegesis has adhered to a traditional, conservative approach to the study of the Bible. This has been especially true with regard to the question of the historicity of the gospels. In recent years, however, Catholic scholars have enjoyed a greater freedom in their research, and have pondered more carefully the values to be found in perspectives such as those of Bultmann and his disciples.

As Protestant exegesis has helped us to appreciate the influence of the primitive Church in the emergence of the gospel and to grasp the eschatological quality of the New Testament proclamation, it is to be hoped that a more exacting and scientific appraisal of the New Testament by Catholic scholars may lead to a keener realization of the inseparability of the Jesus of history and the Christ of Faith.

The *Instruction on the Historical Truth of the Gospels* issued by the Pontifical Biblical Commission on April 21, 1964, in its constructive tone and progressive outlook reflects the advances that have been made in New Testament study by contemporary Catholic scholars, and provides a basis for looking to the future with great expectation. A few excerpts from the Instruction may serve to illustrate this point:

It is highly gratifying that the Church today can number so many faithful sons, possessed of that proficiency in matters biblical which is required at the present time, who have responded to the call of the Supreme Pontiffs and are devoting themselves wholeheartedly and with unflagging energy to their weighty and exacting task. "And all other children of the Church should bear in mind that the efforts of these valiant laborers in the vineyard of the Lord are to be judged not only with fairness and justice, but also with the greatest of charity" (*Divino afflante Spiritu,* E. B., p. 564), for even interpreters of the highest reputation, such as Jerome himself, in their endeavors to clear up certain more difficult points, have on occasion arrived at results which were far from happy. (Cf. *Spiritus Paraclitus,* E. B., p. 451.) [1]

The Commission goes on to make the following points:

1. The Catholic exegete, under the guidance of the Church, must turn to account all the resources for the understanding of the sacred text which have been put at his disposal by previous interpreters, especially the holy Fathers and Doctors of the Church, whose labors it is for him to take up and to carry on. In order to bring out with fullest clarity the enduring truth and authority of the Gospels he must, whilst carefully observing the rules of rational and of Catholic hermeneutics, make skillful use of the new aids to exegesis, especially those which the historical method, taken in its widest sense, has provided; that method, namely, which minutely investigates sources, determining their nature and bearing, and availing itself of the findings of textual criticism, literary criticism, and linguistic studies ....

In appropriate cases the interpreter is free to seek out what sound elements there are in "the Method of Form History,"

---

1. *Instruction on the Historical Truth of the Gospels,* authorized English translation as published in the *Catholic Biblical Quarterly,* July 1964, p. 305.

and these he can duly make use of to gain a fuller understanding of the Gospels. He must be circumspect in doing so, however, because the method in question is often found alloyed with principles of a philosophical or theological nature which are quite inadmissible . . . .

2. In order to determine correctly the trustworthiness of what is transmitted in the Gospels, the interpreter must take careful note of the three stages of tradition by which the teaching and the life of Jesus have come down to us. [2]

These three stages are summed up as follows:

Christ our Lord attached to himself certain chosen disciples who had followed him from the beginning, who had seen his works and had heard his words, and thus were qualified to become witnesses of his life and teaching . . . .

The Apostles bearing testimony to Jesus, proclaimed first and foremost the death and resurrection of the Lord, faithfully recounting his life and words and, as regards the manner of their preaching, taking into account the circumstances of their hearers. After Jesus had risen from the dead, and when his divinity was clearly perceived, the faith of the disciples, far from blotting out the remembrance of the events that had happened, rather consolidated it, since their faith was based on what Jesus had done and taught . . . . It need not be denied that the Apostles, when handing on to their hearers the things which in actual fact the Lord had said and done, did so in the light of that fuller understanding which they enjoyed as a result of being schooled by the glorious things accomplished in Christ, and of being illumined by the Spirit of Truth . . . they in turn interpreted his (Jesus') words and deeds according to the needs of their hearers.

In so doing they deployed various manners of speaking: catecheses, narratives, testimonies, hymns, doxologies, prayers

---

2. *Ibid.*, pp. 306-7.

and any other such literary forms as were customarily employed in Sacred Scripture and by people of that time.

The sacred authors, for the benefit of the churches, took this earliest body of instruction, which had been handed on orally at first and then in writing — for many soon set their hands to "drawing up a narrative" (cf. Lk. 1:1) of matters concern- the Lord Jesus — and set it down in the four Gospels. In doing this each of them followed a method suitable to the special purpose which he had in view.... For, out of the material which they had received, the sacred authors selected especially those items which were adapted to the varied circumstances of the faithful as well as to the end which they themselves wished to attain; ... since the meaning of a statement depends, amongst other things, on the place which it has in a given sequence, the Evangelists, in handing on the words or the deeds of our Savior, explained them for the advantage of their readers by respectively setting them, one Evangelist in one context, another in another.... For the truth of the narrative is not affected in the slightest by the fact that the Evangelists report the sayings or the doings of our Lord in a different order, and that they use different words to express what He said, not keeping to the very letter, but nevertheless preserving the sense....

Unless the exegete, then, pays attention to all those factors which have a bearing on the origin and composition of the Gospels, and makes due use of the acceptable findings of modern research, he will fail in his duty of ascertaining what the intentions of the sacred writers were, and what it is that they have actually said. The results of recent study have made it clear that the teachings and the life of Jesus were not simply recounted for the mere purpose of being kept in remembrance, but were "preached" in such a way as to furnish the Church with the foundation on which to build up faith and morals. It follows that the interpreter who subjects the testimony of the Evangelists to persevering scrutiny will be in a position to shed further light on the enduring theological value of the Gospels, and to throw into clearest relief the vital importance of the Church's interpretation. [3]

The Instruction adds the observation that there remain many problems to be investigated, many serious questions to be answered. It encourages the Catholic exegete to exercise freely his intelligence and skill in carrying out this task which is of the gravest significance. But it also cautions the interpreter to bear in mind, while he makes use of all the scientific instruments at his disposal, "that when the Apostles proclaimed the Good Tidings they were filled with the Holy Spirit, that the Gospels were written under the inspiration of the Holy Spirit, and that it was he who preserved their authors immune from all error." [4]

It will be noted that the Instruction published by the Biblical Commission lays special stress on the three stages involved in the formation of the gospels. Because an understanding of the way in which the gospels were formed has a great deal to do with appreciating the historicity of Jesus himself, it is essential to our purpose to consider more adequately the question of how the life and teachings of Jesus Christ have been handed down to us.

A. THE FORMATION OF THE GOSPELS

A schematic "reconstruction of the development of the gospel material, from the period of oral tradition to that of the canonical gospels, made in the spirit of the recent *Instruction of the Pontifical Commission*" has been proffered by G. T. Montague, S.M., in his article "The Emergence of the Gospels." [5] Since his approach is quite typical of that being used by Catholic New Testament scholars today, we offer a synopsis of his presentation here.

Biblical scholarship distinguishes three successive stages in the formation of our gospels: (1) a lengthy period of oral tradition;

---

3. *Ibid.,* pp. 307-9.
4. *Ibid.,* p. 310.
5. G. T. Montague, S.M., "The Emergence of the Gospels," *The Bible Today,* November 1964, pp. 892-904.

(2) the writing of the first sketches; (3) the final composition of each of the canonical gosepls. How did each of these stages contribute to the ultimate form of the gospels?

The Period of Oral Tradition

We know that approximately thirty years elapsed between the Ascension of Jesus and the writing of the gospel of Mark which the majority of commentators hold to be the oldest of the gospels. During much of this period, therefore, the works of Jesus and the words he had spoken were transmitted orally. St. Paul's letters, some of which were written before our gospels, indicate that the gospel was handed down in oral form to the Christians with whom he had contact. [6] The prologue of Luke's gospel mentions the "tradition" handed down by the original eyewitnesses and servants of the Word. [7] If the Gospel existed in oral form for so long a time, this fact imposes upon us two questions: (a) How did the various material about Christ find its way into the oral tradition? (b) How did oral tradition shape the form of this material?

a) In response to the first question, New Testament research has shown that practical needs had much to do with the choice of materials. The apostles and disciples had received from Christ the commission to preach the gospel. This meant that first of all the Jews had to be convinced that Jesus "in his life and death, and resurrection, was really the culmination of all the sacred history of the people of God." [8]

Since the original Christian community regarded the resurrection as the redemptive event par excellence, the eyewitness accounts of the Lord's resurrection assumed primary importance. The oral tradition naturally conserved this testimony as an essential part of the preaching about Jesus.

But to explain the significance of the resurrection, it was

---

6. Cf. I Cor. 15:1-11.
7. Lk. 1:1.
8. Montague, *op. cit.,* p. 893.

necessary to give some introductory material concerned with the life and death of Jesus that led up to it. Thus a sketch of his public ministry was included as a background for the recounting of the passion, death, and resurrection.

As these central points of the history of our Lord were related over and over, in a type of catechetical approach, they gradually began to fall into a pattern. We encounter what is perhaps the classic instance of this pattern in the sermons of Peter, which are reflected above all by the gospel of Mark, but whose general outline is embraced also by Matthew and Luke. First, there is the preparation of Jesus for his ministry, and his baptism in Judea; this is followed by the ministry in Galilee; next comes the journey from Galilee to Jerusalem; then follow the events of Holy Week. It is also Peter's sermons [9] that reveal to us the nucleus of the first preaching about Christ, the kerygma: Jesus of Nazareth — attested to by God through many miracles — delivered up according to divine plan — rejected and crucified by the Jews — raised from the dead by God who had sent him in fulfillment of what he had promised through the prophets. The same basic schema underlies the speech of Stephen [10] and the catechesis of Paul.[11]

Besides being sent forth to announce the gospel, the first Christians were commanded by Christ to celebrate the Eucharistic meal: "Do this in remembrance of me." This gave rise to another need: when the community assembled for "the breaking of the bread," they desired to relive as exactly as possible the events of that Last Supper. Again the memories of eyewitnesses were repeated over and over, so that very soon a more or less stereotyped account of the institution of the Eucharist appeared. This account thus emerged from the primitive Christian liturgy, a liturgy that exercised an important influence on the shaping of the entirety of the narrations of the passion.

The importance of the Eucharist was such that some of the

---

9. Cf. Acts 2:3.
10. Acts 10.
11. Cf. Acts 13.

other events in the life of Jesus were remembered and conserved primarily because of their bearing on its institution. For example, because the gestures of Christ and his miraculous intervention to provide nourishment were appreciated as prefigurations of the Eucharistic banquet, the story of the multiplication of the loaves was retold time and again as part of the oral tradition.

A considerable amount of the gospel material is comprised of "Pronouncement Stories." When a practical problem would arise in the early Chritsian community, the question was naturally asked: what did Jesus say that might help us resolve this difficulty? One of Jesus' sayings would then be recalled and used in a story which accented his solution to the problem.

We might mention a few of the issues that had to be faced. To fulfill their mission it was necessary for the disciples to circulate with "publicans and sinners." This type of behavior had to be justified against the attacks of the Jews. Thus some of the encounters of Jesus with the Jews and what he said on these occasions were brought to mind. The question of whether or not the followers of Jesus should pay taxes may lie behind the preservation of the statement: "Render to Caesar the things that are Caesar's . . . ." [12] The Christian practice of observing Sunday as the Lord's Day probably contributed to the emphasis placed on the fact that "the Son of Man is Lord even of the Sabbath." [13] The mutual relations between the Christians themselves and their need to resolve conflicts doubtlessly had something to do with the conservation of our Lord's words on fraternal charity. This could very well explain why in Matthew 18 we read an entire sequence of episodes revealing how we should deal with our neighbor.

Another literary form that was quite important was the miracle story. The accounts of the miracles of Jesus were used for several purposes. They were valuable in preaching because they confirmed the authenticity of Jesus as the emissary of God, and

---

12. Mk. 12:13.
13. Mk. 2:27-28.

in certain instances pointed to his divine origin. Matthew and Luke handle Jesus' miracles in such a manner as to place in relief his great compassion, and hence to portray him as being identical with the Suffering Servant of Yahweh. [14] His miracles of "touch" were cherished by the Church as symbolical of his spiritual healing power exercised through the sacraments.

A special problem is created by the traditions underlying the first two chapters of Matthew and Luke. At first the infancy of Jesus, being so far removed from the central events of Holy Week and not having any special value for preaching, did not hold a great deal of interest for the Church. But gradually the question of the origin of Jesus took on importance. In this way the fact of the Virgin birth and the role played by Mary began to come to light. Since according to the Jewish concept of history, which included an awareness of God's plan to save his people, all of the past had its influence on the present and foreshadowed it, it was a frequent practice to describe the saving events of the present (in this case the infancy of Jesus) in terms of God's interventions to save his people in the past. Hence, Old Testament events and thought patterns became very much a part of the narration of the first years of Jesus. For instance, in Matthew the rescue of Jesus (the new Moses?) from Herod is reminiscent of the infant Moses' escape from the edict of the Pharaoh. [15] And in Luke the interventions of the angel Gabriel recall vividly the appearances of the same angel in Daniel.

In summing up the first section of his article, Montague observes that:

> these few examples, and they are far from being exhaustive, suffice to illustrate the variety of literary forms found in the Gospels. They reflect the complexity of the life of the early Church, for it was in this life and of this life that they were born. Not that the basic materials were created by the Church; the Gospels cannot be explained without the historical

---

14. Cf. Is. 53; Mt. 8:16 ff.
15. Ex. 1:22.

person of Jesus at their center. But the practical needs of the Church did dictate what was important to keep. [16]

b) Our second question was directed to the problem of how oral tradition contributed to the *shaping* of the gospel material. Montague remarks that much of the latter is found to be in oral style. "The discourses of our Lord, his pronouncements and his sayings, constantly reveal an oral style." [17]   In the gospel "declarations" this style is especially apparent in the rhythm of phrases and the use of parallelism. The same oral style is characteristic of the gospel "narratives." The stories are not composed of balanced sentences and subordinate clauses, as would be the case if they had originated in written form; rather, the narratives abound in brief sentences and abrupt clauses which are not subordinated, but simply connected by and . . . and . . . and.

The mark of oral style is also imprinted upon the gospels by various techniques employed to aid in memorization. There is frequent use of alliteration, assonance, play on words; "inclusion," a literary arrangement by which a discourse begins and concludes with the same word or idea, often occurs; repetition of key words was another favorite device; finally, there was the use of "hook words": the same word served as a basis for connecting declarations which in themselves had no relationship in content.

The fact that parallel accounts of the same event recounted in two or more gospels sometimes display significant differences can also on occasion be traced to the influence of oral tradition. In some cases "the preachers of the Gospel did not hesitate to adapt the words of Jesus to the psychology and customs of their hearers. Their interest in the words of Jesus was not for what those words meant to the hearers of a remote Palestine town but for what they meant *here and now* . . ." to the audience being addressed. [18] The original message of Jesus was substantially

---

16. Montague, *op. cit.,* p. 897.
17. *Ibid.,* p. 897.
18. *Ibid.,* p. 900.

preserved, but in being communicated to a new group of hearers, it was adapted in the way he himself would have done. Those who proclaimed the gospel felt that making use of this freedom was the only way to remain faithful to the message of Jesus.

As Montague indicates, "we find two tendencies in the apostolic preaching: a scrupulous fidelity to the message of Jesus, a reverence for his words, a desire to have them as they fell from his own lips; and yet a simple and unabashed freedom in adapting them to the living situation in the Church." [19] This twofold tendency helps explain why at times the words the gospel tradition gives us are those of Jesus himself, while in other instances words which are attributed to Jesus are in reality simply the Church's more explicit interpretation of some portion of his teaching. We can understand the Church's taking this liberty if we appreciate its conviction that it was preaching a *living* message, and that it had received the Holy Spirit precisely for the purpose of enabling it "to bring out the fullness of meaning in Jesus' words and deeds." [20]

It was not possible, however, for the early Church to continue for a very long time without coming up against the need to commit to writing certain elements of the oral tradition. The gospels as we have them today betray the presence of sections which in written form pre-existed the actual gospels. This brings us, then, to the second stage of the formation of the gospels.

The History of the Composition of the First Written Sketches

Between the period which witnessed the condensation of oral tradition and the ultimate stage in which the gospels in their final form emerged, there was an intermediary period rather complex in nature. Oral tradition was not simply traced down and put into writing by the evangelists, any more than they merely recorded what they themselves had witnessed and remembered.

Here and there, according to specific needs, parts of the oral

---

19. *Ibid.*
20. *Ibid.*, p. 901.

tradition were placed in written form. For example, since the account of the passion and death of Christ was so vital to the cult of the first Christians, it must have been committed to writing at an early date, for as Montague observes: "it was desirable to have a written form which could be regularly followed, and in which many of the details could be preserved." [21]

Prior to the composition of the gospels, various communities also found it useful to gather together in a written document several episodes pertaining to some particular aspect of our Lord's life. Thus the apologetical aim of demonstrating how the Master was unjustly pursued by the hatred of those who were unwilling to accept his doctrine resulted in the collection of a series of *controversies* over the Law between Jesus and the Scribes and Pharisees and the people. We find a collection of this kind inserted in Mark's gospel, 2:1-3:6.

Lists of the important *miracles* of the Lord were also drawn up, no doubt as aids in preaching. Perhaps one of these was used in the composition of chapter 8, verses 1 to 17 of Matthew's gospel. At other times the *teachings* of Christ were grouped into written sketches. As instances of this we have the Sermon on the Mount, Matthew 5:1-7:28, which is a collection of instructions of our Lord arranged to give the effect of a "typical" sermon, and the "section on the loaves," Mark 6:31-8:26. The discernment of these written sections which pre-existed the gospels is of definite importance, because they reveal to us central issues upon which the primitive communities focused their attention.

It might be objected: how can these "pre-written" sections be recognized in the gospels? How do we know that artificial groupings are not simply the result of the work done by the evangelists themselves upon the oral traditions passed on to them? As a matter of fact, in the past several years the trend known in biblical terminology as *Redaktions-geschichte,* a study of the way in which the gospels themselves were redacted, has intimated that possibly the evangelists have made more of a contribution

---

21. *Ibid.*

to the formation of the gospels than was believed in the recent past dominated by the *Formgeschichte* perspective. [22]

But to answer the question, there is a variety of evidence pointing to the existence of written sources anterior to the gospels. Luke himself testifies that such documents circulated among the disciples of Christ, [23] and in his gospel he obviously makes use of such sources: for instance, the section concerned with the journey from Galilee to Jerusalem, in which we find an abundance of material not related by any of the other gospels, Luke 9:51-18: 14; and in the Acts: a document describing the original community at Jerusalem, the Acts of Peter, the Acts of Philip, etc. One of the things that most clearly shows that Luke uses and even intertwines written sources placed in his hands, is the presence of occasional apparent contradictions in his text. [24] When we come to realize that he is combining different sources which offer divergent viewpoints, the "contradictions" become intelligible. Moreover, when we are suddenly transported in Luke's gospel from his eloquent Greek to a style that is awkward and frequently suggests an Aramaic substratum, it seems quite reasonable to conclude that Luke is quoting from one of his written sources.

There are still other indications of the evangelist's use of pre-existent written sources. Often in reading the gospels we encounter sudden "jumps"; if the evangelist himself were composing according to information he had received through oral tradition, it seems that he would have furnished smoother transitions from one passage to another. The abrupt "jumps" show that he desires to be faithful to the written sources he is following, and so he does not alter them in combining them. And then, certain elements appear in rather strange places in the synoptic discourses. Not even the use of the "hook word" can explain the juxtaposition of some statements which in themselves are not related. In these cases we must surmise that the evangelist had

---

22. Cf. Barnabas M. Ahern, C.P., "The Gospels in Light of Modern Research," *Chicago Studies*, Spring 1962, pp. 5-16.

23. Lk. 1:1.

24. Cf. Luke's treatment of the Council of Jerusalem in Acts 15.

come across a saying of Jesus which he wished to preserve, and simply had to fit it in as best he could.

What we have been saying might be clarified by considering more at length a particular episode from the gospel of Matthew, an episode which is perfectly isolated from the context surrounding it. The complete lack of relationship of this passage, Matthew 8:1-4, with what precedes and follows it indicates that it must have been an independent literary unit which Matthew chose to insert at this point. In Matthew 8:1 we see that Jesus has terminated the Sermon on the Mount, 7:28, and descends from the mountain. But verse 2 tells us that while Jesus is being followed by a great crowd, a leper approaches him. Jesus heals him and commands him not to say anything to anyone about this. Historically speaking, it is extremely unlikely that a leper would come to Jesus while he was surrounded by a crowd; and why the directive: "Say nothing to anyone"? Verse 5, "As he entered Capharnaum . . ." suddenly takes us to a totally different scene. When we find the same story of the cure of the leper in Mark's gospel, 1:40-45, but in a very different context — and probably the authentic one — we are confirmed in our belief that Matthew 8:1-4 represents the insertion of a pre-existent written account of one of our Lord's miracles.

We have by no means presented the full complexity of the problem of the written sources with which the evangelists worked, but a single closing observation must suffice for our consideration of this aspect of the formation of the gospels. Not only did the writers of the gospels make use of written documents, these very documents in some cases had their own involved history. To illustrate, the Sermon on the Mount was not necessarily one document which Matthew incorporated; he could have composed it by selecting material from several written sources at his disposal, or parts of it could have already been written down independently and put together by someone else before finding their way into the hands of Matthew. The study of the prehistory of what could be called the "prologue" of the Sermon, the Beatitudes, is in itself quite a task. J. Dupont has presented evidence that in their original form, the Beatitudes constituted a proclamation of a prophetic type, announcing the realization of the messianic promises. [25] In Luke the teaching assumes a sapiential demeanor; in Matthew the appeal is to more of a moral ideal of perfection. Hence, the traditions behind the gospels were adapted to the needs and the preoccupations of the milieux in which present texts ultimately were fixed. This adaptation, as we have noted previously, reveals the consciousness which the first Christians had of the living value possessed by the words of the Lord.

We have now examined two phases in the development of the gospels. We have seen the contribution made by oral tradition and have observed how parts of this tradition were committed to writing. No doubt, there was even further literary contact between many of the written sources before they came to serve the purposes of the evangelists. But eventually the task fell upon the men we know as Mark, Matthew, Luke, and John to collect the essential oral tradition, to seek out and sort the written documentation, and finally to produce our gospels. Let us now reflect for a few moments on that role played by our composers in the last stage of the formation of the gospels.

The Inspired Contribution of Each Evangelist

The article of Montague delineates very succinctly and yet quite clearly the way in which we should evaluate the personal work of the evangelists. We quote from his conclusions at some length. [26]

> At this point we are in a position to appreciate better the situation in which each evangelist found himself when he undertook to write. Only John and Matthew had been intimate associates of Jesus, and our present canonical *Matthew* is the work of some later editor. Each evangelist found himself faced with a wealth of oral traditions, handed down for

---

25. J. Dupont, *Les Béatitudes, I. Le problème littéraire: Les deux versions du Sermon sur la montagne et des Beatitudes*, Bruges-Louvain, 1958.

26. Montague, *op. cit.*, pp. 902-4.

thirty or forty years in different communities and representing different preoccupations as well as different traditions. He also had at hand written sketches of varied provenance. Some of these were large, self-contained units; others were highly fragmentary. It was a question of organizing this material in view of the particular author's purpose.

Mark's plan is as simple as his narrative; he depends largely on the graphic souvenirs of Peter to relate the facts which show Jesus to be the Son of God.

His gospel seems to fall naturally into two main sections. The first extends from 1:14 to 8:30; it could be designated "the mystery of the Messiah," for it terminates with the confession of Peter that Jesus is the Christ (8:29). The second covers 8:31 to 16:8; it might be entitled "the mystery of the Son of Man," and seems to find its focal point in the centurion's confession on Calvary: "Truly this man was the Son of God!" (15:39). Thus for Mark, the economy of revelation can be broken down into two characteristic periods, one in which Jesus revealed himself to a few privileged individuals as the Messiah, while jealously guarding the secret from others, and another in which his mysterious mission as Son of Man is proclaimed to all.

The redactor of *Matthew* had *Mark* to work with, plus a wealth of discourse material. He eliminates many of Mark's graphic narrative details as irrelevant, and groups his materials in a highly artificial and artistic way, with a distinct taste for symmetry — in fact, the whole structure of his Gospel shows a symmetrical paralleling of narrative and sermon leading up to, and away from, the central section — the parables of the Kingdom (chap. 13) — which reflect Matthew's central interest. Jesus is the Emanuel of the messianic age, and his Church is the Kingdom. It is in *Matthew* particularly that we find guidelines for the life of the Church. Little wonder then that *Matthew* should become the favorite Gospel in the early Church, used more than any other for preaching and liturgy.

Luke is, of course, the evangelist of the Gentiles. Possessed of a delicate and sympathetic soul, combining the fineness of an artist with the science and skill of a physician, he more than any other has the interest of a Gentile historian. The event of Jesus and the Church must be inscribed in universal history, the reign of the Caesars and the Romans and Judean governors. Of all the evangelists he has the greatest sense of chronology. He arranges his material so as to bring out the progressive development of the public ministry. But here too the data is organized around a somewhat artificial plan — geography. He wishes to show how the Good News progressed from Jesus' baptism in the Jordan, to Galilee in his ministry there, and then in an almost liturgical procession as he journeyed from Galilee to Jerusalem to consummate his work.

Not pertaining to the "synoptic" gospels, the gospel of John constitutes a case apart. Although the general structure is the same, Jesus begins his ministry after his meeting with John the Baptist — succeeded by activities in Galilee and in Jerusalem — the passion and the resurrection, it is clear that John had his own purpose in writing and is not preoccupied with his predecessors. Feuillet is of the opinion that the fourth gospel seems to be presented as divisible into two books, the first of which, chapters 1 to 12, could be termed "the Book of Signs" and the second, chapters 13 to 20 or 21, "the Book of the Passion." The evangelist views the entire public life of Jesus through the prism of his "Hour," the "Hour" par excellence of Christ being his passion, the setting in motion of his return to his Father, his true glorification. The existence of Jesus, therefore, is partitioned by John into two major periods, the one leading up to the coming of his "Hour," the other dealing with its actual presence. The preparatory manifestation of the Christ, the Word Incarnate, in the course of his public ministry is followed by his supreme manifestation in his life of suffering and glory. John's gospel can indeed be qualified as dynamic, as it describes a relentlessly intensifying movement toward eschatological consummation. [27]

---

27. Cf. A. Feuillet, *Introduction à la Bible*, Vol. 2, p. 624.

Montague continues:

Space does not permit developing each Gospel in detail.
Suffice it to say that each author brought to the Gospel tradition
his own personal touch, used by God in setting down the
apostolic tradition. The picture each evangelist gives us is
not a photograph, but a portrait: each evangelist wished to
bring out some brilliant feature of his Lord.

From what has been said, we see that we cannot expect to
find in the Gospels a biography of Jesus . . . . The Gospels
were not written in that way. They were rather the combining of disparate elements from various periods of Jesus'
life, as they had been handed down orally.

. . . We must not, therefore, conceive of the Gospels *merely*
as documents of history nor *merely* as documents of faith.
They are both, inextricably both. On the one hand, the
Gospels testify to faith in Jesus; they are written by believers
for believers (Lk. 1:2). On the other hand, there is the
constant affirmation that the kerygma is true only in the
measure that the facts are true: "If Christ has not risen, vain
then is our preaching and vain too is your faith" (I Cor. 15:
14). . . .

The inseparable union of history and faith in the Gospels can
be understood only if we realize that the word of God is
preached, not as a dead letter, but as a living reality. The first
missionaries realized this when they adapted the message to
their particular audiences and drove home to their hearers,
not only what Jesus said and did, but what he is saying
and doing right now in the proclamation. Our reading of
the Gospel or hearing it preached is, therefore, anything but
a pastime to titillate our curiosity, literary or historical. It is,
in its very nature, the placing of ourselves in a situation where
the saving acts of a personal God challenge us to choose.
To accept not just the facts but their significance is to believe . . . .

Fortunately for us, the evangelists (and behind them the early Church) give us not only the facts but also what they mean. Thus, we might ... say that the Gospels are portraits that tell us no less about Jesus because they are portraits, but more. That *more* which the pale eye of science cannot see, the loving eye of the spouse of Christ has caught and etched into the portraits she has painted for her children. If we would see all she saw, we too must love. [28]

B. THE HISTORICAL VALUE OF THE GOSPELS

The preceding analysis of the process of the formation of the gospels casts some light upon the question of the historicity of Jesus, and gives evidence to substantiate the assertion that there are no just grounds for divorcing the Jesus of history from the Christ of faith. The oral traditions, the first written sketches, and the gospels in their final form were all directed toward one goal: portraying the Jesus who actually lived, died, and rose from the dead in the most faithful and adequate manner possible.

How could the simple, unsophisticated fishermen of Galilee create a mythical Christ, much less suffer and die for one? How could a community of devoted Jews bring upon themselves excommunication from the religion of their birth and their nation, in order to create an ideology which in many respects was foreign to their most revered traditions? If as much creative liberty were allowed the community and the evangelists as is inferred by such authors as Bultmann, how can this be reconciled with the obvious and sincere attempt made to preserve intact the traditions about Jesus which had been carefully handed down from the very beginning?

But there are other points which can also be made in support of the historical value of the gospels. In the nineteenth century a definition of the "historical" was framed which required that all truly scientific history be founded on documentary evidence furnished by eyewitnesses. When critics proposed that the gospels

28. Montague, *op. cit.*, p. 904.

are not eyewitness accounts, naturally the historicity of the writings of the evangelists was brought into question.

According to this notion of history, unless the evangelists themselves had witnessed the events recounted in their gospels, then the latter could not be trusted as reliable historical documents. This criterion for the "historical," however, has itself now been abandoned. It came to be considered unsatisfactory by the students of profane history even prior to being esteemed defective by the critics of sacred history. Thus, as John L. McKenzie, S.J., has reasoned,

> The historical character of the Gospels is not assured by a demonstration that they are written by Matthew, Mark, Luke, and John, just as it is not weakened if they are not the work of these four men. The question of 'genuinity' in the classic sense of the word is irrelevant to the historical character of the Gospels. Modern interpreters, therefore, look now not to the individual authors (of whom Mark and Luke have withstood criticism), but to the source on which the authors of the Gospels depended whoever they were: the proclamation of Jesus by the first generation of the Church, the living memory of Jesus. The historical value of the Gospels turns not upon whether the individual authors were 'informed and veracious,' but on whether the primitive church was informed and veracious. [29]

Why isn't it particularly important whether or not the four men to whom the gospels are attributed actually wrote them? Although what has been said already at least implicitly answers this question, perhaps a few additional remarks could clarify the matter. As we have seen, the gospels are rooted in tradition, and the origin, character, and functioning of tradition is basically a *social* phenomenon. This means that no individual, not even an evangelist, could authenticate the gospel message. Only the community of the early Christian Church could do this.

---

29. John L. McKenzie, S.J., "Pastoral Apologetics and Modern Exegesis," *Chicago Studies,* Fall 1962, p. 160.

Hence, the composers of the gospels, of the Synoptics in particular, display only a limited amount of individuality. Luke, for example, when he progresses beyond his introductory material, sacrifices his own identity to his material and writes in what can be identified as the "evangelical style." Moreover, as McKenzie remarks, "the three Synoptic Gospels, when set against other ancient literatures, exhibit distinctive common traits; and these traits come from no individual writer. It is the merit of Form Criticism that it has identified the source of evangelical style as the preaching and teaching of the early Church. This Church is in a true and proper sense the author of the Gospel." [30]

Observe that emphasis is placed on the fact that the Church authors the Gospel and not the gospels. Recent New Testament exegesis has shown very convincingly that we should speak of the Gospel before talking about the gospels. As there is "one Lord, one Faith, one Baptism," [31] there is also fundamentally only one Gospel. But who constitutes the Church which stands behind this Faith, this Gospel?

It is by no means an anonymous crowd retailing bits of gossip at random; it is the eyewitnesses and ministers of the word (Lk. 1:2), the witnesses of the Resurrection who were with the company from the baptism of John to the day when the Lord was taken up (Acts 1:21-22). The Gospel is the work of the men who knew Jesus personally and had heard his entire preaching: and the early Church was perfectly aware that its testimony of Jesus could rest upon no other source. In the apostolic witness it had the only link between Jesus and those who believed in him because of this witness. The security of faith did not repose upon individual persons, however unimpeachable their information and veracity, but upon the entire apostolic witness, the group which had no other principle of unity besides Jesus himself. The existence of the Church was the supreme witness to the reality of Jesus. [32]

---

32. McKenzie, *op. cit.*, p. 164.
30. *Ibid.*, p. 163.
31. Eph. 4:6.

Because the apostolic witness plays such a vital part in the formation and authentication of our gospels, then, if we wish to appreciate the gospels for what they are, we must endeavor to "see" Jesus Christ as the apostles and first disciples "saw" him. For the Christ whom they experienced could not really be grasped by human vision, nor could what he was be expressed in human language. They could only relate what he said, sometimes elaborating upon the original words, in such a way as to proclaim their faith in who he was and is. The historical Jesus, because he was the God-Man, transcended their every effort to portray him. This is the Lord and Christ whom we should strive to attain as we meditate the gospels.

When we take the trouble to gaze beneath the surface of the gospels, we discover so much more about our Lord. We begin to see him as the first Christians did, we begin to *sense* what they were trying to enunciate through their traditions. The external deeds of our Lord take on new significance, his words assume new depths of meaning. His miraculous cures reveal not only a compassionate human heart, but a divine power capable of spiritually healing the soul as well as physically ministering to the ills of the body. When Jesus cured the deaf, he bestowed the capacity not only to hear, but to hear his Word; when he loosed the tongue of the mute, he communicated the power to proclaim the coming of the Messiah; when he gave sight to the blind, he opened their eyes to the light of the world. For the early Church, and for the evangelists, therefore, the miracles of Jesus constituted a revelation of his power as the messianic Son of God to save mankind.

Barnabas Ahern has admirably summarized and illustrated the foregoing observations:

> Gospel study, therefore, means work on three levels. (Those of the evangelist — the community — the life of the historical Jesus.) [33] It is only when we view its message from the perspectives of the evangelist's insight and the Church's under-

---

33. Comments thus placed in parenthesis are observations on the part of the present author.

standing that we too, under the light of the Holy Spirit, shall come to appreciate the full, rich meaning of Christ's words and deeds during the days of his earthly life.

An example may help to make this clear. The floor of the ocean is littered with sea shells. Only some of these are swept onto the shore. There the wind and rain smooth away sharp edges. The sunlight brings out rich coloring. A man finds them there, gathers them up and forms them into a vase, beautiful in shape and color. To appreciate the exquisite beauty of the vase we not only gaze at its whole contour and color pattern but we study also the graceful turn and delicate tint of every shell.

It is the same with the gospels. Our Lord's life was like an ocean bed filled with words and deeds in such abundance that books could not contain them. Only some of these reached the shore of the primitive community. There the wind and light of the Spirit shaped the telling of each deed and illumined its deep meaning. The evangelists gathered together these living memories and molded them into a gospel under the light of the Spirit. No two gospels are the same; each has its own contour and coloring.

To measure the truth and to appreciate the beauty of the gospel we cannot be content to study merely the formative work of the evangelist and the overall impression of his literary composition. We must also study each unit in the gospel, as we would study each shell in a vase, to discover what the Holy Spirit disclosed to the Church — the full meaning of each event and the vital significance of each word in the life of Jesus. [34]

As Ahern has indicated, it is not enough to concentrate one's attention on the overall historical value of the gospels and the general relationship between Jesus the historical person and the Christ of faith, while failing to examine in detail more specific areas in order to ascertain whether the gospels

34. Ahern, *op. cit.,* p. 16.

can stand the test of a still more probing literary and historical critique. We shall, therefore, now direct our thought to a more detailed kind of study of more narrowly defined areas. Our approach here will be neither very thorough nor very profound, but we hope it will be illustrative of the way in which refined biblical procedures can help to substantiate the historicity of particular assertions about persons and events to which the New Testament bears witness. The subject matter selected will include: the historical value of Luke 9:51 — 18:14; the historicity of the gospel of John; and the problem posed by the texts concerned with the resurrection.

Luke As a Historian

The section of the gospel of Luke extending from 9:51 to 18: 14, entitled by some "The Great Journey to Jerusalem," is possibly the most interesting part of this version of the Synoptics. When compared with Mark and Matthew, the information it contains is perceptibly original. It narrates the story of an evangelization carried out by Christ and the disciples as they progressed determinedly from Galilee to Jerusalem. The material which Luke has collected for us here is truly marvelous.

The tone is given from the very first as Jesus "sets his face to go up to Jerusalem," 9:51, and sends messengers to prepare the way ahead of him. In chapter 10, Luke relates a mission upon which Christ sends seventy-two disciples. In chapter 9 (vv. 1-6) he had told of a similar mission entrusted to "the Twelve." Mark (chap 6) and Matthew (chap. 10) record the mission given to "the Twelve," but say nothing about the seventy-two disciples. Luke's description of the mission of the seventy-two, moreover, is in several respects more closely akin to Mark and Matthew's narration of the mission of "the Twelve" than is his own account of the latter mission.

Chapter 10 also presents to us the story of the Good Samaritan, in a parable which has conveyed to Christianity perhaps better than any other passage the teaching of Jesus on fraternal charity, a parable which we find in Luke alone. Immediately after this (and seemingly very much out of geographical context, for we are abruptly transported to a town which Luke purposely does not name, but which we know through John, chapter 11, has to be Bethany just outside of Jerusalem), Luke has conserved the beautiful episode of the "busy" Martha and her sister Mary at the feet of Jesus. Again, if it were not for Luke, an irreplaceable revelation of an aspect of the Lord's character and wisdom would have been lost to us.

Our Lord's instructions on prayer are set forth in chapter 11. Luke gives his own version of the prayer the Lord composes for his followers; and he has his particular variation of the way in which Jesus taught the importance of perseverance in prayer, 11:5-8.

In 11:27-28 we encounter an interesting interlude which we have also received solely from Luke: "As he said this, a woman in the crowd raised her voice and said to him, 'Blessed is the womb that bore you, and the breasts that you sucked!' But he said, 'Blessed rather are those who hear the word of God and keep it!'" As one reads this, can he refrain from asking himself: Who might Luke's source have been here? Who would have heard these almost incidental words, words which certainly have no bearing on the context in which they occur, and kept them in her heart?

Most of Luke's chapter 12 has its parallels in Matthew, but even here we catch a glimpse of his sensitivity as he captures for us in verse 32 this fleeting gleam of our Lord's tenderness: "Fear not, little flock, for it is your Father's good pleasure to give you the kingdom."

One of Christ's miracles is described in chapter 13: a woman who had become completely stooped because of a "spirit of infirmity" with which she had suffered for eighteen years is freed by Jesus from her affliction. Luke is careful to observe that the woman does not request the miracle, she does not come to the Lord; the initiative is his, as at the very sight of her he is moved with compassion, calls out to her, and heals her, "and she praised God." Only Luke tells us of this miracle.

In 13:13 Luke strikes once more the dominant theme he wishes to keep before us throughout this section: "I must go on my way today and tomorrow and the day following; for it cannot be that a prophet should perish away from Jerusalem."

Luke has kept for every generation of Christians a unique lesson in totally unselfish generosity in chapter 14, verses 12 to 14:

> When you give a dinner or banquet, do not invite your friends or your brothers or your kinsmen or rich neighbors, lest they also invite you in return, and you be repaid. But when you give a feast, invite the poor, the maimed, the lame, the blind, and you will be blessed, because they cannot repay you. You will be repaid at the resurrection of the just.

Chapter 15 constitutes without a doubt one of the most original and exquisite portions of the gospel of Luke. It comprises three stories designed to paint in the most vivid imaginable colors the unlimited desire with which the Father desires the repentance of the sinner. Who is not familiar with the quest for the lost sheep (also in Mt., chap. 18), the frantic search for the misplaced coin, the incomparable scene of the father with his prodigal son?

Although chapter 16 contains several sayings of Jesus concerned with the Law which are similar to declarations found in Matthew, once again we discover two parables which Luke alone has traced down. There is the mystifying story of the clever bursar who cheated his master but received praise for his guile, because the prudence he displayed gave evidence that "the sons of this world are wiser in their own generation than the sons of light" (16:8). Is not the conclusion of this verse reminiscent of the terminology we usually think of as being characteristic of John?

Next we are greeted with the pathetic tale of the rich man and Lazarus. Perhaps there is a veiled reference here to the Risen Christ and the reason he appeared only to his own followers: "If they do not hear Moses and the prophets, neither will they be convinced if someone should rise from the dead" (16:31).

We are reminded for a third time of the theme of the journey to Jerusalem in chapter 17: "On the way to Jerusalem he was passing along between Samaria and Galilee" (17:11). Possibly the mention of the word "Samaria" provides Luke with the occasion to bring to our attention the account of the Lord's miraculous healing of ten lepers. Recall that in chapter 10 it was the good *Samaritan* alone who displayed love for his neighbor. Now, in chapter 17, as we approach the end of this special section of Luke's, the only leper who returns to thank Jesus is a *Samaritan*. Can we help but think that this emphasis must reflect both Luke's source and preoccupation with his Gentile audience?

Before resuming a more systematic contact with Mark and Matthew in chapter 18, verse 15, Luke leaves us with two original parables; the first returns to the recommendation of perseverance in prayer, as it almost humourously depicts a persistent widow who ultimately obtains justice by practically driving a judge to the point of distraction; the second holds up for admiration the humble prayer of the Publican as contrasted with the haughty self-assertion on the part of the Pharisee. This lesson in humility is employed by Luke as a connecting link which enables him to rejoin the other two Synoptics as they proclaim the necessity of childlike confidence and sincerity in adherence to Jesus: "But Jesus called them to him, saying, 'Let the children come to me, and do not hinder them; for to such belongs the kingdom of God.' " [35]

Throughout this résumé of the great journey of evangelization, passages have been singled out which reveal the originality of Luke. In these pages Luke makes us wonder at the wealth of his information, and the portrait of Christ which emerges from this section is truly noble. A question, nevertheless, intrudes its way into our mind. Where did Luke find all of this material? How could such an extensive amount of the

---

35. Lk. 18:16; Mk. 10:14; Mt. 19:14.

teaching of Jesus and about him have escaped the notice of
the other two early evangelists? Are we not actually in the
presence of several chapters which are almost in their entirety
due to the creative literary efforts of Luke?

Aside from the fact that in the remainder of his gospel, and
in the Acts of the Apostles, it is quite clear that Luke is most
faithful to his sources and in general shows little tendency to
"create," and beyond the observations that have been made
earlier about the control exercised over the evangelical tradition
by the early Church, other indications can be cited which reinforce
our confidence in the historical value of this section in Luke.
These have been delineated most acutely by Lucien Cerfaux. [36]

Monsignor Cerfaux mentions that there exists a number
of hypothetical explanations of the origin of the second part
of Luke's account of the public life, that is, 9:51 — 18:14. Some
consider it as a homogeneous source which parallels Mark and
the collections of sayings of the Lord known as the *Logia*. Others
esteem that it represents the initial attempt of Luke to write
a complete gospel, and when he came in contact with the gospel
of Mark he retouched it. It is Cerfaux's opinion that the evangelist worked personally upon a variety of memories to which
he had access. [37]

As Luke traveled about, he had the opportunity of meeting
many of the disciples who did not belong to the immediate circle
of "the Twelve." He also thought it worthwhile to question
the women of Galilee: Mary, Joanna, Susanna. From the way
in which he uses the material he gathered from his conversations,
we can infer that there existed "a gospel of the disciples," that is,
a gospel distinct from that of the Twelve (Mark and Matthew).
He has synthesized this data, situating it in the framework of
a long journey of evangelization as Jesus proceeded from Galilee
along the edge of Samaria toward Jerusalem. The witnesses
in question informed Luke that during this period Jesus recruited

---

36. L. Cerfaux, *La voix vivante de l'Évangile au début de l'Eglise,*
Casterman, Tournai, 1956, pp. 75-83.
37. *Ibid.,* p. 80.

new disciples and prepared for the time when the growing force of Christianity would spread beyond the narrow confines of Jerusalem and Galilee.

If this important incision in Luke's gospel begins with several episodes of individual vocations, followed by the designation of the seventy-two disciples, much along the lines of the summoning and commissioning of the Twelve, this is not without significance. At least two things are suggested: like the mission of the Twelve, the mission of these disciples is based on the authority and the command of the Lord; in the figure of the "seventy-two" we are led to think of the evangelization of the nations, and the universality of the Christian mission.

The ensuing text centers on the teaching of Jesus: mercy, that of God and that of the Christian; trustful prayer; humility; the right usage of possessions. There are some critics who maintain that these instructions could not have come from our Lord, that they go beyond the type of religion he preached. But how can such a position be justified? When Christ accords more importance to the charity of the good Samaritan than to the observance of the priests and levites, does this any more than illustrate the pronouncement we read in Matthew: "I desire mercy and not sacrifice"? [38] Are not the traits recorded by Luke represented in Matthew's Sermon on the Mount? Yet, Cerfaux does draw an important distinction:

> The great difference lies in the fact that in the Sermon on the Mount the attitudes of the Christian are directed by the fundamental message of the Kingdom of God, while, in the gospel of the disciples, they are detached from this message and praised for their own sake. In this sense progress has taken place. But two years of preaching separate the mission along the borders of Galilee from the beginning of the public life. The doctrine of the Galilean Master has been stripped of the Jewish formulas which were limiting

---

38. Mt. 9:13; 12:7.

> Hence, a continuity can be detected between the other Synoptics
> its scope and appeal; henceforth it expresses a universal religion,
> it expresses sentiments and virtues which will be the basis
> of Christianity. [39]

and Luke, even when he is at the height of his originality. Furthermore, if Luke were "inventing" the section under consideration,
this would be for the purpose of theologizing. But, as the
structure and content of the Acts makes clear, Luke has very little
interest in formulating a theology. If he attributes a great deal
of value to the manifestations of the Holy Spirit, if he takes
careful note of the importance attached by the Lord to prayer,
if he insists upon evangelical poverty, this is but an emphatic
concentration upon certain points belonging to the common
tradition, and hardly amounts to a theology. Cerfaux hints that
all of this might be better comprehended if we would view it
as the work of a "neophyte" who came to the Christian faith
from the gentility and who remarked, more keenly than the
apostles, what was most original in the Christian message. [40]

The question of the "seventy-two," however, could be examined more thoroughly. Who were they? Did they actually
exist as such, or does their story merely have its origin in a
synthesis fabricated by Luke as an organ through which to
communicate the information he had collected?

Cerfaux notes that the book of the Acts reveals a definite
interest of Luke's in certain men whom he designates the "early
disciples." Among their number are included Philip the evangelist, Cleophas and his companion (known as the "disciples from
Emmaüs"), Mnason of Cyprus (Acts 21:16), Manaen (Acts
13:1), and perhaps Barnabas, Stephen, and others. It will be
remembered that the community of brethren assembled at the
moment of Pentecost was one hundred and twenty in number
(Acts 1:15). Besides the Twelve, the relatives of Jesus, and
the holy women, this would imply in addition the presence of at
least eighty other disciples. We also know from the Acts, 6:1,
that the original community at Jerusalem was comprised not only

---

39. Cerfaux, *op. cit.*, p. 77.
40. *Ibid.*, p. 78.

of "Hebrews" but also of "Hellenists," Jews who had come more thoroughly under the influence of the Gentile culture. It would not seem too unlikely that there is a relationship between the disciples enumerated among the "one hundred and twenty," the "Hellenists," and the "seventy-two."

The apostles being from Galilee and being more or less simple, rugged Jews, uncontaminated by Hellenism, their prejudice was understandably in favor of the "Hebrews." It is not to be wondered at, then, that the common tradition deriving from the Twelve more or less neglected these "secondary" disciples and credited small importance to the second period of evangelization, that which rubbed shoulders with the Samaritan, and indeed the Greek world.

According to Cerfaux,

Luke did not share the scruples of the common tradition and he was skillful at making effective use of reliable information. Since he proves himself to be perfectly competent when treating of the common tradition (that of the Twelve) — where we are able to verify his work — we can only conclude that his efforts are of equal veracity when he deals with the tradition of the disciples. I do not believe that Luke ever invents; he formulated for himself a documentation coming from the disciples of Jesus; and why should this documentation, simply because it differs from the tradition of the Twelve and goes beyond it, be subject to caution? [41]

As he concludes his remarks on the gospel of Luke, Cerfaux "yields to the temptation of quoting Aimé Puech [42] in praise of our evangelist." It would seem no sin to follow him into temptation:

What is most interesting is that Luke possesses art, a delicate art, all the more delicate in that it is above all, though not exclusively, instinctive. The new character of true Christian

---

41. *Ibid.*, p. 79.

42. *Ibid.*, p. 82. Cerfaux quotes: Aimé Puech, *Histoire de la litterature grecque chrétienne*, I, Paris, 1928, p. 115 f.

art, under all of its forms, already appears distinctly with
him: it is *the soul.* Everything about him is natural, living,
and touching. Not that he seeks realism, strictly speaking; in
him, as in Matthew, many of the concrete details which Mark
gives, especially in the miracle accounts, disappear or are toned
down. His manner is thoroughly interior; he prefers the
psychological to the picturesque. He excels in discerning and
indicating with expressive sobriety the secret movements of
the heart . . . . In the account of the young man of Naïm
who is raised from the dead, he is "the *only* son". . . and his
mother was *"a widow"* (7:12). Almost immediately after-
wards comes the phrase: "and he *gave him to his mother"* (7:
15).

In the parable of the good Samaritan, note the simple details:
the oil and the wine which the charitable passerby poured
over the wounds (10:34); the *mule* upon which he conducted
the injured man to the inn; the two denarii which he gave the
innkeeper the next day upon departing (10:35); in that of
the prodigal son: the *swine* which the unfortunate had to
take care of and the *pods* for which he battled them (15:16);
the brief interior discourse, so touching in its simplicity, in
which his repentance is expressed (15:18-20); the fatted
calf which the father has slaughtered upon his return (15-23).
All of this is noteworthy, but is not the narration in which
Luke has inculcated the greatest persuasive finesse and the
height of irresistible gentleness the episode of the Pilgrims of
Emmaüs, which should be cited in its entirety, from the first
word: *And they were talking between themselves of all that
had happened, and behold, while they were speaking and
raising questions, Jesus in person approached and went along
the road with them* (24:14-15) to the last: *and they said
to each other: Were not our hearts burning within us while
he was speaking to us along the way, and while he explained
the Scriptures to us?"* (24:32).

In these exquisite passages, even more than in the Gospel
of the infancy, Luke reveals the whole of himself to us, along

with his innate sensitivity which the influence of Christ, so well comprehended, had rendered still more acute and more seductive. It is evident that in whatever manner the basic tradition had been transmitted to him, the form it receives here is proper to him. This is not at all a matter of *invention,* at least intentional; it is certain that Luke too greatly respected the history which he related to allow himself to fall into the temptation of embellishing it . . . it is a question of an *interpretation* of this history, an interpretation which is truer and more profound than the most sagacious of critiques has been capable of grasping. This is *poetry* and *truth.*

If Luke interpreted the Gospel, if he transformed it, it was not to write his own theology, [43] it was not to prescind from the historical Jesus; rather it was to grace us with a deeper insight into the gentleness and the glory of the Jesus of history.

The Historicity of John

Thus far our study has focused more or less completely upon the Synoptic Gospels. Although we have applied our remarks about the gospel tradition and its bearing upon the historical Jesus almost exclusively to Mark, Matthew, and Luke, the same observations have their relevancy to the gospel of John. As a gospel, however, John's is a document which is unique. As C. H. Dodd has written, neither in the New Testament nor elsewhere does there exist any book really comparable to the Fourth Gospel. [44] We shall, therefore, devote special consideration to John.

Throughout the history of Christianity the great difference between the Synoptics and the gospel of John has been frequent-

---

43. This does not mean there is altogether lacking a certain theological element in Luke. Actually, in each of the Synoptics the material, that is, the words and actions of Jesus, is "organized" so that the essential message can be put across according to the plan of the evangelist.

44. C. H. Dodd, *The Interpretation of the Fourth Gospel,* Cambridge, 1953, p. 6.

ly noted. The former have generally been regarded as being more faithful to the biography of Jesus, while John's has been called the "spiritual" gospel, having furnished the Fathers with ample material for their allegories. If the historical reliability of any of the gospels should be difficult to establish, then, it would be John's. Before bringing forward our arguments in support of the historicity of John, suppose we take a glance at some of the problems involved. We shall frequently use as our guide through this complex issue a second article by Raymond Brown. [45]

What are some of the fundamental differences between the Synoptic tradition and John? From the very outset the originality of John appears in the "Hymn to the Logos." Both the vocabulary and the content of the Johannine prologue lack any clear parallel in earlier evangelical traditions. What is the source of this mystical canticle sung in praise of the Word?

The Johannine picture enhances the figure of John the Baptist far beyond what we find in the Synoptics. The discourses attributed to Jesus by John seem quite different from the style of speech employed by our Lord in the other gospels. John preaches an eschatology which is already "realized" (the last days are here *now*), while the Synoptics seem to speak of an eschatology looking only to the second coming of Christ. There are many chronological discrepancies: in the first gospels Jesus travels to Jerusalem only once, his ministry could hardly have lasted more than one year; in John there are frequent trips to Jerusalem, three Passovers, and a ministry that must have required at least two years; the Synoptics have the Last Supper occurring on the fifteenth of Nison, John on the fourteenth.

And what has become of all the parables of Jesus, with which we grew familiar in the other gospels? The only "parables" we find in John are really allegories: "The Good Shepherd" and "The Vine and the Branches," and even these have a different

---

45. R. E. Brown, S.S., "The Problem of Historicity in John," *Catholic Biblical Quarterly*, January 1962, pp. 1-14. For more recent development of Brown's thought with respect to John; cf. *The Gospel According to John, I-XII, Anchor Bible*, Doubleday & Company, Garden City, N.Y. 1965.

motif from the stories we find in the tradition of "the Twelve."
And the miracles? Even when a miracle account in John seems
to coincide with an event related in the Synoptics, details in the
description are changed, usually with the result that a more
spiritual or symbolical effect is achieved (cf. the multiplication
of the loaves, John, chapter 6, or the cure of the son of the
Roman official, John, chapter 4).

But perhaps most important, what accounts for the strange
terminology John uses? Where does he get his abstract language:
the Word? the dualism of light and darkness? the notion of
rebirth? the clear emphasis on the Divinity of the Only-begotten?
his theology of the Name?

As if these conflicts did not constitute enough of a problem,
sometimes even the "similarities" between John and the Synoptics
give rise to difficulties. Thus it is maintained by some that in
certain passages John is not giving a description of an actual
event, but is merely combining elements garnered from the Synoptics for the purpose of exposing one of his theological notions. "A
good example would be the story of the raising of Lazarus. This
would have been put together from the Synoptic raising narratives
(son of widow of Naim in Luke, chapter 7; Jairus' daughter in
Mark, chapter 5), the story of Martha and Mary (Lk. 10:38-42),
and the parable of Lazarus and the rich man (Lk. 16:19-31)." [46]

These difficulties along with others of the same species have
served to make the gospel of John a prime target for Bible critics
since the middle of the nineteenth century. Thus Strauss (*Life
of Jesus,* 1835-1836) saw it as the product of a theologian re-
furbishing myths; for the school of Tubingen it was a theological
writing from about 170 A.D., intended to reconcile Petrine and
Pauline traditions, and Gnosticism; Renan (*Life of Jesus,* 1863)
was more moderate, for after having paid a careful visit to the
Holy Land, he was quite impressed by the harmony between the
Fourth Gospel and the nature of the Palestinian countryside;
Loisy felt he could prove that "John's" gospel was the work
of a Christian of the second century who had nothing in common

---

46. *Ibid.,* pp. 5-6.

with the son of Zebedee; the gospel itself? it is merely an allegorical composition, an exposition of mystical theology devoid of all historical value.

As regards the actual perspective, however, notwithstanding the attempt of Bultmann to reduce the Fourth Gospel to a form of second century Mandaean Gnosticism, "it is incontestable in effect that, for several decades, the sympathy of the critics has grown more favorable toward the traditional position with respect to the antiquity of the Fourth Gospel, its deeply Semitic character, its literary unity, as well as its independence of Hellenism or oriental Gnosticism." [47] Later we shall see a few of the reasons for this change of feeling, but for the moment let us attend to the question of how we should envision the gospel of John as contrasted with the other three.

In early Christianity it was contended by some of the Fathers — Clement of Alexandria, for instance — that John had desired to complete the account of the Synoptics; that is, he endeavored to fill in a number of details of the portrait of Christ passed over by or unknown to the other evangelists. Some of the recent commentators, of a more conservative inclination, have continued to support this "complementary" theory. Completely opposed to this view is the "supplantory" thesis of A. Windisch: John was quite dissatisfied with the imperfections of the Synoptics, and so he dedicated himself to composing a document which would replace them. [48]

Neither of these extreme opinions is valid. There seems to be more of a basis for regarding:

> the fourth gospel as *an autonomous writing,* fully intelligible in itself, and not as a mosaic of disjointed accounts between which should be inserted those of the synoptics. On the other hand, John does not reject the synoptics: he pursues his own path in making, as he himself says (20:30-31), a selection among the events of the existence of Jesus, which compels us to believe that he did not regard as unacceptable what he

---

47. A. Feuillet, *Introduction à la Bible,* Vol. 2, pp. 617-18.
48. A. Windisch, *Johannes und die Synoptiker,* Leipzig, 1926.

did not use. It is more difficult to say whether he was directly familiar with and utilized his predecessors. Bultmann and Gardner-Smith deny it; most authors are of the opposite opinion . . . ." [49]

Many aspects of John would suggest contact with the Synoptics: a number of his chronological indications seem to be designed to show how his narratives can be linked with the older accounts; certain instances of silence or abbreviations in the Fourth Gospel presuppose a knowledge of the Synoptics. Thus there are mentioned simply in passing the baptism of Jesus, 1:32, the imprisonment of John the Baptist, 3:24, the Twelve, 6:67, Barabbas, 18: 40; these references would be meaningless without a background furnished by the other gospels. Further evidence of contact is demonstrable in such things as the clear parallelism between John 6 and 7 and Mark 6:34 — 10:1; or the frequent affinities between John and Luke, especially in the account of the Passion.

"Today, moreover," writes Feuillet, "there is a stronger and stronger tendency to pose the problem of the relations of John with the Synoptics on a broader base than merely the literary dependency of the more recent writings on those which are older. What John knew or supposed to be known to his readers was possibly not so much specific writings as the great living tradition. He himself represents a tradition parallel to that of the Synoptics, contemporary to the latter, in some respects even more archaic, and capable of having influenced it as much as having been influenced by it . . .," [50] for the Fourth Gospel was only gradually elaborated, being preached for a considerable number of years before receiving its definitive redaction.

The factors we have observed can help to reinforce our faith in John's gospel. The fact that John sometimes uses and at other times presupposes the Synoptic tradition indicates a desire on his part to remain faithful to the Great Tradition. The fact that it can be shown with a high degree of certitude that on occasion Luke is dependent on the Johannine preaching and

---

49. Feuillet, *op. cit.*, p. 677.
50. *Ibid.*, p. 678.

ambient gives some idea of the force exerted by the latter long
before the final composition of the gospel. Furthermore, our
quandary is greatly lessened by the realization that the Synoptics
no more pretend to be biographies or "histories" in the modern
sense than does the last gospel. As we have remarked earlier,
Mark, Matthew and Luke refer themselves to the primitive tradition preserved by the Church from eyewitness accounts, but each
does so in his own way with his own intentions. Thus we can
say that each of the evangelists was affected to some extent by
theological preoccupations. Hence, for example, if the chronological notations of the Johannine and Synoptic traditions don't
agree, this simply testifies to a lack of concern for "biographical"
dating, and not to a lack of historicity in either tradition. But
let us look a little closer at some of the details of the gospel of
John, and study more critically a few of the apparent "conflicts"
with the Synoptics.

Throughout his gospel, John frequently mentions the names
of places and gives exact locations, in fact he does this more than
do the other gospels. It was once contended that "the author"
either created these names to serve him in the fabrication of allegories, or, writing under the pseudo-identity of John, he inserted
names, titles, etc., to give the impression that he was a native
of Palestine and thereby lend to his composition a more authentic
ring. Recent archaeological discoveries, however, have proved
the actual existence of sites named by John, for example the
pool of Bethzatha (5:2), and penetrating analysis of his gospel
has for all practical purposes dispelled the notion that John
(or the actual author) might have artificially woven names into
his accounts to make them appear more genuine. [51]

The inference is that the material of the Fourth Gospel
essentially derives from a Palestinian Jew. Further study reveals
that this man must have been an eyewitness, a disciple ("the one
whom Jesus loved"), an apostle, the son of Zebedee, John. This
means that even though it undoubtedly received its ultimate form
from an editor or editors other than John, the Fourth Gospel

---

51. Cf. Brown, *op. cit.*, pp. 1-2.

is substantially his work and deserves the confidence due the testimony of an apostle, a very special apostle.

Again, if we delve more sensitively into the texts, we begin to see that some of the variations between John and the Synoptics are not so significant as they may have seemed. Previously we spoke of the way in which the figure of the Baptist is more exalted by John than by the others. "But if we get behind the gospel sense to the historical details of the Baptist's actual ministry, the two traditions present the Baptist in the same light of primitive eschatological expectation." [52] That is, if we look beyond the *interpretation* each gospel gives to certain events of John's life, to the historical skeleton of the events themselves, we observe that all the gospels give us the same reality: John the Baptist, a man sent by God to preach to the people repentance and baptism in preparation for the proximate coming of the time of the Messiah.

With regard to the problem posed by the long discourses in John, there is no questioning the fact that they differ greatly from the style of speech used by Jesus in the Synoptics. No doubt we witness in these discourses the imprint of John's qualities as a theologian and contemplative. The consequences of this admission, however, should not be exaggerated. Thus, major themes presented in the Synoptics are also accented in John, though in a different manner; for example, in the former the "Kingdom of God" is preached by Jesus through parables, in John it is present in Jesus. [53] Moreover, many of the metaphors employed by John (the shepherd, the vine, the gate) are also characteristic of the parables of Mark, Matthew, and Luke. It might also be pointed out that most of the time John's discourses are placed in a definite geographical setting and linked to precise historical circumstances.

They display none of the qualities of the carefully designed compositions of Greek rhetoric; on the contrary, they remind

---

52. *Ibid.*, pp. 3-4.

53. Brown refers to "Le thème littéraire parabolique dans l'Évangile de saint Jean," *Recueil Lucien Cerfaux*, Louvain, 1954, Vol. 2, pp.17-26, *ibid.*, p. 4.

us of the preaching of the prophets of Israel, especially that of Jeremiah contradicted, threatened with prison and even death, and obliged to defend himself against hateful adversaries. It is most likely that Christ did have extremely vibrant discussions of this same kind with the Jews. [54]

The different eschatological outlooks? John's proclamation of a "realized" eschatology would seem to be just as faithful to the doctrine of Christ as is the Synoptic view. There is a good chance Jesus actually preached that "the Hour is *now*," the last times have already begun; for, as Brown mentions, "while the Synoptics seem to emphasize a parousia eschatology, careful studies like those of Feuillet [55] show that in the Synoptic tradition there has been a certain reinterpretation of Jesus' own eschatology which, in some aspects, was truly a realized eschatology." [56]

If we devote more than a cursory perusal to the chronological discrepancies between the Synoptics and John, our faith in the reliability of John is increased still more. Actually, rather than contradicting his predecessors in this domain, John seems to complement them. The latter have Jesus coming to Jerusalem only at the end of his public ministry; unless, as John indicates, in reality Jesus visited Jerusalem on numerous occasions and was well known there, the entire Passion becomes an enigma and passages like Mark 11:2-3 are rendered senseless. It is quite likely, then, that the Johannine chronology of Jesus' public life is closer to the historical truth than that of the Synoptics. Moreover, only John's chronology of the Passion, which places the death of our Lord prior to the official eating of the paschal lamb, has historical likelihood. [57]

When we examine the ensemble of the differences between the Synoptics and John, therefore, we must conclude that the "conflicts" are not as pronounced as some critics have insisted,

---

54. Feuillet, *op. cit.*, p. 668.

55. "Les origines et la signification de Mt. 10:23b," *Catholic Biblical Quarterly*, 1961, pp. 182-98.

56. Brown, *op. cit.*, p. 4.

57. For a different view on this matter cf. the thesis of A. Jaubert, *The Date of the Last Supper*, Alba House, Staten Island, N.Y., 1965.

and the case against the historicity of John is appreciably weakened. Even if the mystical genius of John has contributed a great deal to the literary presentation of the Fourth Gospel, this should not dispose us unfavorably toward accepting as true what John has to tell us.

If, for instance, in studying a miracle narrated by John we notice that it obviously has symbolical overtones, we should not immediately jump to the conclusion that it must be nothing but symbolical. In effect, the author, just as do the Synoptics, leaves us with the distinct impression that the miracles of Christ were "signs" the reality of which was absolutely indispensable if they were to be acknowledged as guarantees of the validity of his words and the legitimacy of his claims.

With regard to the miracle of the raising of Lazarus, John 11, to which we referred earlier, it is curious that a miracle so wondrous should not even have been alluded to in the Synoptics. But is this any more startling than the Synoptics' failing to speak of the multiple trips of Jesus to Jerusalem and his ministry there, even though the latter have every chance of being historical? If John did invent the miracle of Lazarus' resurrection for didactic purposes, why did he enter so many details which contribute nothing to the symbolism or doctrinal message, and yet seem so true to life? Merely to add realism to his account? Why does he have Jesus stop "about two miles away" from the home of Martha and Mary? Why does he have Martha come out to Jesus almost stealthily and alone? Why does Martha then have to go back to Mary and call her "quietly" away? These observations by John do not seem to add significantly to the meaning of the raising of Lazarus, but they do fit quite well into an historical situation in which the time of the Passion has approached and Jesus knows himself to be in extreme danger in the environs of Jerusalem. We might also observe that if the Synoptics do not describe the raising of Lazarus, they do relate other resurrections, and that of Lazarus at Bethany possibly could have been omitted because it did not lend itself readily to their general plan.

In any event, even if the seeming contradictions between John and the Synoptics can be more or less reconciled, even if the special qualities of John's miracle stories and discourses can be justified, there still remains to be resolved what is perhaps the key problem and the most pertinent question of all: what is the source of the more original elements of the theology enunciated by John? Where do the themes of the Incarnate Logos, of the opposition between light and darkness, etc., come from? Could they in fact be owed to the influence of oriental Gnosticism upon the evangelist?

Those commentators who have proposed that John is substantially a Gnostic work, usually date the appearance of the Fourth Gospel near the end of the second century when Gnosticism was beginning to flourish. Several discoveries made during our century, however, have antiquated this opinion. The discovery in Egypt of the *Papyrus Egerton 2* [58] and the study of the *Papyrus Rylands 457* have given good reason to believe that the gospel of John was already known in Egypt at the beginning of the second century; [59] this, along with the publishing of the *Papyrus Bodmer II,* a manuscript containing the first fourteen chapters of John almost in their entirety and dating from about the year 200 A.D., has for all practical purposes confirmed with certitude that the Fourth Gospel must have received its final recension some time before the turn of the first century. If John's gospel appeared this early, then it would appear that it must have influenced the Gnostic documents rather than vice versa.

Secondly, the unearthing of Gnostic writings such as the *"Gospel of Truth (Evangelium Veritatis),"* a late second century document proffering a Valentinian type of Gnosticism, has given evidence that the Fourth Gospel is radically distinct in its doctrine from the Gnostic brand of thought to which some critics had assimilated it. For example, one of the major themes of the *Gospel of Truth* is "the fall of the spirits": according to this theme certain spiritual beings, very badly mistaking the true nature of God, found themselves enveloped by fog and completely lost

---

58. Cf. H. I. Bell and T. C. Skeat, *The New Gospel Fragments,* Manchester, 1935.

59. Cf. C. H. Roberts, *An Unpublished Fragment of the Fourth Gospel in the John Rylands Library,* Manchester, 1935.

sight of the divine realities; wandering about aimlessly, they fell and were imprisoned in matter; their only chance for salvation was through the *Logos,* the Word, who could enable them to regain consciousness of their true nature so that they could return to heaven. It is obvious enough that such a theme is quite foreign to the thought of John.

A third development which has helped emancipate the gospel of John from those who would reduce it to Gnostic Hellenism is the discovery (dating from 1947) of a number of documents at Qumrân. The content of these writings, particularly the *Manual of Discipline,* the *Sadokite Document,* the *Thanksgiving Hymns,* the *Scroll of the War of the Sons of Light with the Sons of Darkness,* and the *Commentary on Habakkuk,* has clarified the authentic Palestinian character of the Johannine tradition.

> The abstract language, the dualism of light and darkness, and other features which once seemed to rule out Palestinian origin now help to confirm it. For much of the very same vocabulary, mentality, and theological outlook found in John, is found also at Qumrân both before and during Christ's time. A real Palestinian background has been discovered against which the Jesus of John can be plausibly pictured. [60]

There is general agreement today, therefore, that the Fourth Gospel, as much as the other three, takes as its point of departure the apostolic kerygma. Nonetheless, the gospel was elaborated in a particular milieu, and it possesses certain themes and pre-occupations which must, at least in part, owe their place in the evangelist's presentation to the interests and intellectual climate of the people for whom it was destined. In order to appreciate more fully the gospel of John, then, it is essential to probe painstakingly into its background. Although we cannot attempt to do that here, we can bring to the reader's attention a few of the results obtained through this type of research.

In our summary of this aspect of the problem of the sources affecting the formulation of John's gospel, we shall often refer

---

60. Brown, *op. cit.,* p. 2.

to articles by F. M. Braun [61] and G. Quispel. [62] The former is concerned with showing the affinities between John, the Hermetic writings, and the documents of the Qumrân community. The latter points out how John could have been influenced by pre-Gnostic trends of thought exemplified in the traditions of certain unorthodox Jewish sects existing at the commencement of the Christian era.

From the outset Braun remarks: "It is plain that John has written in a special language and with a special sensitivity, both of which are directed to the religious aspirations which traversed the world of antiquity. The problem of his relations with these currents of thought is one of the most complicated which we could possibly approach." [63] We shall try to disengage the main features of Braun's study, but necessarily in a somewhat oversimplified fashion.

It is to be noted initially that the Fourth Gospel depends above all on the species of Judaism we find reflected in the Bible, that its author was preoccupied with placing the mystery of Christ in the perspective of the Old Testament. Throughout the gospel the Scriptures are used with such frequency and delicacy that we would have to presuppose their having been profoundly assimilated by the evangelist. Besides implicit allusions, to the messianic King, to the Prophet who had been announced, to classical themes like the Word, the Light, the Vine, the Shepherd, there are at least twenty explicit scriptural references introduced by such formulas as "Is it not written in the Law?" "As Scripture says . . . ."

But much more than simply citing the Old Testament, John sees the entire New Alliance as a prolongation of the earlier covenant between God and his people. Thus he shows how the events of the liberation of God's chosen race recorded in Exodus are but shadows of the salvation wrought in the coming Jesus;

61. F. M. Braun, "L'arrière-fond du quatrième évangile," *L'Évangile de Jean,* Desclée de Brouwer, 1958, pp. 179-96.

62. G. Quispel, "L'Évangile de Jean et la Gnose," *L'Évangile de Jean,* Desclée de Brouwer, 1958, pp. 197-208.

63. Braun, *op. cit.,* p. 179.

think of these references in the gospel to the escape from Egypt: the divine presence signified by the luminous cloud which enveloped the meeting tent, 1:14, the Law transmitted through Moses, 1:17, the paschal lamb immolated at the time of the exit from Egypt, 1:36; 19-36, the lifting up of the bronze serpent, 3:14; 12:32, the manna descended from heaven, 6:31-33, the rock struck by Moses, 7:38, perhaps even the pillar of clouds, 8:12; 12:35. This usage of Old Testament realities was John's way of saying that in Christ there was effected at last the true passage from captivity to the freedom of sons of God, from the darkness of sin to true light.

In the past, John's representation of Jesus as the Incarnate *Logos* was a major argument forwarded by critics to prove that he had Hellenized the gospel. But even here a Judaic concept may be at the root of John's thought pattern, for in the context of the last gospel it would appear that it is the Hebraic *Word* that is in view. [64] Are not the very first words of the Prologue: *In the beginning was the Logos* ... obviously inspired by the Priestly document which introduces Genesis: *In the beginning God created heaven and earth* ... (Gen. 1:1)?

Moreover, the creation account continues with the regularly repeated formula: And God *said* ... and it was so. Is this not the concept contained in the psalmist's chant "By the *Word* of the Lord the heavens were made ..." (Ps. 33:6). "The *Word* of God, assuredly, is the Bible's expression for creative power. John appears to have been content to develop this idea along the line of the wisdom literature, in particular Proverbs and Sirach"; [65] it is especially with these books that the Prologue has many elements in common. Thus, Wisdom is the most ancient of all that is, it dwells in the intimacy of God, a pure emanation of his glory, yet playing a role in creation; it seeks an abode among men and finds one in Israel. God loves only those in whom it dwells: theirs is the grace and mercy reserved for the elect. While we cannot deduce from these parallels an immediate

64. Cf. M. E. Boismard, *Le prologue de saint Jean,* Lectio Divina 11, Paris, 1953, pp. 109-154.

65. Braun, *op. cit.,* p. 182.

textual dependence of John on sapiential literature, they certainly suggest that themes current in the Jewish teaching of his time did exercise a general influence on an author who desired to remain faithful to the traditions of his nation.

Be this as it may, the Fourth Gospel has unquestionably drawn from sources other than the Old Testament and orthodox Judaism. Careful study has given cause to surmise that the pseudo-epigraphical literature which can be traced to the period beginning with the epoch of the Maccabees and extending to the end of the second century A.D., was to some degree known to the evangelist and used by him.

Henoch, Jubilees, The Assumption of Moses, The Apocalypse of Baruch, the oldest parts of the third book of the *Sibylline Oracles,* and the *Fourth Book of Esdras* are among the pseudo-epigraphical works which contain texts bearing a marked resemblance to some of the material of John, notably in their emphasis on apocalyptical and eschatological themes. (*The Testament of the Twelve Patriarchs* might also be included in this list, but with hesitation, since the date of origin of this writing is highly disputed, and it is certain that the primitive text has at least been altered by Christian interpolations.)

In John's gospel Jesus is presented as the agent of a great revelation. He has been sent to reveal secrets of celestial origin, secrets which no one can unveil unless he has come from on high. Now, this would seem to be the role of the Son of Man, mentioned in the books of *Daniel and Henoch* as the one who would establish the perpetual kingdom of the last times. Besides, the doctrine of the Son of Man, the resurrection on the last day, final judgment, and eternal life are concepts which we find the best supported in the apocalyptical literature to which we have referred.

Among all the pseudo-epigraphical Jewish writings, the *Testament of the Twelve Patriarchs* displays the most numerous and precise points of contact with John's first epistle, Apocalypse, and Gospel. Both one and the other deploy the notions of light versus darkness, truth versus the lie, eternal life, true judgment, living water, the spirit of truth. Even though the *Testament* does suffer from Christian interpolations, and it can only cautiously be compared with the Johannine literature, there is no doubt that this document depends on the literary and spiritual milieu which has been revealed to us by the Qumrân texts mentioned above; moreover, there is a definite affinity between the latter and the writings of John. This signifies that both the *Testament* and the Qumrân literature can give us an insight into the intellectual and religious climate which John must have taken into account in his writing.

With regard to the themes recurring in the Qumrân texts, Braun remarks:

> How can we help being struck first of all by the ideas: faith, judgment, eternal life, knowledge, the light of life, the holy spirit or spirit of truth, which occur with equal frequency (at Qumrân and) in the Fourth Gospel? This is but a first impression. In the one and the other there is the same kind of dualism opposing light to darkness, life to death, truth to deceit, tracing them to the contrary action exercised upon men by the angel of darkness or Mastêma (Satan) and the angel of light — who in the Gospel is replaced by the Savior. The section of the *Manual* consecrated to the theme of the two spirits and the two ways most closely corresponds to the epistle in which can be noted in particular the two ways of light and of darkness (1:6, 7; 2:9-11), the two spirits of truth and of error (4:1-6), and the evil world under the power of Satan, from which we must separate ourselves entirely (2:15-17; 2:1-13; 4:4-5; 5:10). [66]

The similarity between the concepts and terminology of John and the texts of Qumrân is too patent and too frequent to have resulted from mere accident. Some type of intimate contact, either direct or through the agency of a common ambient of thought, must be presupposed. We must be wary, however, of several pitfalls. Not too much can be deduced from the use of identical terms, for words like "light," "darkness," "truth," "life," and "spirit" appear not only in the Qumrân documents and in

---

66. *Ibid.*, pp. 187-88.

John, they appertain to the basic vocabulary of the Jewish literature of the period.

Furthermore, it would be an error to fail to consider the way in which various contexts, both proximate and remote, can give to similar expressions divergent senses. Hence, the background of the Fourth Gospel could include not only the Qumrân material, but also could embrace influences filtering through from such sources as even the more heterodox sects and rabbinical traditions strictly so called. The manner in which John shows his familiarity with the principles professed in the rabbinical schools (cf. 8:17; 7:22-23), and with the subtleties of the casuistry of the Pharisees, as well as his treatment of the Thora in which he proclaims that Christ is the realization of all that the rabbis pretended to find in the Law (cf. 1:17), would tend to confirm this thesis.

Does the fact that John's spirit is so permeated by the Scriptures, that the gospel is visibly familiar with the apocalyptical literature of Qumrân or of other milieux, and that the author was not unaware of many of the fine points of the Law so popular with the rabbis, imply that the Fourth Gospel owes nothing to Hellenic religion? Not in the least. For example, Dodd has shown very convincingly [67] that John and Philo [68] can be compared on more than one point, even though there are radical differences between the Johannine *Logos* and *Logos* presented by Philo. Moreover, the body of Hermetic writings dedicated to the revelations of Hermes Trismegistus furnishes an even better basis for comparing Hellenism and the Johannine tradition. Thus, literary contacts between John and *Poimandrès,* tract I, dating from about 125 A.D., the *Secret Discourses Concerning Regeneration and the Rule of Silence,* tract XIII, and *Asclepius* are practically undeniable.

According to *Poimandrès,* God or the great *Noûs* is light and life; he gave birth to the *Logos* at the same time as to the primordial Man, to whom was remitted all power. Through

---

67. Dodd, *op. cit.,* pp. 54-73.
68. Philo was a Hellenized Jew of Alexandria, born about 30 B.C.

him humans can be saved from their miserable carnal condition. Those who love their body remain locked in darkness; those who manage to free themselves from it begin their return to the Father and their ascent to light and life. Poimandrès offers himself as their guide: by his words he teaches them the secret of deliverance from darkness and from death... Holy is God... who through the *Logos* has established everything that exists; to him are raised pure sacrifices of words, offered by pious souls. As for him to whom the revelation is supposed to have been made, who has believed and who attests his belief, he is invested with the mission of imparting it to his brothers, victims of ignorance. [69]

The resemblance between the terminology used here, and to a lesser extent the ideas signified through the words, and the gospel of John, particularly in the Prologue, is most striking. In both we see God creating and offering salvation, in terms of light, life, and liberation from darkness, in conjunction with an intermediary. In both emphasis is placed on the importance of knowledge, of belief, and of witness.

Although the cosmology, anthropology, and soteriology of the pessimistic Hermetic Gnosis as represented by *Poimandrès* and the other works cited above are thoroughly distinct from the perspective of the Fourth Gospel, the similarities between these works and John are too numerous and too salient to be dismissed lightly as coincidental. What, then, was the nature of the contact that must be presupposed?

The Hermetic religious current encountered the influence of the Septuagint and other Jewish writings and, therefore, a certain number of parallels between John and Hermetism can be explained by the fact that both drew from a common source. While there can be no literary dependence of John on the discourses of Hermes because the former received its final edition an appreciable time before the latter, it remains plausible that the Hermetic writings could have extracted some of their notions from the Fourth Gospel. There must also be taken into consideration the

---

69. Braun, *op. cit.*, p. 191.

possibility that the manuscripts through which the Hermetic discourses have been made known to us could have been subject to interpolations on the part of Christians.

It is Braun's contention that the discovery of two Hermetic treatises in the Gnostic library of Nag Hamadi in Upper Egypt has made it impossible to question that a definite influence was exerted by Hermetism upon the Christian form of Gnosticism. There had to have been some contact between Christianity and the Hellenic religions, and the influence would have been reciprocal rather than merely unilateral. In any event, Hermetism could be looked upon, according to the formula of Festugière, as a *spiritual Koinè,* that is, a body of popular theological terms and concepts pervading the religious atmosphere of the milieu in which John was composed. From the dawn of the Christian era this religious "language" was spread throughout the Hellenic world, and it is very unlikely that certain elements in the Fourth Gospel are unrelated to its impact.

The fact that Hellenized Jews from the diaspora frequently found occasion to visit Jerusalem on pilgrimage adds to the possibility of Palestine's having been infiltered by Greek religious ideas. Moreover, certain spiritual groups in Palestine seem to have been especially receptive to at least some of the Hermetic views on the problem of salvation. For instance, Josephus has given us sufficient information about the community of the Essenes to lead us to believe that this Jewish sect embraced the Platonic doctrine of the soul being a prisoner of the body and several other notions characteristic of the Alexandrian ambient.

Braun sums up his position in the following manner:

It has not been proved that the author of the Fourth Gospel was in direct contact with the community of Qumrân nor that he was familiar with its books. But what we can affirm without exaggeration is that where John and Hermetism coincide, the background of these writings and that of the Fourth Gospel is noticeably alike. The conclusion which results from the examination of the Dead Sea Scrolls, therefore, is that it would be rash to seek elsewhere than in Palestine the milieu to which John is the most closely attached.

This does not, however, exclude a more immediate dependency of the evangelist with respect to religious paganism. Having become attentive to the aspirations of the souls of the elite to whom the philosophy and mysticism of Alexandria offered their method of salvation, his thought, his vocabulary, his style could have received therefrom a certain enriching; in addition, in its ultimate form John's gospel could owe something to retouching on the part of disciples who had come in more intimate contact with Hellenism than he. [70]

What would have passed from the Judean milieu into the Gospel would be a selection of themes and phrases which were common enough in the spirituality of the epoch, as well as the feeling for the religious aspirations which were being propagated in the ancient world. John found there a source of inspiration ... which he did not use to Hellenize the apostolic kerygma through questionable compromises, but to show to souls anxious for their salvation and at the same time enamoured with the concepts of light and truth, that Jesus is the Light and that it suffices to believe in him in order to receive the fullness of life. [71]

Quispel [72] has maintained that while it is erroneous to think John borrowed directly from Gnosticism, it can be admitted that the Fourth Gospel does bear the traces of an anthropological climate which we can classify as "pre-Gnostic," a climate which can be identified with a current running through heterodox Judaism. Perhaps a brief examination of a few of the texts or themes which come to us from these Jewish sects will help to confirm this thesis.

Three relatively ancient sources constitute at the present time our principal point of contact with the unorthodox Jewish tra-

---

70. *Ibid.*, p. 195.
71. *Ibid.*, p. 196.
72. Quispel, *op. cit.*, p. 198.

ditions: *III Enoch, The Apocalypse of Abraham,* and the information conserved by Sharastani and Al Qirqisani concerning the sect of the *Magharias.* Might a study of these documents give us a profounder grasp of the overall backgound of John's gospel?

In the *Third Book of Enoch* we read an interesting series of notations about *Métratron,* "the lesser Yahweh." "This is Metratron, My servant. I made him a prince and a ruler over all the princes of My kingdoms and over all the children of heaven . . . . And every command that he utters in My Name you are to observe and fulfill (X:3)." "And He called me the lesser Yahweh in the presence of all His heavenly household: as it is written (Ex. 23:21): 'For My Name is in him' (XII:5)." "And I put upon him of My honor, My majesty and the splendor of My glory that is upon My Throne of Glory. I called him the lesser Yahweh (YHWH), the Prince of the Presence, the Knower of Secrets: for every secret I reveal to him as a father and all mysteries declared I unto him in uprightness (XLVIII:7)." [73]

In several respects *Métratron* reminds us of the *Logos* of John: his role is to manifest God and to conduct men to the divine throne; he is associated with God in a very close and apparently unique way; great power is given to him in the Name of God; he is to reveal great mysteries; Yahweh is related to him as a Father. Compare the above texts with John 17: 11-12: "And I now am no more in the world, but they are in the world, and I am coming to You. Holy Father, keep them in Your Name, which You have given me, that they may be one, even as we are one. While I was with them, I kept them in Your Name, which You have given me . . . ."

The Apocalypse of Abraham, originating in Palestine between 70 and 120 A.D., is representative of doctrines which are less developed than those of *III Enoch.* In the *Apocalypse* we read the following passage devoted to the Angel of the Lord (a passage reminiscent of Ezekiel's vision, 1:26 ff.):

"And while I was still lying with my face on the earth, I heard the voice of the Holy One speaking: 'Go, Jaoel, and by

---

73. As quoted by Quispel, pp. 199-200.

means of my ineffable Name raise me yonder man, and strengthen him (so that he recover) from his trembling.' And the angel came, whom he had sent to me, in the likeness of a man, and grasped me by my right hand, and set me upon my feet, and said to me: '... I am called Jaoel by Him who moves that which exists with me on the seventh expanse upon the firmament, a power in virtue of the ineffable Name that is dwelling in me . . . . (X)' " [74]

Jaoel, the Angel of the Lord, is, as we have intimated, comparable to the "Man" of Ezekiel. He is sent to men by God. He is to be found at the side of God, on the throne of the divine glory, but it seems he is to be distinguished from God Himself. Once again the theology of the "Name" appears.

Affinities with John can be discerned not only in *Enoch* and the *Apocalypse,* but also in the tenets of the sect of the Magharias. The members of this group held resolutely to the absolute transcendence of God; hence, they refused to attribute to God the texts from the Bible which contained the least anthropomorphism. These they would apply to "the Angel of Yahweh." This Angel is not God in the strictest sense, and yet he is described as being so close to God that his divine character is indisputable. [75] He is the bearer of the Name of Yahweh. He assumes as applying to himself all the scriptural references which employ human images in speaking of God: for example, Isaiah 6:1; Ezekiel 1:26. He is conceived of as possessing the qualities of the Messiah. In brief, the Magharias thought of the Messiah as a divine Adam (Man), the Lord of the Angels and the Angel of Yahweh. He is the Envoy, the *apostolos* of God, whom God has given a special Name and whose coming, an exodus from a glorious and celestial condition, is equivalent to the coming of God Himself.

From the preceding data Quispel concludes "to the presence of a pre-Gnostic Jewish current, esoteric though it was, which speculated about the existence, the nature, and the role of a divine Being called Angel of Yahweh, prince of light, invested

---

74. As quoted by Quispel, p. 201.
75. *Ibid.,* p. 202.

by the supreme God with the possession of the divine Name,
and charged by God to be His apostle to men, His messenger,
His elect, His lieutenant, His Messiah." [76] Now, we also observe
this line of thought not only in the gospel of John, but in the
Gospel of Truth, which is representative of Valentinian Gnosis,
and in *The Book of Jeû* which depicts for us quite another type
of Gnosticism.

The following passages give some idea of the theology of the
Son of God developed in the *Gospel of Truth*:

> When, therefore, it pleased Him that His beloved Son should
> be his Name and when He gave him this Name, he who has
> come forth from the Depths has spoken of His secrets, knowing
> that the Father is absolute Goodness. Also He has sent him
> for this reason, that he might speak on the matter of the Place
> and of his place of repose whence he had come forth, and
> that he might glorify the Plérôma, the grandeur of his Name
> and the delightfulness of the Father;

> Who, then, was able to enunciate for him a name, the great
> Name, if not He alone, to whom this Name belongs, and the
> Sons of the Name, those upon whom reposes the Name of
> the Father (and who) reciprocally repose in His Name? Since
> the Father is unbegotten, it is He alone who has begotten him
> for Himself as a Name before He produced the Aeons, so
> that the Name of the Father would be over their head as Lord,
> he who is the authentic Name, firm in his authority, in his
> perfect power.

> Thus the Word of the Father advances into the All, being
> the Fruit of His Heart and figure of His Will; nevertheless,
> he confirms the All, he effects there a choice and, what is
> more, he dons the form of the All. [77]

These few excerpts give us some idea of the Valentinian
theology of the Son and of the Name of God. From all eternity

---

76. *Ibid.*, p. 204.
77. *Ibid.*

God has begotten His Son. He has given him His Name so that he might rule certain lower creatures as their Lord (*Kúrios,* practically the Koinè equivalent of *Yahweh*). These creatures, the aeons, repose in the Son.

Several concepts analogous to these are met in *The Book of Jeû,* especially where this writing speaks of the hidden *Logos* of Yahweh. Jeû proceeds from God. He is himself God. He has received from God his name, and this name, Jeû, is but the transcription of YHW, Yahweh. In uttering the divine name, Jeû produced the Universe. He is also the king of "the treasure of light," and elsewhere is called "the great Man."

Now, in the gospel of John we encounter once again a theology of the Name. Christ reveals the Name of God: "I have manifested Your Name to the men whom You have given me . . . (Jn. 17:6)"; more than this, He Himself *is* the Name (John 12:23: "The hour has come for the Son of Man to be glorified"; and John 12:28: " 'Father, glorify Your Name.' Then a voice came from heaven, 'I have glorified it, and I shall glorify it again' ").

Among various points which can be adduced to support this identification, we cite the following:

1. John's gospel forcefully emphasizes that Jesus performed his miracles in the Name of his Father. He proved in this way that he had come in the Name of his Father. As a result of certain of these miracles many persons believed in the *Name* of *Jesus.*

2. In Exodus 3:14 the expression "I AM" is practically the equivalent of the Name of God. Throughout John's gospel Jesus often applies this expression (*egō eimi*) to himself. [78]

3. It would even seem that the use of *Logos* in the Prologue of John is related to the theology of the Name. This term must have been comprehended by the readers of the gospel without difficulty, because it was a sufficiently familiar messianic title. Moreover, in other passages it is a fact that the Johannine writings identify *Logos* (Word) and *Onoma* (Name). [79] This is perhaps

---

78. Cf. Jn. 8:58.
79. Cf. Jn. 1:12; Apoc. 19:13.

not unrelated to the rabbinical practice of referring to the Name of God as *memra,* that is, *Logos.*

Thus, for John Jesus is not only the fulfillment of the Old Testament promises, he also realizes everything that was postulated by the esoteric traditions for the one whom God had begotten to bear his Name: he is the Man of Ezekiel, who has existed from all eternity; and, like the Son of Man of the Jewish traditions, [80] he is the Judge of the last times: "For as the Father has life in himself, so he has granted the Son also to have life in himself, and has given him authority to execute judgment, because he is the Son of Man" (Jn. 5:26-27).

If we read perceptively through the gospel of John, the *Gospel of Truth,* and *The Book of Jeû,* then, we notice at least one thing that all have in common: an incorporation of elements accented in the heterodox Jewish sects of the age. The contention that these extraordinary Jewish traditions played an important role in the birth of what we can call a pregnosticism would, therefore, seem to be justified. This pregnosis formed a part of the religious atmosphere, the *spiritual Koinè,* of the milieu in which *John* was composed, and very probably appealed to the evangelist as offering an advantageous medium for conveying the truth about the light of the world, the Word of God.

Quispel concludes:

It appears to me that the problem of *John* and Gnosticism has in recent years received a largely new clarification. On the one hand, the scrolls of the Dead Sea have taught us that the *Gospel of John* must be understood from the perspective of Jewish pregnosis. To be sure, the manuscripts of the "Essenes" give us hardly any information touching upon the preexisting Messiah, even though John the Baptist preached him. But this lack has now been filled by the *Gospel of Truth.* If we combine the speculations on the name contained in this writing with the data of esoteric Judaism and the pre-Christian beliefs of the Magharias . . . , it would seem

---

80. Cf. *I Enoch.*

that these sources contain an abundant amount of material which can be compared with the Fourth Gospel, and which can shed considerable light upon it.

We do not, then, find ourselves in the presence of a concept foreign to Judaism when the Fourth Gospel teaches the Man-God. All the efforts to fall back upon Iranian, Gnostic, or Hellenic data to support the contrary are irrelevant. As soon as we recognize, for one thing, that the Messiah is the divine Adam, the Man-God of Ezekiel 1:26, and for another, that he is the bearer of the Name and, consequently, the Lord, the *Kurios,* we recognize the divinity of Christ. Once we have proceeded this far, it becomes impossible to see how the Christian dogma (of Christ's divinity) has in reality departed from the kerygma of the Fourth Gospel, a kerygma so closely akin to the messianic expectations of the Jewish People. Jesus of Nazareth is the manifestation of the Divine Being. The Apostle who was instructed by the Baptist and who was well known to the High Priest, the Apostle who had familiarized himself with the language of the rabbis and was initiated to the experience of the Jewish religious communities, proclaims this Credo in the language of Canaan. [81]

What is the upshot of the remarks and observations which have been made about the qualities of John's gospel? A summary of our study of the historicity of John might be helpful here. We began by focusing our attention on what appear to be contradictions between John and the Synoptics. We noted that recent biblical research has made great progress towards the resolution of this problem, especially by showing that while Mark, Matthew, and Luke give us one tradition and John gives us another which, at least to a significant degree, was independently formed, both give us the same historical Jesus Christ.

The differences in terminology and in theological perspective, in particular those which have been discussed in relation to a possible Gnostic influence upon John, can be satisfactorily explained, but only by taking into account a complex variety of

---

81. Quispel, *op. cit.,* p. 208.

factors: the more or less autonomous evolution of the traditions, the originality of the temperament and purpose of each evangelist, the disparate character of the recipients of each gospel, the religious climate of the author's milieu, the time differential between the first stages of the formation of each tradition and its final redaction. Each of these aspects of the overall problem having been examined, our conclusion is that the *Gospel of John* is truly historical, as well as deeply mystical, and that this historicity rests upon the solid foundation of faithfulness to the apostolic kerygma.

One note of caution, however, should be sounded: the "historicity" of John (as well as of the Synoptics) does have its limits. Although John tells us of the words and deeds of Jesus, he does not attempt to arrange them in such a way as to produce a history, his main intent always being to reveal to us the *meaning* of what the Word came to do, and what he in fact achieved. Some of John's chronological indications, for example the mention of various feasts, may help us to know a little more about the Jesus of history, but we should avoid trying to deduce too much from the few details John brings into his gospel. It is generally accepted by exegetes, moreover, that John received its final form from a redactor other than the original evangelist. "This editor seems to have worked with a basic tradition stemming from John himself, and to have added other Johannine pericopes wherever they seemed to match the context." [82] This has resulted in a number of passages in John possessing a composite quality, that is, they represent a sequence that is literary rather than historical. This does not mean that the information transmitted in such passages is not historical, nor that the doctrine is not in conformity with what Jesus actually taught, but that the material is presented in a theological rather than chronological or historical order.

Assuredly, we do meet the real Jesus in the Fourth Gospel. In effect, it could be argued that John presents to us more fully

---

82. Brown, *op. cit.*, p. 10.

than do any of the other evangelists the *reality* of our Lord, for his view is that of the beloved disciple whose great Faith was able to penetrate profoundly into the mystery of the Man-God. But it is only after exhaustive reflection upon each element of John's portrait of his Master that we can properly appreciate not only the Master, but also the disciple whom he loved.

The Authenticity of the Resurrection

In our brief analysis of parts of Luke's gospel and in our consideration of John, we have seen that while both of these gospels possess their own unique characteristics, still they remain faithful to the basic apostolic kerygma and to history. But now, again by way of illustration more than thorough study, let us attend to a special and all-important problem which involves all four gospels. In large part, whether or not the gospels are to be taken seriously depends upon how this problem is resolved.

As we have seen earlier, some intellectuals, notably those of the Bultmannian school of thought, are of the opinion that Jesus did not, as a matter of historical fact, rise from the dead. To support this thesis they begin by accepting the "fact" that to modern man the resurrection is incredible because it is unscientific. Human beings simply do not rise from the dead. Since Jesus could not have risen, therefore, the New Testament must mean something else by the resurrection of Christ, and it is this "interpretation" which must be sifted out through demythologization.

Once having assumed this position, scholars following this line of thought produce other evidence to substantiate their conviction. They propose that there are irreconcilable contradictions between the accounts of the resurrection attributed to various witnesses, and hence these accounts cannot be taken literally (historically). They further maintain that the notion of the resurrection entered Christianity through contact with pagan mythologies, so that disciples succeeding the apostolic generation gradually came to believe that Christ actually rose. They conclude that one of the tasks of Christian exegesis today should be to demonstrate that through faith we accept the resurrection not as a fact of history, but as the eschatological dimension of the crucifixion of the Lord. Jesus died, yet he lives on as we accept the implications of his victorious death in our lives here and now.

While this point of view may have some value in rendering the mystery of Jesus more present to our daily existence, the reduction of the resurrection to an almost purely symbolical dimension hardly seems to meet the needs of many "modern" men, not to mention the fact that the above "interpretation" scarcely does justice to the testimony of the New Testament.

Not all men of faith and intelligence are ready to admit that the historicity of the resurrection is both incredible and irrelevant. Listen to the testimony of several contemporary Catholic writers.

Paul Claudel is of the persuasion that the reality of the Lord's resurrection assures us of the fullness of human and supernatural existence which our own will bring: "Human love will continue. Our Savior's assurance is formal: 'There where I am, you also will be.' Our life after death will thus be his life. In the world beyond we shall not be exiled; there will be no radical change. We shall pass from the world of effects to the world of cause. Instead of seeing reality in terms of its effects, we shall see it — in God — in terms of cause." [83]

For Gabriel Marcel:

> The world today can be endured only if one's spirit is riveted on this hope (in the Resurrection). For us Christians living today, something especially influences us to believe in the resurrection of the body: what we know the body endured in the concentration camps. One feels that human flesh has undergone such intolerable outrage that it must receive some kind of reparation in glory.... I believe life today is unendurable if one's spirit is not rooted in this hope of our Creed. If this hope were shared by a greater number, perhaps

---

83. *The Resurrection of the Body*, Claudel cited in an introduction by Denise Barrat; a collection published by Fides Publishers, Notre Dame, Ind., 1964, p. 1.

a respect for the flesh and for the body, so terribly lacking in our time, would be restored. [84]

R. P. d'Quince insists:

For the Christian, the resurrection is integration in the Body of Christ, which is something wholly different from the seasonal renewal of vegetation (a reference to the typical sense of resurrection in primitive biological mythologies). Basically we believe in the resurrection of the dead because Christ rose again. St. Thomas has correctly noted the unique character of the resurrection of Christ, at once a miracle and a mystery.... The loss of hope in the resurrection is related to our sense of faith. There is too strong a tendency to reduce faith to a purely moral and sociological content.... We see the resurrection too much as a reward, a little like children who expect a good mark after they have done their work well. But the resurrection is a religious and not a moral thought. It is the Savior resurrected, it is creation redeemed, it is "the restoration of all things in Christ." [85]

In his excellent biblical study of the resurrection, F. X. Durrwell adds emphasis to the central importance of the fact of Christ's having been raised up by God:

The believer's entire faith centers upon this divine fact (the fact that God raised up a man, Christ Jesus, for our salvation, lifting him to his true divine life, in the total gift of the Holy Spirit). It is briefly defined as "faith in the operation of God who hath raised him up from the dead" (Col. 2:12; cf. Rom. 10: 9; I Cor. 15:2 ff.; II Cor. 4:13-14; Eph. 1:19; I Th. 4:14). It believes in God whose will to save us is affirmed in the resurrection of Christ and who judges the world in Christ. So essential is Christ's resurrection to our faith, that if he had not risen, that faith would be simply a dream, void of meaning (I Cor. 15: 14-15).

---

84. *Ibid.,* pp. 3-4.
85. *Ibid.,* pp. 7, 9.

Thus the object of our faith is not God in his serene essence, a God standing in motionless perfection, but the person of God who breaks into our history through the justifying and judgment-giving act of the Resurrection, who obliges us to make a decision, and radically changes the course of our destiny. [86]

John L. Mckenzie, in *The Power and the Wisdom,* writes in a similar vein:

The power of love is seen in the death of Jesus; it is seen more fully in his resurrection. For love is a communication of self; and the Christian is not identified with God in Jesus Christ unless he is identified with Jesus risen. Death is the end of a life and of a world; the resurrection is the beginning of a new life and a new world. If Christ has not been raised, you are still in your sins (I Cor. 15:17). The Christian shares the saving act; he dies with Christ, he rises with Christ. Only then is he fully identified with Christ. For Christ lives. The life of the Christian is not the imitation of a dead hero — and it is worth noticing that it can become just that. The Christian lives in Christ, and Christ lives in the Christian.

The theological value of the resurrection, it must be confessed, has been somewhat obscured by its apologetic value; the resurrection has become the major weapon in the apologetic armory. On the hypothesis that we need apologetics, this is a useful treatment of the resurrection; but it is not the New Testament use. The resurrection of Jesus is attested entirely by a few chosen witnesses; the risen Jesus did not reveal himself to the same public which had known the historical Jesus — if I may use the term here. If Jesus had wished an apologetic demonstration, a public manifestation would certainly have done it; and it would have made the task of the apologete much

---

86. F. X. Durrwell, C.Ss.R., *The Resurrection,* translated by R. Sheed, Sheed & Ward, New York, 1960, p. 333.

easier. The resurrection is the climax of the saving act, and it must be seen as such before anything else. It is an object of faith before it is an object of demonstration. [87]

Belief in the reality of the resurrection of Jesus is not outmoded, then, nor is it unnecessary. On the contrary, if we exclude the resurrection, we eliminate the one doctrine which, more than any other, enables Christianity to bestow upon life in today's world meaning and hope. If the resurrection of Christ is difficult for modern man to accept, this testifies only to the intensity of modern man's need to believe in the resurrection, and not to the improbability of Jesus' having risen.

But it is not enough to state that modern man needs to believe in the resurrection, for critics can object: yes, it is precisely because man is dissatisfied with the conditions of this life and seeks consolation in the thought of immortality that he has invented the doctrine of the resurrection for Christ, and for himself!

The veracity of the witnesses to the resurrection of Jesus must be tested, the real meaning and genuineness of their testimony must be deciphered. This is not an easy task, and it is not our intention to attempt it here, at least in a very profound or thorough way. We can, however, bring to the reader's attention several points which help to show that our faith in the resurrection is reasonable and not blind and to delineate its significance. To do this we must first of all study and compare the very texts in which we find the testimony of those who encountered the Risen Lord.

In Mark 16:1-8 we see Mary Magdalene, Mary the mother of James, and Salome going to the tomb of Jesus early on the first day of the week. They discover the empty tomb and are told by a young man dressed in a white robe: "Do not be startled. You seek Jesus of Nazareth, who was crucified. He has risen, he is not here." The women are then directed to inform the disciples, Peter in particular, that Jesus will precede them into Galilee.

---

87. John L. McKenzie, S.J., *The Power and The Wisdom,* Bruce Publishing Company, Milwaukee, 1965, pp. 118-19.

"And they went out and fled from the tomb; for trembling and astonishment had overcome them; and they did not say anything to anyone, for they were afraid."

Matthew 28:1-20 gives us a different version, one which varies from Mark in some details, and adds other details. Only Mary Magdalene and "the other Mary" are observed coming to the tomb. An earthquake occurs, an angel rolls back the stone and petrifies the guard; the angel then addresses the women: "Do not be afraid, for I know that you seek Jesus who was crucified. He is not here, for he has risen as he said." Again the women are instructed to tell the disciples (Matthew does not mention Peter here) of the resurrection and are advised that they will see Jesus in Galilee. "So they departed quickly from the tomb with fear and great joy, and ran to tell his disciples." Along the way, Matthew has the women meeting Jesus himself: "Jesus met them and said, 'Hail!' And they came up and took hold of his feet and worshipped him." But Jesus issues a command similar to that of the angel: "Do not be afraid. Go and tell my brothers to go to Galilee, and there they will see me."

Matthew next seems to indulge in a bit of apologetics: in the infant years of Christianity the story had been spread among the Jews that Jesus had not truly risen, the disciples had come to the tomb and stolen the body, and this was the reason the tomb was found empty. Matthew takes the trouble to trace this rumor to the chief priests and the elders.

The scene suddenly shifts to Galilee. There, on a mountain, the gospel of Matthew rushes to a close: the presence of the "eleven disciples" is noted; "and when *they* saw him they worshipped him"; but the evangelist is careful to add: "some doubted." Jesus utters his final command, assures them that "I am with you always, even until the consummation of the Age," and the gospel ends.

The account of the resurrection as recorded in Luke (23: 55 — 24:53) gives clear evidence of the influence of a tradition distinct from that followed by Mark and Matthew. It is "the women who had come with him from Galilee" who come to the tomb. This time they are greeted by *two* men in dazzling apparel.

The latter seem to chide the women: "Why do you seek the living among the dead? Remember that he told you, while he was still in Galilee, that the Son of Man must be delivered into the hands of sinful men, and be crucified, and on the third day rise." With no further directions from these messengers, the women "returning from the tomb, told all this to the eleven and to all the rest." Luke then identifies the witnesses: "Mary Magdalene and Johanna and Mary the mother of James and the other women with them." The apostles, however, did not yet believe them.

Abruptly then Luke transports us to the road to Emmaüs, and relates the well-known encounter between the Risen Lord and two of his disciples. In the course of the conversation one of the disciples mentions the experience of the women in the morning, and notes that some of the other disciples had gone out and seen the empty tomb. There is no mention whatsoever of the women having seen Jesus himself. Jesus vanishes from the sight of the two disciples as they recognize him "in the breaking of the bread." When the disciples return to Jerusalem to tell their story, they are greeted by "the eleven gathered together and those who were with them, who said, 'The Lord has risen indeed, and has appeared to Simon!' "

At this moment Jesus appears to the entire group in Jerusalem. He assures them that he is no spirit, and to prove the reality of his flesh he partakes of a piece of broiled fish. After this, Jesus instructs them to remain in the city until they are "clothed with power from on High"; then the group is led out as far as Bethany, Jesus blesses them and "departs," and "they returned to Jerusalem with great joy, and were continually in the Temple blessing God." Thus Luke concludes the first volume of his history of the origins of Christianity.

While in his gospel Luke creates the impression that Jesus departs from his disciples for the last time on the very day of the resurrection, in the book of the Acts he adds several details which show that in his gospel he was actually telescoping the final contacts of the Lord with his nascent Church: "To them he presented himself alive after his Passion by many proofs, appearing to them during forty days, and speaking of the kingdom of God." Only after this period do the disciples gather with Jesus for the last time; on this occasion the Holy Spirit is promised explicitly, and the mission is conferred: "You shall be my witnesses in Jerusalem and in all Judea and Samaria and to the ends of the earth." For the first time, also, the Ascension is described: "As they were looking on, he was lifted up, and a cloud took him out of their sight."

In the gospel of John (20:1-31) still another version of the resurrection account is presented to us, once again with its own peculiarities and new information. Before sunrise Mary Magdalene, alone, comes to the tomb. Having found it deserted, she immediately hastens to Simon Peter and "the other disciple, the one whom Jesus loved"; she exclaims: "They have taken the Lord out of the tomb, and *we* do not know where they have laid him." Peter and the other disciples then witness the empty tomb themselves. The disciples return wonderingly to their homes, but Mary remains at the tomb, in tears. At this instant she sees two angels in white; they simply ask her: "Woman, why are you weeping?" She answers, turns around, and sees Jesus whom, like the disciples from Emmaus, she fails to recognize. He repeats the question voiced by the angels: "Woman, why are you weeping?" And when he calls her by name, "Mary!" she knows him, "Rabboni!" Although nothing is mentioned of Mary's having embraced his feet, Jesus dictates the mysterious command: "Do not hold me, for I have not yet ascended to the Father; but go to my brethren and say to them: I am ascending to my Father, and your Father, to my God and your God." So Mary announces to the disciples: "I have seen the Lord."

The scene moves forthwith to a house in Jerusalem, on the evening of the same day. Jesus appears to the disciples and greets them with the phrase "Peace be with you"; according to John's account, he emphasizes the reality of his identity by showing the disciples his hands and side. Next, the Lord once again communicates his peace, and issues the mission: "As the Father has sent me, even so I send you," and breathes upon them the Holy Spirit, for the forgiveness of sins.

Eight days later the disciples are apparently still concealing themselves in the same house. On this occasion the doubtful Thomas is in their company, and the Lord seems to appear especially for his benefit. To the latter's dramatic confession "My Lord and my God!" Jesus gently replies: "Blessed are those who have not seen and yet believe."

On this note the evangelist appears to conclude his gospel. "Now Jesus did many other signs in the presence of the disciples, which are not written in this book; but these are written that you may believe that Jesus is the Christ, the Son of God, and that believing, you may have life in his Name."

Let us return now to Mark 16:9-20. In point of fact, Mark's gospel ends with verse 8. Some ancient manuscripts, however, add after verse 8 (and others after verse 20): "But they reported briefly to Peter and those with him all that they had been told. And after this, Jesus himself sent out by means of them, from east to west, the sacred and imperishable proclamation of eternal salvation." Without going into the problem of the origin and value of this addition, we can say that it obviously represents an early Christian attempt to clear up the curious silence of the women recorded in Mark 16:8: "and they did not say anything to anyone," as well as to include the notion of the spread of the gospel to the entire world.

Verses 9 to 20 constitute a distinct and complex problem. Suffice it to remark that they constitute a later contribution of an author or authors very likely different from the original evangelist. Verses 9 to 11 provide a summary of John's account of Mary Magdalene's testimony. Verses 12 to 13 appear to be a reference to Luke's two disciples from Emmaus; yet, in Luke when the two disciples return, the others exclaim that "indeed the Lord has risen, and has appeared to Simon," while the annex to Mark professes that "the disciples" went back and told the rest, but "they did not believe them." In verse 14, when the Lord "afterward" appears to the eleven, he does not try to prove himself, as in Luke, nor is he the essence of kindness as in John; rather, "he chastised them for their unbelief and hardness of heart because they had not believed those who saw him after he had risen."

There follows the command to preach the gospel to the world and to baptize all who believe, as in Matthew. But another note of harshness is added: "He who does not believe will be condemned." Verses 17 to 18 make reference to the miraculous powers accompanying those who believe, the implication being that nothing can withstand those who accept the Gospel and proclaim it, and that the authenticity of this preaching will be guaranteed by signs; in this we are reminded of Acts 2:4; 3:6; 5:12, 15, 16.

Finally, the appendix to Mark culminates in a proclamation of the Ascension, reminiscent of what we read at the conclusion of Luke's gospel and at the debut of Acts, but culminating with the special grandeur of a Christian witness that has achieved a fuller insight into the meaning of the event to which it testifies: "So then the Lord Jesus, after he had spoken to them, was taken up into heaven, and took his seat at the right hand of God. And they went forth and preached everywhere, while the Lord worked with them and confirmed the message by the signs that attended it. Amen."

Not only the gospel of Mark but also that of John has a second "conclusion," for many scriptural authorities see in chapter 21 of John a later addition to the primitive Johannine gospel on the part of a disciple or disciples of John; that is, the material in chapter 21 does stem from the apostle John's testimony to the risen Christ, but it is given in a highly redactional form attributable to the final editor of the Fourth Gospel.

In John 21 the locale is no longer Jerusalem, but the shoreline of the Sea of Tiberias, in the New Testament more frequently called the "Sea of Galilee." Jesus reveals himself to "Simon Peter, Thomas called the Twin, Nathanael of Cana in Galilee, the sons of Zebedee, and two others of his disciples." The group had been fishing all night, and having failed to catch anything, were coming in, at daybreak. While they were still about a hundred yards out, Jesus called to them from the shore. They did not recognize him, yet at his command they once more dropped their nets into the water, and took in a tremendous catch of fish. At this, "the disciple whom Jesus loved" realized that it was the Lord.

It is interesting to note that earlier in his gospel John omits any reference to the miraculous draught of fishes connected by Luke (5: 1-11) with the vocation of Simon and the sons of Zebedee, and Simon Peter's confession: "Depart from me, for I am a sinful man, O *Lord."* Nevertheless, the Johannine account we are now considering seems to presuppose this miracle, for it is precisely through this sign that "the Lord" is discovered.

One is tempted to think that the author of this tradition has taken an event historically associated with the calling of Peter, James, and John, and transposed it to this moment so that it might serve to introduce the Lord's final words to Peter and his definitive enunciation of the mission of the shepherd of the apostles.

Yet, the details of the narrative are so precise, so vivid, so typical: Peter throwing himself into the water and thrashing his way to Jesus; the observation that the boat was about a hundred yards out; the charcoal fire with fish and bread Jesus had already prepared for them; the one hundred and fifty-three fish; the net which was not torn. Can we be convinced by the conjecture that all of this was merely invented to give a tone of realism to the tale?

John 21:14 observes: "This was now the third time that Jesus was revealed to the disciples after he was raised from the dead." With this apparition in Galilee, the second conclusion to the gospel of John is terminated, as the disciple of the evangelist bears witness: "But there are also many other things which Jesus did; were every one of them to be written, I suppose that the world itself could not contain the books that would have to be written."

This, then, is our summary of what the four gospels and the book of the Acts have to tell us about the Risen Christ. We have, in effect, taken inventory of the various reports of encounter with Jesus after his resurrection. No doubt, it was this testimony which was at the base of the Petrine kerygma: My dear Israelites, hear me well . . . Jesus the Nazoraion . . .

this man whom, having been delivered to you according to the plan fixed in the divine foreknowledge, you have brought to death by crucifying him through the hands of the pagans, God has raised up in delivering him from the throes of death, because it was not truly possible that it hold him in its power . . . . This Jesus, God raised up, *and of that we all are witnesses.* (Cf. Acts 2:22-24, 32.)

We summon as our last witness the Apostle Paul: "Now, I would remind you, my brothers, that . . . I have transmitted to you, as teachings of the greatest importance, that which I myself have received, namely: that the Christ died for our sins, according to the Scriptures, then he was placed in the tomb and on the third day he rose, in accordance with the Scriptures, and that he was seen by Cephas, next by the Twelve, and then he was seen at one and the same time by more than five hundred of the brothers, most of whom are still living today, although a few have died. Afterward, in the time that followed, he was seen by James, then by all the apostles; but last of all, after everyone else, as to a child untimely born, he appeared even to me" (I Cor. 15:1-8).

Having examined the evidence conserved in favor of the resurrection, we must now attempt to render some kind of verdict as to its value. To initiate our critique, we must first of all acknowledge the presence of several difficulties which are real, although possibly not as significant as they may seem. Concerning the testimony of and about the women: did Mary Magdalene come to the tomb alone, as John appears to say? Was she accompanied by "the other Mary," as Matthew indicates? Or by "Mary the mother of James, and Salome," as Mark declares, or by all the women who had followed Jesus from Galilee, as we learn from Luke? Did the women find only the empty tomb? Or did they see one young man? Or was it two angels? Did the women keep silence, or did they rush to the disciples and relate their experience? Did Jesus appear to Mary Magdalene, or to the entire group of women, or to either?

Concerning the testimony of the disciples: did they see Jesus in Jerusalem that night, or did he, according to his word,

go ahead of them into Galilee? Was it in Galilee or outside
of Jerusalem that the disciples saw Jesus for the last time? Did
the group of disciples believe the two from Emmaus, or didn't
they? If the actual site of Emmaus (as seems to be most likely)
is twenty miles from Jerusalem and not the seven suggested
by Luke, how could the disciples walk there and back in such
a brief span of time?

The disciples of Emmaus recognize Jesus in "the breaking
of the bread" (apparently a Eucharistic reference), and yet
we were not told of any disciple other than the Twelve being
present at the Lord's Supper! In Jerusalem did Jesus wish the
disciples his "peace" and prove to them how real he was, or
did he rebuke them for their lack of faith? Why isn't such an
important manifestation as the apparition to the "more than
five hundred of the brothers at one time" mentioned by Paul
cited in any of the gospels?

Did Jesus give his followers their final instructions and then
slip quietly away, never again to reappear, as might be inferred
from the conclusions of Matthew and John, or did he depart
from this earth in a dramatic ascension such as that described
by Luke? These and other difficulties unfold as we confront
the resurrection accounts one with another. For, depending upon
which account we study, the answer to each question differs.
There cannot be any doubt, taken as they stand, that the resurrection accounts are definitely in conflict. But are these conflicts
sufficiently serious to justify modern man's skepticism about the
resurrection itself?

It would be interesting to have at hand a scientific psychological
study of the modern mind, a study conducted to determine whether
this mind is really more critical and objective than were the
minds of the predecessors of the contemporary generation, or
whether modern man is just as credulous and gullible as most
of his ancestors have been. A superficial examination of this
question produces only ambiguous evidence. If we reflect on
the techniques used by most popular advertising today, for instance, they seem for the most part to be aimed at an almost
incredibly uncritical audience. Truth or exactness of witness

has no meaning in this domain. Again, if we look at the many scandals in the area of contemporary politics, and the fraud and deceit current in the judiciary — judges accepting bribes, witnesses flagrantly perjuring themselves, etc — we discover little concern for the truth.

On the other hand, if we turn to the "critical" sciences which propose for themselves the task of objectively and microscopically contemplating the properties of matter or of thought, the quest for the truth is almost infinitely demanding in the norms it sets. All data is tested and retested, and even after lengthy research if it is confessed to be "certain," it is regarded as "certain" only until more is learned.

Or again, if a decision has to be reached and steps have to be taken which will affect a majority and cost the members of this group some sacrifice, the matter will be weighed quite diligently and at great length, lest a rash or false judgment be passed. We need think only of the great turmoil which has arisen over attempts to initiate a civil rights program for the correction of the racial injustice which has for so long been taken for granted in American society.

These observations of several rather banal characteristics of the society in which we live may very well point to a tendency of the modern mind to be prone to rationalize away anything that places demands on us, while it is all too ready to condescend to whatever enables us to elude our responsibilities as sons of God. If the testimony we hear gives us consolation and comfort, we are ready to receive it; if it challenges us to a commitment which involves a risk of ourselves, it will be accepted, if it is accepted at all, only after the most arduous scrutiny.

It is more than likely under this perspective that we should search for the roots of modern man's inclination to deem the resurrection incredible, and not so much from the viewpoint of the influence of scientific criticism upon the engagement demanded by faith. The scientific attitude of the leaders of modern man certainly has a significant role to play, but it may be questioned whether in the overall picture its effect is the primary source of the doubts that plague the religious spirit of the present world.

To the world in which Christ rose from the dead, the resurrection was a boon. Such an astounding victory, such a marvelous proclamation of love offered unheard-of hope and consolation to the multitude of souls for whom life, at best, was
a tortured lot, and for whom death opened the door only to
nebulous darkness. Is it any wonder that this world should have
come to herald the Risen Lord? Yet we know that even this
world did not accept the doctrine of the resurrection without
hesitation and struggle. When Paul proclaimed the resurrection
on the Areopagus, the learned Greeks saluted him with mockery
(Acts 17:32). The first Christians were esteemed and martyred
as fools, as annoying unbelievers; the doctrine of the resurrection
ultimately triumphed not because paganism found it consoling,
but because paganism found it harder and harder to doubt the
blood of Christians. A myth might be comfortable to live by,
but who would die for nothing but a myth?

The situation of the modern world is quite different, so
different that, paradoxically enough, the resurrection rather than
being a comforting doctrine, to a great many constitutes a threat.
To a world permeated by *relativism,* the resurrection, taken as
a historical fact, instead of a mere religious symbol, appears
to stand for a complex of values based on *absolutes.* If the
resurrection can be reduced to mythology, then why can't the
entirety of the New Testament message be accommodated to
the situation of modern man, emptied of all absolute content
and rendered as relative as this situation itself? But if Christ
actually rose, does this not render an absolute value to the
testimony of his witnesses? Does not such a resurrection imply
not only joyous victory, but also the reality of the Justice and
Judgment to come? Is not the assertion "not a jot of the Law
will pass away" given a fuller meaning?

Modern man, at least among many of our more "advanced"
Western peoples, despite the brand of misery his comfort breeds,
considers himself relatively well fixed, comfortable, secure. At
least this is the illusion he constantly strives to project before
himself. He needs no myth of a heavenly reward to compensate
for his present anguish. Tranquilizers will do to carry him from

one diversion to the next. For the thoughtful "believer," who cannot bring himself to discard the New Testament entirely, or simply ignore it, a convenient solution is found in "reinterpreting," in "demythologizing," in diluting faith to a vague expectation of some sort of "eschatological fulfillment," and in reducing moral responsibility to the ethics of what is demanded by love-in-situation.

We have no intention of excluding here the very real need for "reinterpretation" and "demythologization," nor do we reject the validity of an existential or situational perspective in the field of moral judgment. But we do challenge the excesses to which these approaches so readily and subtly lead. Above all, we wish to make the point that the resurrection taken seriously (that is, as historical fact) means the New Testament taken seriously. [88] It means that the inexorable imperative of the Lord "He who does not accept his cross and follow me is not worthy of me (Mt. 10:38)" cannot be watered down or evaded. If the resurrection of Christ is real, his demands are real, and he demands that we die in order to live (Mt. 10:39). Modern man is not particularly eager to accede to such a categorical vocation, and thus he is psychologically ripe for rooting out the least flaw in the testimony to the resurrection as fact. He requires that this witness be submitted to the severest of tests.

Is there a justification for expecting the quality of the testimony of the first Christians to measure up to the standards we set for historians or biographers today? Yes and no. We have every right to expect to hear the *truth* from any and every witness. But we have no right to impose the *form* through which that truth is conveyed. The preceding study of the nature of the gospels

---

88. We do not infer that exegetes such as those of the Bultmannian school do not take the New Testament seriously; moreover, they too desire to evoke from the modern Christian a complete commitment to Christ. The point is, once the resurrection is deprived of its historical quality, its facticity, the "absolute" value of the entire New Testament as divine revelation is called into doubt and its message reduced to relativism. Now, how can the average person commit himself absolutely to a body of relative "truths" whose ultimate significance is forever shifting?

should have made it sufficiently clear that there is not merely one form of witness to Christ in the New Testament; there are many forms, sometimes found in a pure state, more often intermingled, and almost always to some degree foreign to our own patterns of thought.

In addition, it must be remembered that the apostles and disciples of Jesus were not trying to transmit to us just any truth, but a Divine Truth which of itself transcended their every effort to express it. We are wrong, therefore, to require that every detail in each of the resurrection accounts be in agreement with what is stated in all of the other accounts. Unhappily for us, who delight in having our problems resolved by neat, simple, orderly, and consistent pre-packaged solutions, any endeavor to smooth out the rough spots in the testimony to the resurrection, any effort to reconcile the contradictions in detail, is predestined to flounder. For such aspirations ignore the true purpose and miss the point of the resurrection tradition. Perhaps if we look a little more deeply into the heart of the message of Jesus' being raised from the dead, we shall better appreciate this.

First of all, two pertinent facts ought to be mentioned which increase our confidence in the witnesses of the resurrection. An appreciable period of time elapsed between Easter Sunday and the writing of the gospels, say, thirty years for Mark, about seventy years for the final edition of John. If the resurrection were from the very outset an invention, fabricated for theological or apologetical reasons, why weren't at least a few ornamental details also contrived across the years, to give greater glory to the narration of this triumph of the Lord?

The risen Christ took an unprecedented place in the spirit and in the life of the disciples. Through his resurrection he was consecrated in all of his prerogatives: The Elect of the Divinity, the Head, who had conquered death and who conducted to Life. It was in this atmosphere of triumph that the earliest traditions were established, whence came forth the gospels. We would be within our rights to expect writings of a style elevated to meet the level of the reality; and indeed if they were redacted thirty years or more later, the tone should have been lifted to correspond to the pitch of belief. Now such was not the case: not the least amplification was substituted for, or even added to the simple memory of the original facts. [89]

The same sober, factual tone runs through all of the reports of the resurrection, whether they are redacted by the Synoptics or by John. Hardly any more color is given to the happenings of Easter than to the laconic descriptions of the passion. There are, to be sure, the tears of Mary Magdalene, her tender "Rabboni," the dazzling array of the angels, Peter's "Lord, You know everything, You know I love you," and the ascension. To some extent the reports incorporating these features may manifest the creative talent of the evangelists or those behind the tradition they give us, as they strive to portray in an emphatic but restrained way how greatly the followers of Jesus loved him, in his humanity and in his divinity. But in general, the tone of all the accounts is rather matter-of-fact.

Again, we know that the later evangelists depended upon those who preceded them, or at least made use of common sources. Now, if the composers of the resurrection accounts felt free to invent, and if they were trying to fabricate a story which would convince their hearers, why didn't they take the trouble to erase the obvious conflicts between the various stories? The very persistence of these variations in the testimony is an indication of the reliability of the evangelists and of the Christian community which placed its seal of approval on their gospels: their major goal is loyally to preserve the tradition of the resurrection as they received it, not to write a logically coherent treatise on the resurrection. If they word their version of the tradition in such a way as to achieve a particular kind of theological impact, they do not thus betray the reality of the event itself; rather this is their way of highlighting some aspect of the inexhaustible riches of the person of Christ.

We can, moreover, trace a general line of development of the

89. P. R. Bernard, O.P., *The Mystery of Jesus*, Alba House, Staten Island, N.Y., 1966, Vol. 2, p. 451.

events which followed the resurrection; this sequence seems to
be attested in one way or another in all of the resurrection accounts,
and has every chance of being historically valid.

Early on the morning of the first Easter, a number of the
women who had been closest to Jesus came out to finish the
task of the embalmment. They found the tomb empty. In returning to tell the apostles and other disciples of this startling turn
of events, it is most likely that they split up, so as not to draw
attention to the location where the followers of Christ were
concealing themselves. Thus it is quite possible that some
could have made their way to the apostles and announced to
them the empty tomb, while Mary Magdalene, and perhaps several
of the others, could have been favored by a meeting with the Risen
Lord along the way. Some of the men, led by Peter and John,
came out to see the tomb for themselves. They then went back
to Jerusalem in wonderment.

Sometime later, it makes little difference whether it was
actually the day of the resurrection or not, Jesus appeared to
two disciples outside of Jerusalem, causing them to return to
the city. This was followed by other apparitions in the environs
of Jerusalem: to Peter, possibly to James, conceivably to some
of the other apostles individually, and no doubt on several occasions
to the assembled disciples. Some "believed" even before they
themselves had witnessed the Risen Christ (Jn. 20:8), others who
had not seen him would not believe (Jn. 20:25), and still others,
even though they did see him, thought they were seeing only
a ghost (Mt. 28:17; Mk. 16:14; Lk. 24:37).

Because Jesus had many other disciples from the region of
Galilee, who were not to be found in Jerusalem, but who also
were to share in the joy of the resurrection, the scene of apparitions
shifted to Galilee. Here the Risen Lord was able to meet with
larger groups of his followers, and to give them their final instructions in a more leisurely fashion than would have been
possible in Jerusalem.

While the above is but a more or less probable conjectural
reconstruction of the actual order of events, everything else
remains much less certain. The ascension accounts in the gospels

and Acts are so colored by the theological orientation of the writers responsible for them that it is impossible to decipher objectively and without speculation the historical reality behind them. It is possible that Jesus addressed his last words to his disciples in Galilee, told them to go back to Jerusalem and await the fulfillment of the promise of the Father, and departed from them. It is equally possible that, having ordered some of them to return to Jerusalem, he appeared to them for the last time outside of the city, and thence ascended to his heavenly Father. Such details matter little. It is the theological message of the ascension that the evangelists want us to appreciate: after having completed his work on earth, the Lord ascended to the side of his Father, there to reign over his kingdom forever. He left behind him his apostles, his Church, to work in union with him in the world, until the day when the kingdom of heaven and the kingdom of earth would be totally one.

For a person who is willing to believe in the resurrection, to believe that it is possible, to believe that God could love man so much, what has been said in the preceding paragraphs should help to alleviate the feeling of insecurity which might be aroused by the "contradictions" in the resurrection accounts. There is no reason to be disturbed by the different ways in which the gospels tell us of the resurrection. Once we realize how complex was the evolution of these accounts, and how diversified the traditions from which they were drawn, the amazing thing is the strikingly similar tones in which they give us the same reality of the person of Jesus after his resurrection. (We might mention in passing a recent interpretation of the resurrection presented by G. W. H. Lampe in *The Resurrection,* Mowbrays, London, 1966. Bothered by the contradictions in the testimony and the fact that Paul does not mention the empty tomb, Lampe suggests that the corpse of Christ was not resurrected. The resurrection was an objective event, but only in that the risen, *incorporeal* Christ appeared to the apostles.

Such an interpretation, in our opinion, exemplifies too rationalistic an approach to the New Testament evidence, deducing far too much from far too little. Furthermore, it deprives the resurrection of what is perhaps its most vital significance: it is not merely the soul of man that will endure, for it is not merely the spirit of Christ — but the *whole* Christ — who survives; it is the body *in its very corporality* that will be glorified and, reunited with the soul, be one with the Lord forever. Indeed, do we not have in the mystery of the resurrection divine affirmation of the ultimate dignity and value of the corporeal, the material, even in the here and now?)

* * *

Rather than the attack on the resurrection accounts from the viewpoint of their inconsistencies, possibly a more disconcerting challenge to belief in the resurrection is to be found in the notion that the entire story was an invention based on religious conceptions gleaned from pagan mythology. The problem of the origin of belief in the phenomenon of resurrection, as well as the history of this doctrine as it has been accepted and taught by religions other than Judaism and Christianity, is much too involved to be treated in a work such as ours, but we can make a few remarks relevant to the influence which pagan notions concerned with immortality may have had on the Christian presentation of its faith in the resurrection of the Lord and in the future resurrection of all men.

In pre-Christian times and even prior to the appearance of the Israelites, there was no dearth of theories about the afterlife. In primitive agrarian societies the life-death cycle was closely related to gods who died and rose. Death was looked upon as a prerequisite for generation of new life. The chief of a tribe or the king (god) of a people was often looked upon, in Egypt for example, as incorporating in himself the destiny of his people. H. Cornélis, O.P., in his study of primitive conceptions of the resurrection of the body,[90] describes this attitude:

When the chief dies, the tribe itself in some way dies. Thus

---

90. H. Cornélis, O.P., *The Resurrection of the Body,* as indicated above, p. 28.

it is imperative that the chief be resurrected, even though in another world, in such a state that his function in life continues to be carried out. On the one hand the chief reincarnates part of himself in his descendants; on the other hand, he rejoins the gods, or at least his forefathers, in a place where he continues his beneficent action.

Often the resurrection affected only the god himself and did not apply to the believers. Also, the personality of the god frequently more or less dissolved with his death, he survived, but only as assimilated to the functioning of the cosmos. In certain instances, however, the gods seem to have had more of a personal survival, by which their subjects were benefitted. By way of illustration,

> the solar gods ... are more often savior gods, themselves "saved" through a victory of truth over the dark words of an enemy of cosmic dimension.... The dramatic action in which they find themselves engaged makes them strongly delineated personalities, even where the gods, as in the Indo-Iranian domain, had a general tendency to be only hypostatized functions. See, for example, the portrayal of the personage of Indra in the Indian veda and of Mithra in Iran. When, through these "mysteries," the faithful participate in the glorious deed of a god, this can lead in principle to a more individualized idea of the salvation of souls after death.[91]

These observations, however, are immediately qualified by Cornélis as he adds:

> This generally complete and coherent outline can be utilized as a valid explanation only here and there, where one can assemble proof that the progress of concrete religious thought has indeed developed along this line, and there seems to have been no case in which the proofs have been completely established. [92]

---

91. *Ibid.*, p. 29.
92. *Ibid.*

Although the Egyptians possessed a relatively highly developed eschatology and there was a close and prolonged relationship between Israel and Egypt during almost all of the periods of the history of the Hebrew people, it does not seem that Egyptian ideas about the afterlife, judgment, and resurrection, as expressed in the myth of Osiris for instance, exercised much of an influence on the chosen people. "If the Egyptian belief had any influence on the formulation of the eschatological beliefs of Judaism and Christianity, it was in the elaboration of the idea of a particular judgment." [93] In effect, "we can only be surprised that there is so little similarity between their (Israel and Egypt's) eschatological conceptions . . . . We should note, however, that the two peoples had a similar idea of the dignity and the importance of the *body* in assuring the survival of the 'individual' after death." It is noteworthy that neither the Egyptians nor the Jews practiced cremation, a custom that was frequent enough in the East and had definite religious overtones. [94]

Another ideology about life after death with which Hebrew thought could have had some contact revolves around the Grecian notion of metempsychosis, reincarnation. It cannot be determined with certitude exactly where or when the idea of reincarnation originated. Apparently it developed more or less simultaneously in various places. It would seem to have its roots in an acute human sense of justice. When man observes that the good often lead a praiseworthy life, filled with suffering, yet without recompense, while the evil enjoy a life devoted to self-seeking and pleasure, yet without retribution, he surmises that there must be some way of balancing the scales after this life. In Hellenistic thought a kind of dualism usually offered a solution to the anguish of the just man: the human being is composed of two antagonistic principles, spirit and matter; man's sense of justice is satisfied by admitting that "the spiritual principle, burdened with the moral past of the individual whose continuity

---

93. *Ibid.*, p. 32.
94. *Ibid.*, p. 37.

it assures, is reincarnated after death in this or that womb according to the merits accumulated during its earlier lives." [95]

While the historian of the Jewish wars, Josephus, states that
the Jewish sect of the Essenes, under the influence of Pythagore-
anism, taught a mode of eschatology which included the notion
of metempsychosis, this, even if true, constitutes an isolated
case pertaining to a heterodox group of Jews, and is not indicative
of a possibility that Israel could have received its concept of
the resurrection of the dead from the Hellenic theory of metempsychosis.

> For those who have studied the texts, this hypothesis seems
> absolutely unconvincing, because (in Judaism) the resurrection
> of the dead is not an opinion independent of any religious
> context, or one proceeding mainly from anthropological specu-
> lations. It is an essentially religious doctrine drawing all its
> meaning from a fundamental notion of a justice to be re-
> established by God on a day chosen by him for releasing his
> people from opprobrium and restoring — to the living as
> well as to the dead — the benefit of the unfailing Covenant.
> The doctrine of metempsychosis, on the contrary, derives from
> a well-developed view of the constituent elements of the human
> personality . . . the justice which the law of karma affirms re-
> mains essentially *immanent* (that is, deriving from a determined
> process intrinsic to the cosmos), and has nothing to do with the
> intervention of a transcendent God since it functions very well
> without him. [96]

It is true that the rabbinism of the Jews sometimes suggested
doctrines that seem to parallel aspects of the theory of reincarnation, for example, the preexistence of souls. But more
thorough examination shows these parallels to be of little significance. The theory of transmigration of souls implies a cyclical
view of the cosmos envisioning a process without definite beginning
or end. The Hebrew outlook, however, was what we might

95. *Ibid.,* p. 41.
96. *Ibid.,* p. 42.

term "linear," anticipating at the end of life the sovereign act of a God who would determine each person's state according to what that person's life had been.

The Jewish idea of resurrection of the body, firmly based on the notion of judgment and a decision which cannot be appealed, is thus, despite certain appearances, at the opposite pole from a doctrine of successive reincarnations each of which is a sanction upon the acts of the preceding one. These conceptions are irreconcilable, as an immanent justice contradicts the idea of a judgment of a transcendent God. [97]

It should be added that a dualistic conception of man was foreign to primitive Jewish thought. Only shortly before the Christian era did Judaism begin to hint at a distinction between body and soul in man; up to this time, man in all of his functions was regarded as a totality, a person. And even after a contrast was drawn between body and soul, this was not precisely in the Hellenistic sense of a dualism between matter and spirit. And still later, when St. Paul depicts the "spirit" warring against the "flesh," it is the entire "spiritual" man or the entire "man according to the flesh" that he has in view. Thus, there was little compatible ground between Jewish eschatology and the Hellenic notion of reincarnation.

On this point Cornélis concludes:

To those who would wish to establish a parallel between the hopes of an individual resurrection which the Eleusian mysteries (the principal religious "mysteries" of ancient Greece) or others of like kind awakened among their initiates and the resurrection as it is conceived in the Judaeo-Christian tradition, it is sufficient to recall that if the pagan mind had really been prepared for the apostolic teaching on this point, St. Paul would not have been confronted by mockery on the Areopagus (cf. Acts 17:16 ff.), and Augustine would not have had to declare three and one-half centuries later that the dogma of

---

97. *Ibid.,* pp. 44-45.

the resurrection was still the Christian teaching most violently rejected. [98]

Although the deduction of Cornélis here is possibly too absolutely stated, nevertheless, his point is well made.

If neither Egypt's nor Greece's eschatological beliefs exerted a very formative influence on Israel's faith in the resurrection, could it be that the Semitic culture and religions furnished a more fertile soil from which the chosen people reaped their notions about the afterlife? M. J. Lagrange is rather extravagant in his opinion about the wealth of doctrine related to the resurrection to be found among the Semites and peoples closely akin to them, such as the Babylonians:

"The idea of resurrection is found everywhere, just as the idea of renewal is universal in mythology. More than once there are cases in which the power of the infernal gods (that is, those who imprisoned the deceased in the darkness of the abyss) having been broken, hell casts up its prey .... If one thinks of the extraordinary influence exercised by the Chaldeans in the religious domain and of the number of rather exalted beliefs common to the Semites, one will not be far wrong to place the resurrection of the body among the ideas prevailing in the Semite world about 2000 B.C., and the care taken with sepulture finds in the hope of resurrection a still more complete explanation . . . ." [99]

Cornélis has countered with the observation that the discovery of new facts has altered the picture sketched by Lagrange. Recent research has tended to confirm a profound homogeneity of religious sentiment running throughout the Semitic world. Hence, the major religious tenets of Semite culture would usually meet a favorable reception in contemporary Semitic milieux. But,

through the discoveries of Ras-Shamra we now possess rather extensive remains of a religious literature whose redaction antedates the Bible and which offers evidence about the religion

---

98. *Ibid.*, p. 48.

99. As quoted by Cornélis, pp. 52-53, from *Religion des Sémites*, pp. 294-95.

of a Semitic branch adjacent to the Hebrews. Deciphering these remains difficult, but so far nothing decisively favoring belief in the resurrection of the dead has been found in them. [100]

While it is true that man's death was a problem which perplexed the Semitic spirit and gave rise to speculations about immortality, "except in the case of unusual divine or semidivine personages, no one was thought to escape the confines of Hades," and in Semitic literature "we find no trace of a general resurrection of the dead." [101] There was lacking in the common Semitic tradition, moreover, one basic condition presupposed by a doctrine of the resurrection of the dead which would be comparable to that of Judaism, and this was the idea of an ultimate judgment by God, a judgment progressively extended to "all flesh."

In Israel the expectation of a divine judgment was an important religious theme beginning with the "Day of Yahweh" on which God would pass sentence against the enemies of the chosen people, and culminating in the judgment portrayed with cosmic dimensions in the later apocalyptical literature. When the idea of a universal judgment developed in Judaism, however, "it was normal that the preparatory elements, diffused through the images of 'life' and 'death' that Israel drew from a common Semitic foundation, should crystallize in the doctrine of the resurrection, a corollary of the universal nature of this judgment." [102] Thus, even though it does not seem that Semitic religious current instilled in the Hebrew people a belief in the resurrection of the dead, once this belief had emerged, the culture of the Semites could have contributed to the apocalyptical imagery in which the doctrine was couched.

There remains to be examined a final pattern of eschatological thought, that which was characteristic of the Iranians. Of all the historic religions with which the Judaeo-Christian tradition

---

100. Cornélis, p. 53.
101. *Ibid.*, pp. 55-56.
102. *Ibid.*, p. 56.

was in contact, only the Mazdaism (Zoroastrianism) of ancient Persia had a belief in the resurrection which is really comparable to that of the Bible. [103]

The question of the relationship of Judaism and Mazdaism, however, is extremely difficult to resolve. First, there is a problem of chronology. It is not certain when the founder of this religious current, Zoroaster, lived; the more popular opinion of Iranists places him in the sixth century before Christ, and yet there exists a number of feasible arguments for dating him four hundred years later. Furthermore, it is indisputable that a great portion of the Zoroasterian tradition was formulated at a period considerably posterior to the reformer himself. In many instances then, from a point of view of temporal relationship, Judaic beliefs could have influenced the Iranians, rather than the latter having influenced the religion of Israel.

Secondly, if the religious convictions of the Egyptians, the Greeks, and even the Semites did not contribute a great deal to the Jewish belief in the resurrection, why should Mazdaism, with which Israel had much less contact, wield a very significant influence?

Finally, Iran was such a varied and constantly changing religious world, a world in which many mutually opposed religious beliefs could exist simultaneously, that the task of tracing the development of a doctrine and the influence it exerted on other religions is rendered all the more intricate.

Nonetheless, we cannot help but admit the remarkable similarity between certain aspects of Zoroastrian eschatology and that of Judaism. This is particularly true of the structure of the Iranian and Jewish apocalypses:

> In the former, a cosmic catastrophe, preceded by signs in the heavens, serves as a background of a last universal judgment in which the works of each person are openly manifested. At the end of this judgment the good will be definitively separated from the evil. A general resurrection unites the soul which has endured pain or received reward in a provisional

---

103. Cf. *ibid.,* p. 30.

state, to the body whose matter is restored from the four elements. The resurrection is thus consummated in order to permit the public manifestation of the sentence of judgment and also to integrate the material world, purified by fire, into the final victory of goodness. This resurrection has for its author Saoshyant, the eschatological Savior, held in reserve in the form of a golden seed in a lake where the virgin who gives it birth bathes. Saoshyant begins by awakening the "sleeping" heroes who will help him in his final struggle against the forces of evil. [104]

As Bousset has put it, only in Iran and in the Judaeo-Christian tradition do there exist these three eschatological elements in combination: the destruction of the world by fire, the resurrection of the dead, and the last judgment. [105]

While on the surface this parallelism is most remarkable, when each element of the two eschatologies is studied in depth, as to the time of its origin, the doctrinal position which produced it, and its religious significance, the resemblance between Judaism and Mazdaism is appreciably diluted. With regard to the fire of judgment, for example:

It is impossible to conclude with certainty that the place of fire in the Jewish apocalyptic was a borrowing from Iran, for the fire of the holiness of Yahweh is affirmed as far back as the earliest biblical accounts, and its evolution into an eschatological fire can be explained as an internal development, not needing any contribution from outside. [106]

As to the matter of the resurrection, it is not certain that Zoroaster himself taught the resurrection of the dead, nor can it be absolutely determined when this doctrine appeared for the first time as part of the Iranian religions. Thus, the Judaic belief in the resurrection could have developed independently, in line with the Covenant and God's faithfulness to his promises, being

---

104. *Ibid.,* pp. 67-68.
105. *Rel. des. Jud.,* p. 581.
106. Cornélis, *op. cit.,* p. 74.

only incidentally influenced by Mazdaism, and possibly even exercising its own influence on the latter.

In concluding his study of the resurrection of the body, Cornélis sums up the entire issue very well, evaluating in particular the relationship between Judaism and Mazdaism, and delineating the originality of the Israelitic and then of the Christian belief.

When comparing the religion of Iran and that of the Jews, it is stressed that

> Judaism had in its own premises all that was needed to develop a doctrine of the resurrection, but that certain aspects of this doctrine, particularly those of the apocalyptics, assume cosmological ideas of a breadth new to Israel, which was not naturally gifted in this type of speculation. The broadening perspectives in which the Day of Yahweh occurs could have come about because of ideas introduced through foreign contacts. [107]

It seems that anthropological considerations led the Iranian religions to conclude to a general resurrection in which the whole man, body and soul, would be subject to judgment. On the contrary, the most common reason in all Judaism for faith in the resurrection was that God had made certain promises to the patriarchs, and as centuries passed it became more and more apparent that the perfectly faithful Yahweh could only fulfill his promises through a general resurrection.

> It is impossible to imagine that those upon whom the promise had been personally bestowed would be deprived of its fulfillment. That this belief was at the heart of the authentic tradition of faithful Israel is proved by Christ's argument — at first glance seemingly out of place in a discussion specifically related to the resurrection of the body: " 'I am the God of Abraham and the God of Isaac and the God of Jacob.' He is not the God of the dead, but of the living" (Mt. 22:32). In other words, for Christ, assurance of the resurrection is

---

107. *Ibid.*, pp. 91-92.

founded on the indissoluble bond between God and the *verus israelitus,* created by fidelity to the covenant. [108]

As opposed to the cosmological and anthropological perspectives of Mazdaism or Hellenism, "in the Jewish tradition and in the teaching of Jesus, the question was one of a concrete 'filial' hope not resting upon abstract ethical considerations or anthropological fitness but directly upon faith in the covenant." [109]

With respect to the gospels,

> The introduction of the Son of Man into the history of the chosen people gave it (the judgment), aside from all anthropological speculation, a universal character already grasped by the prophets who were aware of the universal and decisive value of the Word of God, and this fact resulted in removing doubts about the universal nature of the judgment, placing all men *ex aequo,* in terms of a New Covenant. Thus, if the New Testament is more definite about the doctrine of a general resurrection than Judaism, this is due neither to the influence of a more highly developed eschatology nor to the introduction of anthropological categories of Hellenistic origin, but to an understanding of the universal meaning of salvation in Christ. [110]

After the exile Judaism evolved a doctrine of the resurrection, sometimes making use of notions derived from neighboring religions, but always bending these ideas to its own monotheistic prejudice. Nevertheless, even in the time of Christ, Judaism was not unanimous in its adherence to belief in the resurrection. In the declarations of Jesus and in his own resurrection, the doctrine received divine, incontrovertible confirmation, and in the writings of St. Paul the teaching was elaborated not in a philosophical interpretation of man nor in a cosmology, but in a theological view of the destiny to which God has summoned man.

---

108. *Ibid.,* p. 94.
109. *Ibid.*
110. *Ibid.,* p. 95.

According to Cornélis, the *originality* of the Jewish theology of the resurrection cannot be doubted: "The resurrection of the dead is, in the last instance, founded only on God's omnipotence and the act of divine good pleasure which parallels the sovereign and inexplicable act of creation. In the authentic Mosaic tradition, each act God initiated in history has this abrupt character and the act which completes its course is equally sudden." [111] While the majority of the religions which might have exercised some influence on Israel fell into an immanentism stressing an autonomous cosmos containing within itself the energies sufficient to assure the continuation of a cyclic pattern of rebirths, Judaism emphasized the inability of the creature to free himself from his sin and the death it entails, without the gratuitous intervention of the creator who initiates a reborn creation. [112]

Perhaps it might be thought that Cornélis is somewhat conservative in his estimate of the degree to which Judaism borrowed elements of its eschatology from other religious currents, especially that of Zoroastrianism. As a matter of fact, the author avows that he has no illusions about the "compelling" force of his arguments. In light of our present documentation, however, his presentation must be regarded as fundamentally sound and indicative of a truly independent and original strain in the Jewish vision of the last things.

If the Judaic faith in the resurrection, which prepared the way for the acceptance and understanding of the resurrection preached and effected by Jesus Christ, does in reality owe more to ideas originating in "pagan" religions than many authors would care to admit, why should there be anything in this to disquiet us? Certainly, God chose for himself a people which has enjoyed a privileged role in the unfolding of his plan of redemption, but on what grounds can we limit the extent of his revelation to this one people? If this people was specially prepared for the coming of the Savior, why should all other nations have been left totally unprepared? If there are similarities, contacts, and

---

111. *Ibid.*, p. 96.
112. Cf. *Ibid.*, p. 97.

mutual dependencies between Judaism and other religions, does this not simply point to the solidarity of mankind, and demonstrate most emphatically that Jesus is the Lord and Savior of all men?

To recapitulate the preceding pages concerned with the resurrection: we first examined the New Testament testimony to the resurrection of Jesus, and judged it to be basically consistent, despite certain conflicts in details and elaborations reflecting theological preoccupations. Then we concentrated our attention on a summary of the history of the doctrine of the resurrection as taught or at least foreshadowed in Judaism and neighboring religious milieux.

Up to this point we have said little about the doctrine of the resurrection in the religions contemporary to the birth of Christianity, nor have we commented to any extent upon the influence which these systems of belief might have had on the Christian faith in the resurrection. We can only devote a few pages to this complex subject, but perhaps our summary may give some concept of what is involved in the issue.

Of the religions which maintained some sort of belief in the resurrection at the inception of the Christian era, perhaps Mithraism had the best chance of influencing Christianity. Mithra was anciently a god of Persia and India. Because the central sacrament in the cult of Mithra was the sacrifice of the ox, and Zoroaster manifested an abhorrence for the sacrifices of antiquity as well as a great respect for the ox, Mithra was only a minor figure in primitive Zoroastrianism. Nevertheless, by the fifth century B.C., Mithra had assumed the position of the principal Persian deity. He was esteemed to be a god of light and wisdom, closely associated with the sun. As his cult spread through the Middle East to Europe, it developed into the religion known as Mithraism, which was to be one of the foremost competitors of nascent Christianity in the Roman Empire.

Mithraism was characterized by several themes or practices which at least at first sight appear to parallel Christian beliefs. There is a struggle between the powers of light and darkness; Mithra gave to his devotees hope of blessed immortality, the resurrection of the dead forming a part of the creed of Mithraism;

fasting and continence were rigorously prescribed by the religion; the rituals (which were highly secret and reserved to men) included many of the sacramental forms, such as baptism and the sacred banquet, common to the various mystery religions; Mithra presides over the last judgment and will author the conflagration which will consume the world.

Franz Cumont summarizes the Mithraic eschatology in these terms:

> After death, the genie of corruption seizes the corpse, the dark spirits and the heavenly envoys dispute the possession of the soul separated from its corporeal prison. It is submitted to a judgment presided over by Mithra, and if its merits weigh more than its faults in the god's scales, he defends it against the myrmidons of Ahriman who try to carry it into the infernal depths, and he guides it toward the ethereal spaces where Jupiter-Ormuzd sits enthroned in eternal light . . . . The souls of the just go to live in the infinite light, which extends beyond the stars, and, stripped of all sensuality and all covetousness in passing through the planetary spheres, become as pure as the gods whose companions they will be. Yet, at the end of the world, even their bodies will participate in their beatitude because, like the Egyptians, the Persians believed that the whole person should enjoy eternal life. When time is completed, Mithra will redescend from heaven to earth, and will resurrect all men and pour out upon the good a marvelous beverage which will assure them immortality, while the wicked will be annihilated with Ahriman himself in the fire that consumes the universe. [113]

It is interesting to note that Mithraism inculcates a very pronounced type of Iranian *dualism*, reminiscent of the Mandaean and Manichean Gnoses. Nonetheless, it was able to unify its dualism of spirit and matter, in which the soul was the prisoner of the body and liberated by death, with a resurrection of the

---

113. F. Cumont, *Rel. Orient.*, p. 147.

body, a synthesis that certainly seems to imply a rather marked contradiction.

Returning to the matter of resurrection in the New Testament, could Christianity have received its notions about the resurrection of the dead from Mithraism or a similar version of mystery religion? This would not appear to be the case. Despite certain resemblances between Mithraism and some of the features of the Christian persuasion, there is actually no firm foundation on which to base a contention stating such a dependency. Several facts can be adduced in support of this judgment.

In the first place, the Synoptics scarcely present what could be called a "doctrine" or a "theology" of the resurrection. The general resurrection of men is passed over, although it is implied in the last judgment. While the resurrection of Jesus is the climax of these gospels, it is attested not in a doctrinal way but simply as a *fact* witnessed by the followers of Jesus. The apocalyptical passages might remind us of the Iranian eschatology, but they also coincide with the Judaic vision of the end of the world, and in any event, are not particularly related to the observation of the empty tomb and the Risen Lord.

The gospel of John indeed includes a dualism of light and darkness. But in no sense does John give evidence of an opposition between the body and the soul. John does possess something of a theology of resurrection, as he makes Jesus "the Resurrection and the Life" and insistently relates our resurrection to that of the Lord, but when he brings forward his witnesses to the resurrection of Jesus, the factual tone of the Synoptic tradition continues to ring through his theological orchestration. The testimony clearly centers on a person, not on an ideology.

If John does introduce more doctrinal nuances, is this any more than a reflection of the Christian community's growing awareness of the divinity of the person who had risen? Again, as we saw above, John was influenced to a degree by the Hellenistic milieu and thought patterns, and doubtlessly made use of the latter in order to render his gospel more intelligible to the Gentiles;

why, then, should he place emphasis on the resurrection, and thus honor the body, when the corporeal was looked upon with disdain by the Gnosticism of the orientals and the Hellenists?

When the epistles of Paul speak of man's resurrection at the end of time, this event, to be sure, is described in terms of Pauline theology. At times there is even a mythical note in the theophany portrayed:

> For the Lord himself will descend from heaven with a cry of command, with the cry of the archangel, and with the sound of the trumpet of God. And those who have died in Christ will rise first; then we who are living, who are left, will be caught up together with them in the clouds to meet the Lord in the air; and so we shall always be with the Lord. (I Th. 4:16-17.)

The sacraments of the Church and the life of the Christian are placed by Paul in strict dependency upon the resurrection of Jesus: "We were buried therefore with him by baptism into death, so that as Christ was raised from the dead by the glory of the Father, so also we might walk in newness of life" (Rom. 6:4). Our resurrection is a function of his: "For if we have been united with him in a death like his, we shall certainly be united with him in a resurrection like his" (Rom. 6:5). "For as in Adam all die, so also in Christ shall all be made to live. For as by a man came death, by a man has come also the resurrection of the dead" (I Cor. 15:22, 21).

All the same, when Paul speaks of the resurrection of Jesus himself, he does so soberly and without embellishment, once again in the tones of the apostolic kerygma: "For I delivered to you as of primary importance what has also been handed on to me: that Christ died for our sins in accordance with the Scriptures, that he was buried, that he was raised on the third day in accordance with the Scriptures" (I Cor. 15:3-4). Paul, then, in his description of the Lord's resurrection, remains faithful to the simplicity of the primitive gospel tradition; nevertheless, his discussion of the resurrection carries a special conviction, due possibly to his own encounter with the Risen Lord. Although Paul's presentation may with reference to specific passages, particularly in the captivity epistles, be characterized as imaginative, mystical, or even "Hellenistic" (cf. his doctrine on the "Body of Christ," Christ as the "Pleroma," or the "Form of God"), it contains no trace of the extravagances of Mithraism.

In brief, therefore, the New Testament has its sacraments and its "mysteries," but these have little in common with the secret rituals of the mystery religions. On the whole, the Christian faith in the resurrection can be explained in terms of the Judaic tradition of resurrection, the teaching of Jesus and his resurrection from the dead. It is hardly to be excluded, however, that in the proclamation of this resurrection and of its relation to that of men in general, the Christian message could have gradually begun to take more serious account of various "pagan" beliefs concerned with the after life, in order to announce to the world that the resurrection of Jesus Christ, the Lord, was the answer of God to the expectations of *all* mankind.

Finally, some of the similarities between Christianity and a religion like Mithraism could very well be explained by an influence of the former on the latter. During the first three centuries of the Christian era there existed a great deal of "competition" among the various religions. The question of life after death and related eschatological themes played a role of major importance. It was common enough for the various oriental religions to borrow popular beliefs from one another, in their struggle for survival. Perhaps this type of tolerance for accretions could account for the strange combination in Mithraism of a dualism declaring a state of war between soul and body, and a belief in the resurrection of the body. In any event, those authors who seek the origin of the Christian faith in the resurrection in Iranian eschatology or in Hellenistic Gnosis have scant real evidence to accredit their claims.

Having discussed the problem of the *origin* of the doctrine of the resurrection, we now conclude with several observations about the *importance* of this event to the early Church. When we think of Redemption today, we customarily think of the Cross. The passion of Jesus, principally because of the emphasis it received from medieval theology, is regarded by the contemporary Christian as THE instrument of our salvation. This was not the mentality of primitive Christianity. "In the early Church it was not the Passion but the Resurrection which was to the fore. In the apostolic Church the Resurrection dominates all thinking." [114]

Thus, in the book of the Acts, in which we see Christian catechesis in its earliest form, the focal point of the early sermons of the apostles was the resurrection of Christ preached as the definitive salvation event. [115] Nor should this emphasis seem strange to us, for the early Church did not create the doctrine of the resurrection, rather *it was the resurrection of Jesus that gave birth to the Church* and constituted the fundamental belief of the primitive community. [116] Possibly it is because Catholic theology allowed the resurrection gradually to slide away from the center of its interests and became preoccupied with the more tangible events of the tragedy of the passion that modern Christianity has lost the sense of the actuality of the resurrection which was so keenly felt by the original witnesses of the Lord.

To those who saw Jesus after his emergence from the tomb, the resurrection furnished irrefutable evidence that he was indeed the Messiah, the Anointed of Yahweh promised by the prophets. Since the primitive community consisted largely of converted Jews, this was of the greatest importance. After an ignominious death which threw into the gravest doubt all of Jesus' messianic claims, the miracle of Easter morning reverberated as the divine response to any questioning of the authenticity of this, the Envoy of the Father.

Yet, the resurrection was much more than a "proof." It opened the way for a more profound faith in the person who had risen. It is above all after the resurrection that Jesus is

---

114. Barnabas M. Ahern, C.P., *New Horizons,* Fides Publishers (Dome Books), Notre Dame, Ind., 1965, pp. 66-67.

115. Cf. *ibid.,* p. 67.

116. Cf. A. Feuillet, *Introduction à la Bible,* Vol. 2, p. 821; J. Schmitt, *Jésus ressuscité dans la prédication apostolique,* Paris, 1949; also F. X. Durrwell, *op. cit.*

designated not simply as the Christ or Messiah, but as the LORD, as one exercising divine prerogatives. A man had been raised from the dead, but the faith of the apostles came to see through the glory of their Risen Messiah a divine power, a divine personality.

More than the other writers of the New Testament, St. Paul accents the salvific efficacy of the death of Jesus, but he does not envision this death independently of the resurrection which removes its scandal. For Paul, as for John, the death and resurrection comprise one and the same mystery of salvation. By becoming man and dying, Christ who was "in the form of God" humiliated and emptied himself. Through his resurrection he was exalted by the Father, made to reign at his right hand, constituted the head over all things for the Church, the reason for our hope for a glorious inheritance, the firstborn from the dead, the one in whom the fullness of God was pleased to dwell (cf. Phil 2:1-11; Eph. 1:16-23; Col. 1:11-20; Rom. 1:1 ff.).

Like the other evangelists and Paul, John endeavors to show that the foundation of the Christian faith and the ultimate reason why Christians hope for their own resurrection is the resurrection of Jesus. Hence, he underlines the historicity of the event by bearing witness to the empty tomb, by recalling that some of the followers of Jesus even touched him after he had risen, by presenting Jesus having breakfast with his disciples on the shore of Tiberias.

At the same time, however, John adds a new note to the resurrection theme: he remarks that "the disciple whom Jesus loved," after having entered the vacated sepulcher, "saw and *believed*" (Jn. 20:8), even before seeing the Risen Christ. And to Thomas Jesus says: "Blessed are those who have not seen and yet believe" (Jn. 20:29). John's point is clear: for those who were privileged to encounter Jesus after he had thrown off the bonds of death, there was no question of "believing" in the resurrection; on the contrary, it demonstrated to them who Jesus actually was. But for all those who would subsequently enter the Christian ranks, the resurrection of the Lord would not so much constitute a "proof," but would become a part of the faith, a doctrine to be believed by those who had not seen.

We believe, then, that the apostolic testimony to the resurrection is reliable, that it clearly professes to assert a historical fact which had its witnesses. Although this testimony shows the effects of theological arrangement which brings more and more to the surface the divinity of the person of the Lord, it does not betray a dependency on the mythologies of the mystery religions. It was a testimony joyfully and enthusiastically proclaimed in the fervor inspired by the Spirit, but regarded with disdain by the multitudes of the incredulous, and accepted in faith only by a few.

Thus Paul, as his life drew to a close, sadly and yet triumphantly exhorted his beloved son, Timothy, "Remember Jesus Christ, risen from the dead, descended from David, as preached in my gospel, the gospel for which I am suffering and wearing chains like a criminal. But the Word of God is not chained" (II Tim. 2:8-9).

CHAPTER FOUR

THE VALUE OF THE MODERN
APPROACH TO THE NEW TESTAMENT

The Eternal Openness of the Word of God

At the outset of our study, we spoke of that quality of truth by which it is absolute and immutable. The fact was also stressed that truth never can be adequately expressed in human terms and is always conditioned by the circumstances which give birth to its enunciation. In the preceding pages devoted to the reviewing of some of the most vital problems broached by the contemporary analysis of the New Testament, we have tried to illustrate both the absolute character of the Christian belief and the way in which this faith was subject to the influences of the milieux in which it was first preached and accepted.

Modern biblical research, at least as practiced by some, may be guilty of having laid the groundwork for seriously confusing or undermining the spirit of faith by proceeding with an attitude too prone to skepticism and too ready to reduce fact or doctrine to what it considers outdated mythology. But when study of the Bible has been carried out in a spirit both objectively scientific and open to the authentic commitment demanded of the believer, the results have been positive and give reason to hope that future critical research will be even more fruitful. A particular contribution of this type of scholarship which I wish to single out for special emphasis here is the manner in which such research has brought into sharp focus the TRANSCENDENT nature of the Word of God, the truth par excellence.

As was pointed out earlier, when something is objectively true, a certain *absolute* and unchangeable quality is implied. Thus, if it is true that such and such a thing happened, it happened, and not even an infinite power can erase the reality of what occurred. In the *knowing* of the event that happened, however, there is immediate subjectivization and the truth becomes ambiguous; that is, the truth of what occurred will be apprehended in a personal way by each person witnessing the event. Hence, the problem of evaluating the fact which took place, determining whether it was morally good or evil in significance, important or unimportant, unusually meaningful or banal, is inevitably rendered more or less complex because of this personal, subjective factor.

If it can be difficult to ascertain the "truth" of even a commonplace experience, therefore, plainly the attempt to master the truth of divine revelation can be assured of encountering highly involved obstacles, obstacles which without the grace of the Spirit surely would be insurmountable.

Now, while the invaluable contributions to the understanding of the Scriptures made by the Fathers and Doctors of the Church, as well as by other exegetes and students of biblical theology throughout the Christian era should by no means be disparaged, it would seem, nevertheless, that even the greatest minds of the Church have on occasion approached the task of interpreting the Word of God overconfidently, thinking that the temporal-atempoal teachings and commands of the Lord could be simplified, or encapsulated in the expressions of a particular philosophy or theology. On this score, modern biblical criticism has indicated (not only through its positive results, but also through its shortcomings) that the manner of interpreting divine revelation in the past is reproachable on at least two fronts (not that these are the only ones, but they are of special import here).

First of all, in studying the development of the Church's

theology, [1] especially as seen through the wranglings and definitions of the councils, [2] one sometimes gets the feeling that the Word of God is being "manipulated." The Bible seems to serve as a kind of arsenal from which to draw arms marvelously apt for cutting down heretics. It is not infrequently that we find texts extracted from their proper context and without sufficient exegetical justification combined to form the basis for the pronouncement of a definitive statement of faith.

The cause underlying this procedure is evident enough. The bishops of the Church who gathered in council to settle a doctrinal dispute did not have to probe the Scriptures primarily to discover *what* the Church believed. They knew from the living tradition of the Church what was required by faith with respect to a particular doctrinal issue of major importance. The dogma to be defined by a council could have been more or less a foregone conclusion. Scripture was employed, then, not to reveal the dogma, but to help in framing the terminology to express it and to give support to it once it reached the stage of formal definition.

There is no question that whenever this process has been used, it has enjoyed a certain validity. But this does not excuse the procedure from being subject to criticism. The less than scientific assembling of biblical texts tends to diminish confidence in the doctrine being defended. And the absolute merit of arranging texts into arguments from which emerge definitions which purportedly will endure for all time can be challenged.

Our objection is directed not at the truth which is defined, but at the very methodology which produces a definition and partially at the conception of definition implicit in the process. For in certain instances the councils leave us with the impression that the Church has the power of reducing the Bible to little

---

1. It is, of course, Catholic doctrine that we have in view here.
2. For a treatment of this subject from the viewpoint of the relation between the ecumenical councils and renewal of the living Church, cf. Hans Küng, *The Council, Reform and Reunion,* Sheed & Ward, New York, 1961.

more than a very useful tool. Not that the Bible cannot serve
the Church as an instrument, as long as we do not fail to recognize
that its instrumentality is transcendent. But the Word of God
has been betrayed if we are made to labor under the illusion
that the truth of revelation is exhaustible, that it can be put
down once and for all in human terms in a statement that will
never stand in need of being revised. It cannot be assumed that
what is divine can be adequately delimited by what is human.

The failure to appreciate fully the boundless expanses to
which the significance of God's Word is capable of stretching,
the distorted perspective stemming from the underestimation of
the true dimensions of the transcendency of revelation, has in
several respects been detrimental to the Church. It has tended
to make Catholicism woefully complacent in what it has esteemed
to be total possession of the truth. As a corollary to this
position, our orthodoxy has been either condescending or terribly
severe toward those who have been so rash as to differ with the
Citadel of Truth.

Recent advances achieved in biblical studies, ecumenical theology, and related disciplines have done a great deal to dispel the
misconception that revealed truth is ever totally possessed by,
or the singular treasure of any institution. The modern believer
is more aware than ever before that just as the wisdom of God
manifested in his Son is unsearchable, so also the truth of the
Logos prolonged in the Church is ever subject to being newly
apprehended, more profoundly interpreted and differently applied, as the exigencies of the temporal situation evolve. The
will of God as expressed through the divine Son, the revelation
of the Father centered in the person of the Incarnate Word,
is a mystery the depths of which we cannot hope to fathom.

In our consideration of the formation of the gospels, in
our study of their historicity and of their composers' struggle
to present the resurrection, we remarked that the witnesses of
Christ had to face every sort of difficulty in striving to announce
their message to peoples of widely diverse cultures and religious
persuasions, and we noted that the message was adapted to
become more intelligible to the listeners who received it, so

that the true nature of the Lord might be more faithfully conveyed.

Indeed, as we read the closing lines of the New Testament, the atmosphere is dense with the sensation that the apostles and their fellow Christians of the primitive Church endeavored in every conceivable way to portray the full magnificence of the fact and the personage of the Lord, but that even they found themselves inadequate to the task of defining the will of God become one with the flesh of a man.

Is not the Christianity which has succeeded the apostolic age presumptuous, then, if it pretends to do more than carry on the endless work of penetrating to the heart of the eternal mystery, if it dares to define: *"this* is the truth, *all* of the truth"?

Our criticism is not meant to infer that there is no room in the Church for definition or doctrine. Nor does it exclude the possibility of evolution of dogma, the possibility of gaining ground in the understanding of the revealed mysteries, ground from which retreat will never be necessary. Nonetheless, there is a vital difference (admittedly subtle and sometimes difficult to pinpoint) between the absolutes given through revelation and the interpretations of argumentation by which they are frequently circumscribed.

The Question of Hell

An example or two may help to clarify the issue that has been raised. That all men are guilty of sin and are afflicted to some degree by an inclination to evil is a fact attested both by experience and by revelation. It is also indisputably a matter of Christian faith that Jesus Christ is the Savior of all men, having given himself in propitiation for all sin.

When the councils, specifically those of Orange and Trent, offer their resolution of the problem of original sin, however, their statements of what is revealed are overlapped by theological speculations rampant with details mentioned in biblical accounts but never thoroughly weighed and balanced by scientifically critical exegesis. How could all of their definitions, therefore, be accepted as the "ultimate"? Should Canon II of the Second Council of Orange (529), for instance, condemning anyone who "asserts that Adam's transgression injured him alone and not his descendants, or declares that certainly *death of the body only, which is the punishment of sin,* but not sin also, which is the death of the soul, *passed through one man into the whole human race . . ."* [3] be received as the definitive pronouncement on the subject and the only way of expressing the revealed doctrine of man's solidarity in sin?

Or must the definition of the Council of Trent (1545-1563): "If anyone does not confess that the *first* man Adam, when he had transgressed the commandment of God *in Paradise, immediately* lost his *holiness* and *justice* in which he had been established, and that he incurred through the offense of that prevarication the *wrath and indignation* of God and hence the death with which God had previously threatened him . . . let him be anathema" [4] be canonized as the best conceivable explanation of the original relationship between man and God? Is it entirely impossible that the revealed truth of the alienation of mankind from the God of love might be explicable in different terms?

Because the response to these questions on the part of some voices within the confines of the Church would be an adamant and unreserved "Yes! These matters have been permanently decided!" we are exposed today to the declamations of Catholic writers of the brand of Magdalen Goffin:

Why is it that her (Rome's) power to repel is as strong as her power to attract, that the call of antiquity, the claims of logic, all the seductions provided by a beautiful liturgy, frequently beckon in vain, and that hearts and minds, remain, not indifferent indeed, but hostile? The answer given, expressed in one way or another, amounts to this: we cannot love you, we cannot join you, because let your credentials be ever so persuasive, your helps to heaven ever so numerous,

3. D.B. 175, emphasis mine.
4. D.B. 788, emphasis mine.

your liturgy ever so splendid, in practice you invite us to worship a shrunken god." [5]

Or again: "The stupidities, the absurdities of the Roman Catholic Church are there for all to see, Aunt Sallies which any half-educated lout may shatter with a twist of his animal arm." [6]

Mrs. Goffin's barbs may seem overly abrasive and acrid, but perhaps that is at least partially because they rub quite roughly against a very tender spot, and come all too close to exposing a truth which we can only begrudgingly admit.

Almost in the same breath that she utters her harsh invective, however, Mrs. Goffin points to the even greater evil which flows from the reaction to an exaggerated dogmatism requiring credulity rather than faith:

> But the lout does not know that he has been deluded into believing something far more deeply absurd, false, and silly than any broken image which lies grinning on the ground. He has been guilty of that superstition which the Greeks recognized, a too great unbelief, a negative credulity just as gross and far more damaging than its counterpart. He has been seduced by his environment into thinking that the only things which can be true are those which are capable of empirical proof, persuaded that nothing lies beyond the range of rational demonstration. So he denies to religion what he unconsciously affirms every day of his life when he loves another human being or admires the flowers in his garden. [7]

One of the Church's doctrines which Mrs. Goffin criticizes as superstitious or unworthy of God is the belief in a place or state of eternal torment. [8] Her position does not seem necessarily to include a rejection of the doctrine of hell altogether,

---

5. *Objections to Roman Catholicism,* "Reflexions on Superstition and Credulity," J. B. Lippincott Company, Philadelphia and New York, 1965, p. 17.

6. *Ibid.,* p. 46.

7. *Ibid.*

8. *Ibid.,* p. 17.

but might be construed as a refusal to accept the usual meaning attached to "hell."

Traditionally, Catholic theology has always interpreted the "everlasting fire" of the Bible most literally. It is indeed supposed to be a place of eternal torment of the worst kind imaginable. Thus the Athanasian Creed (which may date from as early as the fifth century) declares: "Thence he shall come to judge the living and the dead; at his coming all men have to rise again with their bodies and will render an account of their own deeds: and those who have done good, will go into life everlasting, but those who have done evil, into *eternal fire.*" [9]

And as recently as 1863 we see Pius IX insisting: ". . . God, who clearly beholds, searches, and knows the minds, souls, thoughts and habits of all men, because of his great goodness and mercy, will by no means suffer anyone to be punished with *eternal torment* who has not the guilt of deliberate sin . . . . But, the Catholic dogma that no one can be saved outside the Catholic Church is well known; and also that those who are obstinate toward the authority and definitions of the same Church . . . cannot obtain eternal salvation." [10]

Notwithstanding the above statements which are representative of the official teaching of the Church, it is not impossible that the doctrine of hell be made more plausible and "worthy of God." In the first place, the texts of Scripture could be interpreted more metaphorically and less literally, so that the real significance of "hell" might be allowed to appear.

Some would suggest that hell is not God inflicting torture upon a soul throughout eternity, but is a state of existence brought about by a free will purposely, almost systematically isolating itself from the will to which by destiny it should submit. Could this be what Pierre Teilhard de Chardin had in mind when he wrote:

> Then, in a Creation brought to the paroxysm of its aptitude for union, the Parousia will occur. The unique process of

9. D.B. 40, emphasis mine.
10. D.B. 1677, emphasis mine.

assimilation and synthesis, pursued from the beginning of time, being at length revealed, the universal Christ will appear like a flash of lightning amid the storm-clouds of a slowly consecrated World. The trumpets of the angels are but a weak symbol. It is in the grip of the most powerful organic attraction conceivable (the force which held the Universe together!) that the monads will pour into that place whither they are irrevocably destined by the total maturing of all things and the implacable irreversibility of the whole history of the World — some of them spiritualized matter in the limitless fulfillment of an eternal communion, *and others materialized spirit in the conscious agonies of an interminable decomposition?* [11]

Then, there is an approach which could be considered complementary to the above. Is it altogether beyond the potential of modern biblical research to shed new light on the origin of the concept of hell and thereby lay the foundation for a better appreciation of its real import in Christ's preaching? In studying the doctrine of the resurrection, we noted the wealth of apocalyptical notions pervading the atmosphere of the pre-Christian era. The imagery of a darkened moon, for example, or a sun that will not give its light, or the stars falling from heaven to signal the end of time. These were not images in the least original with the gospels, [12] but were the common patrimony of Judaism [13] and Iranian eschatology as well.

The special importance of fire in the oriental conception of the last things enjoyed a similar history. Its use as a force, or symbol, of purification or chastisement was quite common in the religious literature of the times immediately preceding the dawn of Christianity. Could the sources from which arose belief in a place of everlasting torment inflicted by unquenchable fire furnish us with a key to a modified insight into what Christ really meant by the eternal punishment of hell?

---

11. *The Future of Man,* Harper & Row, New York and Evanston, 1964, p. 307. Emphasis mine.

12. Cf. Mt. 24:29 and parallels.

13. Cf. Ezek. 32:8; Is. 13:10, 24:23; Jl. 2:10, 31.

The question cannot be eluded: is the doctrine which defines hell as a place of eternal punishment, eternal being used in the strictest philosophical sense of absolutely endless, and punishment including the severest kind of spiritual and physical torment, irreversible and without appeal? In other words, is it not conceivable that enlightened by the efforts of biblical scholars and the results of research in related sciences which give us a more thorough comprehension of the background from which the Old and New Testaments emerged, the Church might come to a fuller understanding of the mysterious reality which the Bible tries to depict through its images of fire and brimstone, agony that never ceases, an abyss where the worm dies not, and the fire is inextinguishable? [14]

Let us explore the matter of the climate in which our Lord preached a little more thoroughly. The Jewish people to whom Christ addressed his messages were quite familiar with the theme of the "Wrath of Yahweh." An outpouring of this divine anger was closely associated in their minds with the coming of messianic times and the Day of the Lord. Punishment by fire was also a part of the general ideology of eschatological expectation. Concretely, the fires of Gehenna, that is, the vale of Hinnom, into which the idol-worshiping king Ahaz hurled his children, [15] evoked in the Jewish mind of the times of Jesus an image of the terrible chastisement to be allotted to the perfidious.

Now, one of the features of the revelation brought by Christ was the clarification of the nature of the afterlife. Judaism may have embraced the doctrine of the resurrection of the dead, but its views on the fate awaiting man after his death were still quite uncertain. The belief in Sheol, the gloomy abode of the dead (but not a place of torture or punishment), continued to prevail. An aim of the preaching of Jesus was to emphasize personal responsibility and its relationship to immortality. He wished to show that after death man is not absorbed into infernal

---

14. Cf. Mt. 3:12, 13:30; Mk. 9:43, 48; Lk. 3:17.
15. II Chr. 28:3.

shadows, but continues his relationship with God which is only begun in this life. If man serves his Master well during his earthly existence, he will enter into communion with his heavenly Father; if he is a rebellious child, he will most assuredly suffer punishment. But it is the *character* of this punishment that is in question.

It was customary for the Semite, in teaching, to make use of what we today call "hyperbole," that is, exaggerating a point for the sake of effect. If Christ wanted to tell his people that they were responsible for their acts and would be personally punished for their sins, it would have been most natural for him to do so by making use of the eschatological categories of his time, and by treating them in hyperbolic fashion. This is the only way in which he could have made an impression on the Jews to whom he spoke, Jews so accustomed to the terrifying wrath of Yahweh. If there was to be punishment for sin in the next life, anything less than an everlasting torment of fire for those obstinate in their injustice would have been dismissed as unworthy of the inexorable demands of the all-perfect Godhead.

An analysis of two passages in particular in which Jesus refers to the inextinguishable fires of hell suggests very strongly the deployment of exaggeration for the sake of emphasis. Mark 9:43-44 reads: "And if your hand causes you to sin, cut it off; it is better for you to enter life maimed than with two hands to go to hell, to the unquenchable fire." Is the *everlasting* nature of this *fire* to be interpreted more literally than the command to cut off our hand if it is an occasion of sin for us? [16]

In Matthew 25:41-43 we hear Jesus declare: "Then he will say to those at his left hand, 'Depart from me, you accursed, into the eternal fire prepared for the devil and his angels; for I was hungry and you gave me no food, I was thirsty and you gave me no drink, I was a stranger and you did not welcome me, naked and you did not clothe me, sick and in prison and you did not visit me.' " Did Jesus mean that the penalty for

---

16. Verse 44 is not attested by the best of the ancient manuscripts; verse 48, however, states the identical doctrine of "fire that is not quenched."

failing to love our neighbor sufficiently is endless torment? Or did he wish to announce as forcefully as possible the identity between himself and our neighbor, the great value with which he esteems charity, and the fact that callousness will merit punishment?

If we must adhere to the doctrine, however, that there is a "hell" and it is everlasting, might we not be free to visualize it in some other way than as a fire created by God to torture the guilty? Could not hell be an intense awareness given a person after his death that he had squandered his lifetime, that he had rejected the true meaning of life and totally missed the purpose of earthly existence, that he had wilfully taken the steps which had led him into irreparable error? For there is but one life on earth; taken as a whole it is the one and only chance a man has, and the effects it leaves behind reverberate forever.

In any event, it is evident enough from scriptural data that the words of Jesus concerning hell, or the fires of Gehenna, do have an absolute quality about them and are not merely symbolical. He is certainly revealing that sin committed in this life and not completely forgiven will be punished after death. Moreover, that sin is abhorrent to God and bears with it terrible consequences is unmistakably an essential aspect of the message contained both in the words of the Lord and in the tragic disfiguration of divine innocence through the crucifixion.

Jesus came primarily to save us *for someone,* to manifest the divine love for us and to establish an order through which we might be brought into communion with that love. But this does not exclude the fact that he came also to save us *from something*: from the tragedy of failing to fulfill our destiny here on earth by betraying love in exchange for selfishness. And if in our earthly existence we have rejected the opportunity, afforded us to develop our capacity to love, will it not be this stunted capacity which we shall carry with us, miserably, throughout eternity?

In this sense it seems not only reasonable, but necessary that "hell" be everlasting. On the other hand, does this mean that a person who has thus "lost his soul" by having squandered his life must forever be *totally* separated from God and deprived of all happiness?

We know that the infinite mercy and justice of God cannot inflict a punishment exceeding the limits imposed by the capacity and responsibility of the guilty. Now, can it be persuasively shown that *any* offense of a finite creature, no matter how serious, can be deserving of a chastisement that is not only everlasting, but in a very real sense infinite? Was so severe a penalty as definitive and complete isolation from the Creator and the Savior the *absolute* meaning contained and intended in the admonition: "Depart from me, you accursed, into everlasting fire"?

The Issue of Divorce

Another area of dispute, and one which has the utmost importance in our times, has to do with the Catholic Church's position on divorce. What has become the fixed doctrine of the Church with regard to divorce is the outgrowth of an interpretation of words uttered in a situation vastly different from our own, and a theological development based on a mentality not at all akin to that of the modern Christian.

Christ's ultimatum on the sacredness of the marriage bond was addressed to a culture in which divorce was widely accepted, to a culture in which marriage was not held in particularly high esteem. How could the standard of the time be raised, how could the dignity of matrimonial union be enhanced, how could the rights of woman as a person be assured, unless a new and demanding position be taken? But granted that the decree of Christ left no room for exception *at the time,* does this absolutely mean that it was to be thus *for all time?*

Primitive Christianity saw itself as a categorical rejection of the darkness of the world. It did not look forward to transforming the universe, but endeavored to set the highest of ideals before the world and to draw as many as possible into the system of ideals in preparation for the Parousia of the Lord, which was expected at any moment. Because the lowly state of marriage was regarded as being closely related to the imperfection of the world itself, even one marriage was discouraged, the ideal being virginity (cf. I Cor. 7:8). In such a context, that is, with the lively expectation of the Lord's return and the negative attitude toward marriage, divorce and remarriage between Christians would of course be unthinkable, and the strictest possible interpretation of the Lord's words would be most natural.

In our days, however, when this issue of divorce and remarriage has become such an urgent matter of universal concern, should not this interpretation be subjected to thorough and dispassionate reconsideration by the Catholic Church? If the Catholic Church's traditional position is to stand, must it not be made to stand on a firmer foundation than ever before? And where are we to find such a foundation? Do the few words of Christ on this subject provide a sufficient basis for keeping in force a marital system which exercises a determining (and sometimes extremely detrimental) influence on the spirituality of countless numbers of persons? But, what are the words of Christ? Essentially:

"What therefore God has joined together, let man not put asunder" (Mk. 10:9).

"Whoever divorces his wife and marries another, commits adultery against her; and if she divorces her husband and marries another, she commits adultery" (Mk. 10:11-12).

Matthew repeats the latter with a slightly different nuance: "I say to you that everyone who divorces his wife, *except on the grounds of immorality,* makes of her an adulteress; and he who marries a divorced woman commits adultery" (Mt. 5:32; cf. also Mt. 19:9).

Luke also has his own version: "Every one who divorces his wife and marries another commits adultery, and he who marries a woman divorced from her husband commits adultery" (Lk. 16:18).

Paul reaffirms this charge received from the Lord: ". . . the wife should not separate from her husband (but if she does, let her remain single or else be reconciled to her husband) — and . . .

the husband should not divorce his wife" (I Cor. 7:10-11).
Nevertheless, he immediately adds that lack of faith on the
part of one of the spouses can lead to licit and valid remarriage
for the Christian (I Cor. 7:12-15).

What judgments can be drawn from the preceding testimony?
There is no doubt that Christ is advocating and demanding, in
principle, the *permanency* of marriage. He recognizes and teaches
the good that derives from a marital union in which the spouses
become definitively two in one flesh. But is he commanding
absolute indissolubility of marirage for his own time and for all
time? Is he saying that never is it within the power of the Church
to permit one partner to separate from another and at a later
date remarry, regardless of the reason?

Is it evident beyond question that the texts cited above necessarily require such an interpretation? Furthermore, are there
not other texts which might allow the Church more leeway in the
exercise of its jurisdiction? It would be interesting to see a
thorough discussion of the application of the text governing the
"power of the keys" to this issue. *"Whatever* YOU bind on earth
will be bound in heaven, and *whatever* YOU loose on earth shall
be loosed in heaven" (Mt. 16:19). It would seem that the power
and jurisdiction delegated here is quite universal, extending to
more than simply the forgiving or retaining of sins. And if every
sin of man will be forgiven, except the sin of blasphemy against
the Holy Spirit (Mt. 12:31), must a man live with the mistake
(and not necessarily the sin) of an ill-advised attempt at marriage
throughout his one life on earth? (There is, to be sure, no basis
in tradition for deriving from these texts a power of the Church
to dissolve sacramental marriages. But does this necessarily
imply that God cannot speak to the Church *today* in a new way
through these very texts? The Church can never accept sin, in
this context the evil of divorce. But is it not her role to grant
the sinner the *real* possibility of a new life . . . which in particular
cases might require divorce and remarriage?)

Considering the general tone of the texts we have quoted
and the tenor of the gospels taken as a whole (as they reflect the
merciful and understanding side of Jesus, as well as the *ideal*

he encourages his followers to pursue), it would seem clear that in speaking of marriage, being very conscious of the extremely important effect lasting marriages have upon the spiritual and material welfare of mankind, Jesus vibrantly and absolutely affirms the *permanency* of marriage. But it may be too much to say that he is also defining the *indissolubility* of marriage, rather than simply castigating the practice by which a man divorces his wife to go to another. Is there no distinction between this particular case and the generalization that divorce and remarriage may never be permitted for either party for any reason whatsoever? There are certain features of the texts cited which would lead us to believe that the demands of Jesus were not quite so wide-sweeping.

Why does Matthew add the qualification "except on the grounds of immorality (unchastity)"? This brief insertion has provided subject matter for considerable debate, the interpretation of either party to the debate always serving to confirm the *status quo* position of his Church. One Catholic interpretation is that in the event of unchastity (adultery), a Christian is permitted to divorce his spouse, but this does not mean he may remarry. If we remember, however, that Jesus was addressing a Jewish audience for whom permission to divorce necessarily implied the right to marry someone else, this explanation does not seem particularly compelling.

Other Catholic exegetes have insisted that "immorality" designates the state of concubinage in which a man is cohabitating with his mistress. But, in this case it would not merely be permissible for him to divorce her, it would be his moral obligation to do so. Now, Matthew's text appears to have Christ stating the principle of permanency of marriage and then adding an exception; if "except on the grounds of immorality" referred merely to concubinage, it would appear that Jesus is declaring: "I say to you that everyone who divorces his wife — *unless she is not his wife* — makes of her an adulteress." Does not such an addition, however, seem rather superfluous? (So highly respected an exegete as Rudolf Schnackenburg has recently given new emphasis to the traditional Catholic interpretation of Matthew.

He writes: "If we search for the deeper motives for this radical attitude of Jesus [whose intention was, we recall, to lay an easy yoke on men], we find them primarily in his zeal to win acknowledgment for God's will in its original totality . . . . It is therefore unthinkable that Jesus would have provided for a new mitigation of the divine will by the so-called 'fornication-clause' " (Mt. 5:32; 19:9). In *The Moral Teaching of the New Testament,* p. 79; cf. also C. Spicq, O.P., *Théologie Morale du Nouveau Testament,* vol. 2, p. 555).

Another interpretation of the meaning of "immorality" and the presence of this qualification in Matthew's text has been suggested by other commentators. "Immorality" would signify a violation of chastity, that is, unfaithfulness of one of the spouses. The contention is that Matthew added this limitation to the more rigid precept found in Mark in order to point out to his readers, for whom the observance of so demanding a marital policy in some cases could have been morally impossible, that the words of Jesus, which indeed emphasized the necessity of permanency of marriage, were not meant by him to be as categorical as some would have them interpreted. In certain instances, when one of the partners was seriously unfaithful to the marriage vows, for example, it might be possible for the faithful spouse, in all innocence, to divorce and remarry.

There is nothing new, of course, about this exegesis of Matthew. It represents an interpretation which has long been common among non-Catholic commentators. [17] The question is whether or not the Catholic arguments which have been proposed against this thesis are as conclusive as they might be, or could they profit from a reevaluation undertaken in light of the more recent studies of the New Testament and its milieu?

---

17. *Dictionary of the Bible,* "Marriage," treatment of "Divorce" by C. W. Emmet and J. Paterson, Charles Scribner's Sons, New York, 1963, p. 627. For more recent thought by Catholic authors on the problem of divorce and the law of the Church, cf. I. Lepp and D. Doherty, O.S.B., "The Problem of Divorce and Remarriage," *Marriage,* July 1966, pp. 7-18, and P. Huizing, S.J., "Should the Church's Marriage Laws be Revised?" *Concilium,* Vol. 18, Paulist Press, Glen Rock, N.J., 1966, pp. 165-80.

If the Lord did absolutely forbid divorce and remarriage, without exception, then how are we to justify the teaching of Paul? When St. Paul advises the converted Christian that he is free to marry again if, upon his conversion, he is deserted by his unbelieving spouse, does he not take it upon himself to mollify the Lord's command with a certain leniency?

Christ made no such distinction. His directive was not addressed to baptized Christians, it was uttered to the Pharisees, and to pre-Christians. Today we differentiate between sacramental and non-sacramental marriages, depending on whether or not the two partners to the union are baptized. When at least one of the spouses is not baptized, the marriage is not a sacrament and can be dissolved. But upon what did Paul base his distinction?

To be sure, Paul was cognizant of a great difference between the sanctity of the conjugal bond between two baptized persons who had committed themselves to Christ, and the natural contract existing between "non-believers." But this belief of his was hardly the equivalent of the involved sacramental theology we use today to justify "Pauline" and "Petrine" marriage cases. Apparently it was Paul's conviction that the Lord desired marriage to be a permanent relationship, but that he did not intend to impose upon Christians an impossible burden. Those who believed and were baptized were born into a new life and called to such a high state of perfection that there should not even have been contention among them, much less divorce between Christian partners in marriage. (Toward the end of his life, Paul even goes so far as to *idealize* marriage between Christians as patterned on the union between Christ and his Church. And it is unthinkable that Christ ever be disjoined from his Body, the Church. Eph 5:21 ff.) But the Lord would not require a person, deserted by his infidel spouse because he had become a Christian, to lead thenceforth an unmarried life. It would obviously be very trying to the spirituality and newly found faith of a person accustomed to married life to ask so much of him. The Lord Jesus, in his understanding of the fraility of human

nature, would not ask so much. Could such be the reasoning
of Paul on the precept received from the Lord?

At least partial answers, of course, have been given to
some of the questions which have been raised. Thus, some
would point out that the interpretation of our Lord's words which
we have presented above does not take sufficient notice of the
context in which the words are placed. In Mark 10 and Matthew
19 the situation is plainly one of controversy between the Pharisees
and Jesus. The Pharisees test Jesus by trying to force him to
take sides in a rabbinical dispute. The followers of Rabbi Hillel
permitted divorce for almost any reason whatsoever; the disciples
of Rabbi Shammai insisted that adultery alone furnishes sufficient
grounds for divorce. The Pharisees demand of Jesus: which
is the correct opinion? According to the traditional Catholic
interpretation, the response of Christ transcends the dilemma,
as he declares that in the New Dispensation divorce will never
be permissible, no matter what the grounds. It is argued that this
has to be the meaning of Jesus' proclamation, for why would
the disciples have been so disturbed (cf. Mk. 10:10; Mt. 19:10)
if he were merely assuming a position like that of Rabbi Shammai,
a position that was already familiar to them?

This line of reasoning has its merits, but is it altogether con-
vincing? When Matthew cites our Lord's words in his fifth
chapter, the context is not one of controversy but forms part of
the Sermon on the Mount in which chastity is prescribed and
adultery condemned. If Matthew thus relates Christ's directive
about divorce to adultery in chapter 5, why couldn't the meaning
of the words in chapter 19 be: "You Pharisees know that adultery
is forbidden by the Law; and yet, through your rabbinical haggling
you make a travesty of the Law; through one ruse or another
you find a way to excuse your adultery! But this is not the
will of God. Marriage is a union made holy by God and He
has no sympathy for the mockery you make of it by your quib-
blings!" Jesus emphatically announces that it is the divine will
that marriage be a permanent union, that it be regarded as sacred
and not the prey of Pharisaical hair-splitting — but, is this the

same thing as defining Christian marriage to be absolutely in-dissoluble?

With regard to the amazement of the disciples at the pro-nouncement of Jesus, it might be explicable in this fashion: at the time of Christ the lax opinion proposed by Hillel enjoyed great popularity among the Pharisees and the people. The position of Shammai was esteemed to be overly severe and was not shared by the majority. It is quite possible, then, that the disciples' viewpoint leaned in the direction of the less rigorous attitude toward the sanctity and permanency of marriage. Being used to our Lord's great compassion for the people and sympathy for their weaknesses, the followers of Jesus would very likely have expected him to be a supporter of the leniency of Hillel, at least to a degree. When he took such a firm stand for a very strict interpretation of the Law, an interpretation that seemed to demand still more than Shammai's, there is little wonder that they were troubled.

Whatever the force of these arguments, on one side or the other, one thing is certain: Catholic tradition has interpreted the words of the Lord in their most literal sense, and has absolutely excluded the possibility of divorce and remarriage for baptized Christians. Pius XI, in *Casti Connubii,* 1930, reiterated this position in almost adamant terms. In reference to the suggestion that the Church's laws governing divorce are obsolete and should be brought up to date, he wrote:

> But opposed to all these ravings stands the one most certain law of God, confirmed most fully by Christ, which can be weakened by no decrees of men or decisions of the people, by no will of legislators: "What God hath joined together, let no man put asunder" (Mt. 19:6). And if a man, contrary to this law puts asunder, it is immediately illegal; so rightly, as we have seen more than once, Christ himself has declared: "Everyone that putteth away his wife and marrieth another, committeth adultery, and he that marrieth her that is put away, committeth adultery" (Lk. 16:18). And these words of Christ refer to any marriage whatsoever, even that which

is purely natural and legitimate; for indissolubility is proper
to every true marriage, and whatever pertains to the loosening
of the bond is entirely removed from the good pleasure of the
parties concerned and from every secular power. [18]

Although the Church can dissolve some "natural bond" marriages, nothing earthly can touch a Christian marriage:

> If this stability seems subject to exception, however rare, as
> in the case of certain natural marriages entered into between
> unbelievers, or if between the faithful of Christ, those which
> are valid but not consummated, that exception does not depend
> on the will of man or of any merely human power, but on
> divine law, whose only guardian and interpreter is the Church
> of Christ. Yet, not even such a power can for any cause ever
> affect a Christian marriage which is valid and consummated.
> For, since the marriage contract is fully accomplished in such
> case, so also absolute stability and indissolubility by God's
> will are apparent, which cannot be relaxed by any human
> authority. [19]

Up to the present time, therefore, the Church has applied
our Lord's directives quite rigorously. A Catholic who adheres
to the belief that the Spouse of Christ is infallibly guided by the
Holy Spirit in its solemn interpretations of the Scriptures cannot
question the fact that the Church's application of the precept
of Jesus on marriage and divorce has been correct. An examination of history, and especially of the development of marriage
customs and their effects upon society, only reinforces the Catholic's
persuasion that his Church has justly insisted on the absolute
permanency of marriage throughout its first two thousand years.
Few will fail to acknowledge the evils abounding in a climate
that looks lightly upon the sacredness of the marriage bond. On
the other hand, the contributions made by stable family life to
both the material and spiritual vigor of society are indisputable.

To what conclusion do these reflections bring us? It may

---

18. D.B. 2250.
19. D.B. 2236.

appear that as far as the Catholic Church is concerned the issue has already been irreversibly decided. Divorce has received its unqualified condemnation from Christ, from tradition, and from the experience of mankind itself. But is this an adequate response to the objections which have been raised? Furthermore, there remains what is perhaps the most vexing question of all, a question whose solution is of the most critical importance not only with respect to the issue of divorce, but also in relation to many other problems which the Church of the future will have to face.

Supposing that during the initial period of its history the Church has given to Christ's words the interpretation he desired, the interpretation inspired by his Spirit, does this necessarily mean that the *past* traditional Catholic interpretation is the only one that can be given to his original words, the only one that his Spirit would inspire throughout all time? Could it conceivably be the will of Christ that at this time in our history, for the sake of the spiritual good of a vastly more complex and numerous humanity, a broader interpretation be given to his commandment on divorce? Could he have allowed the evangelical accounts to persist with a certain vagueness, so that at the proper time the Church would see in them a fuller meaning, a wider breadth of vision?

Comparable development of man's understanding of God's revelation has taken place in other instances; why should its possibility be excluded in this case? The gradual revelation of the mystery of the Blessed Trinity illustrates this point. The Hebrews had to learn first of all that there is but one true God. Throughout their history, from Abraham to Christ, this truth was more and more profoundly instilled in their religious consciousness. Once they had rejected forever the temptation of idolatry, however, they could be exposed to the next stage of God's revelation of himself to them, as the Word brought to mankind a knowledge of the threefold personality of the Divinity. Then, conditioned as they were to defend the uniqueness of Yahweh at all costs, the Jews found this doctrine untenable, and to many of them it was not merely heresy, it was blasphemy.

Could a simliar evolution be envisioned with respect to the problem of divorce? It cannot be argued that divorce and remarriage are intrinsically evil. They must be evaluated in relation to the effect they have upon the integrity of marriage and its place in society. Is it unthinkable that with the passage of time this relationship could change in one way or another? After having struggled and sacrificed for centuries to establish as inviolable the principle of the permanency of matrimonial union, could the Church today have reached a threshold at which, while maintaining as forcefully as ever the general principle that marriage is for life, she might allow that in certain cases even Christian marriages may be dissolved in favor of the spiritual good to be obtained for at least some of the parties affected, and ultimately for the Church as a whole?

This is, unfortunately, out of the question, many will unhesitatingly reply. The entire tradition of the Church is too clearly and unreservedly opposed to such a change, and the statements of Pius XI should make this sufficiently clear. But in this complex age of ours in which so many new factors are entering into the picture, can we any longer afford to maintain our preference for looking to the past and a tradition that has in many respects been formulated to Christianize a world very different from our own? When the apostles interpreted Christ's words, they looked for a meaning which would insure the greatest possible spiritual good for the Church of their times. When *we* interpret Christ's words, it sometimes seems that our primary concern is to conform to opinions voiced in the past, rather than to meet the spiritual needs of our own times.

In proceeding this way, do we not run the risk of exchanging life for death, as we strive to preserve the letter and allow the spirit to slip from our grasp? Is the Church necessarily immune to that pharisaical stagnation which Jesus so vehemently condemned? We do not imply a need for rupture with what has been the Church's constant tradition, but we ask whether continuity with the tradition cannot be maintained in a broader framework than has been admissible in the past?

In October of 1965, as the Second Vatican Council began

debate on the section on marriage in the Pastoral Constitution on the Church in the Modern World, quite a stir was created by the Melkite rite Archbishop Elie Zoghbi of Egypt when he asked that the Church examine some of her practices concerning divorce, and reportedly suggested that divorce and remarriage might be sanctionable in such cases as abandonment or mental illness. Following the Archbishop's appeal, the matter was discussed by the United States bishops' ecumenical council press panel. The discussion was covered for the *Natioinal Catholic Reporter* [20] by John P. Donnelly, and a summary of certain remarks made by some of the panelists as Donnelly reports them may add some weight to the arguments that we have proposed.

One line of approach was suggested by John Long of New York, an expert on Eastern Churches on the Vatican Secretariat for Promoting Christian Unity. Long's remarks were reported as follows:

> He noted that in the Byzantine Orthodox Church the only possibilities of divorce are adultery and death.

> Some, he said, have interpreted the word "death" in the sense of "moral death" — that is, long separation, uncertainty as to whether the other party is still alive, incurable disease, even exile to Siberia among the Russians. These were the practices to which Archbishop Zoghbi referred.

> He said the archbishop had in mind this custom going back at least to the sixth century and mentioned specifically in the code of Emperor Justinian. The Byzantines have always accepted this, he said, though Byzantine-rite Catholics are now bound by 1949 legislation against it.

> Father Long said the practice can be traced up to the eleventh century at least, even when Orthodox and Catholic Eastern-rite Churches were united.

> Another instance, he noted, was the practice of the Coptic Church, at least between the sixth and eighth centuries, of allowing divorced and remarried persons to return to the sacra-

---

20. *National Catholic Reporter,* October 6, 1965, p. 6.

ments, "the Church refusing to pronounce on the validity of a second marriage."

He said he considered it particularly significant that during the attempts to heal the schism in the Eastern Church at the Council of Florence (1438-43), "the Orthodox practice of allowing divorce was not even brought up as a stumbling block to unity."

Robert Trisco, professor of Church history at Catholic University of America, singled out another historical precedent:

He said that permission for divorce in case of adultery is to be found in the writings of several of the early Church Fathers of the East, and some even in the Western Church. And in the early Middle Ages the "Penitential of Theodore," Church legislation set down by the Archbishop of Canterbury and followed extensively throughout Britain and northern Europe, allowed divorce and remarriage in the case of a woman's being carried off by a warring tribe.

It was added by another panelist that:

If the Church is going to conduct a meaningful dialogue with the Orthodox, it must reconsider its interpretation of Scripture regarding divorce.

On this point Francis J. McCool, professor at Rome's Pontifical Biblical Institute, continued:

Our teaching is based on the Gospel of Mark —— the oldest of the Gospels on which the others are based. But in Matthew (19:19), though the condemnation of divorce is clear, there seems to be an exception made in the case of "adultery" or "unfaithfulness," depending on the translation. Many think that Matthew's words were meant to be a softening of the doctrine apparently contained in Mark.

At the very minimum, can we not deduce from these observations that the Church's position on divorce and remarriage cannot be considered a closed question? Besides the fact that there seems to be a scriptural and theological basis for an alteration of the Church's doctrine on the indissolubility of marriage, there are also numerous indications in the concrete, everyday life of the present world that the Church's policy toward divorce is going to have to be exposed to some sort of "opening" process, if it is to continue to be the source of soundly based marriages in which spouses and children have the maximum opportunity for mutual promotion and growth in the grace of our Lord.

The doctrine of indissolubility was conceived and promulgated as the true interpretation of Christ's words in an era when it was a much different thing than it is today for a spouse to fulfill his commitment to devote his entire wedded life to the union he contracts with his partner. It is not inferred by this that there has ever been a time when it has been "easy" for the great majority of Christian husbands and wives faithfully to love one another for a lifetime. The exigencies imposed by the principle of permanency of marital union have always presupposed a conquest of self, a readiness to sacrifice, a willingness to combat many disruptive influences coming from the "World." There are, nonetheless, conditions in the contemporary world which make it not only difficult, but in reality morally impossible for a certain number of the faithful (a number that sadly but inevitably seems to be growing) to remain for a lifetime in one marriage.

Among these factors can be counted the following: The first Christians were an élite group, on the whole, truly the elect of God. What they had to sacrifice or to risk sacrificing in order to become Christian often bordered on the heroic. The ordinary troubles of married life would seem small in comparison. The fact that they were willing to venture to make this offering of themselves points to their great spiritual integrity and capacity for responding wholeheartedly to the call of Christ. On the other hand, as Christianity becomes more and more a religion of an innumerable multitude, it is quite natural that many enter its ranks lacking this integrity and capacity, not necessarily through any grave fault of their own, however: frequently they are the products of a situation in which there has been little or no opportunity for spiritual or moral formation.

The age in which we live is characterized by changes that come with startling rapidity, by uncertainty, by insecurity, by restlessness, in a word, by instability. The average young person is more than ever before doubtful about the meaning of life, of what he wants from life and what he should put into it. Without really knowing why, he is made to feel by modern society that in order to be happy he must marry, and marry young. In such a climate it is inevitable that the stability of many marriages will come to rest on a very thin crust.

In the past a man could look forward to pursuing one occupation throughout his lifetime. In the present the average man, throughout the span of years in which he is able to work, has to learn several different types of work in order to remain employed. In the past a careful, leisurely preparation for marriage was the more usual thing. Today social pressures and dating patterns precipitate youths into marriage long before they are ready to sacrifice their independence and accept maturely the responsibilities that accompany married life. In short, there are a great many forces at work in the modern world tending to undermine any kind of stability.

Prior to the last few generations, a generally lower standard of living and more arduous way of life ordinarily saw the development of a more responsible type of youth. The luxuries and ease which have become so widespread in the twentieth-century world have contributed to increasing the desires of young people for the pleasures of marriage, but have diluted their capacity to cope with the multiple problems that are the unavoidable corollary of married life in this world of ours. Thus blinded by desire and softened by living off "the fat of the land," how competent are many of our young people to give that "free and unforced consent" which the marriage vows entail?

The heresies of "love" that run rampant in our society often obscure from those approaching and entering into marriage the demands which it will actually place upon them. Enchanted by the thrill that comes with infatuation, and unable to distinguish the latter from real love or to make the sacrifices necessary for that infatuation to become love, the young couple throw themselves into a world of fantasy, only to awaken to a world of reality with which they are not prepared to cope.

Divorce begets divorce. The children of divorced parents, often having been torn to shreds emotionally, in their personal instability are in many cases prime material for an extremely unsettled marital situation. Starved for love because of the lack of it in their home life, they are anxious at an early age to find a love of their own. But never having known love, they know neither how to give or receive it. And lamentably, there are all too many young people undertaking marriage today with this kind of background militating against their chances for success.

These are factors which circumscribe marriage in the present world. Perhaps to a certain extent they are generalizations which admit of many exceptions, but this does not discount their presence as strongly influential aspects of the dissolution of many marriages. In no sense, however, are they to be condoned or considered "acceptable" merely because they happen to have become so prevalent. Nor will the evil they mirror be exterminated by a lax attitude toward divorce. Quite the contrary, it can only be augmented. The sad state of affairs to which this trend testifies can be ameliorated only by a radical reversal of values, a *metanoia* from the materialism that is devouring the foyer of the vitality of Christianity, the family. The principle of the permanency of marriage is no less "up to date" today than it was when it was pronounced so emphatically by the Lord.

No matter how true this is, however, it also remains a fact that many individuals who are relatively free of any grave guilt in the matter are, nonetheless, tragically ensnared by the evils we have noted. Is it the will of God that they and their children bear the heaviest share of a burden for which they are perhaps the least responsible?

To look at another side of the issue, paradoxical though it seems, unswerving adherence to the absolute stand taken by

Catholicism in the matter of divorce and remarriage has in several ways incubated evils of its own:

There exists a certain type of individual who, consciously or unconsciously, seeks to marry a Catholic because he knows that "Catholics don't believe in divorce." He then feels secure, readily takes his spouse for granted or abuses his marriage in other fashions, being convinced that there is little the other party can do about it. The extreme form of this attitude may be more or less rare, but in lesser degrees it occurs with relative frequency, and if it does not result in divorce, it is certainly a breeder of unhappy family relations.

Unfortunately common is the case of the wife with several children who is deserted by her husband. She cannot remarry, so she must work to suport her family. But regardless of the efforts she makes, she cannot be a mother and father at the same time, and it is a rare feat when the children are brought up properly.

Or sometimes a wife is almost entirely responsible for destroying a marriage. Perhaps she has entered the marriage for deeply selfish reasons, and not with sincerity or love. She does not want the responsibilities that accompany marriage and refuses to give the cooperation essential for successful conjugal union. Despite all of the efforts of the husband to meet her demands or to help her perfect herself, she continually does more to frustrate the marital relationship, finally demanding that she be "let out" through divorce. The husband is left to himself, possibly with several children to raise, expected to lead a good spiritual life and provide his children not only with a father's discipline, but also a mother's attentiveness.

Again, there are those who marry prematurely, perhaps because of premarital pregnancy, or out of spite for someone else, or because of an almost neurotic eagerness to be married induced by diverse causes, or because of childish fascination for the "loved" one, or for any number of other puerile reasons which have little to do with the real nature of marriage and the species of total commitment it presupposes. Often these "unions" are practically predestined to dissolution from the moment they are contracted. Although one wonders in cases such as these whether a true marriage even exists, in practice the Church holds such marriages to be forever valid, only rarely finding a remedy for the mistakes of the young.

Must the door be unconditionally closed to those who in a very real sense are *victims* of other persons, or sometimes of circumstances or background? Is the welfare of their souls to be sacrificed more or less to a preoccupation for maintaining without exception a principle enunciated by the Savior for the good of souls? Is it certain that today this kind of absolute interpretation of our Lord's words is required to assure the stability of marriage and the good order of society?

But what becomes of those who cannot find the strength to bend to the interpretation of the Church, and after divorce remarry? There are some who, after divorce, try to accede to the demands of the Church. They endeavor through a life of prayer, dedication to the work of the Church, frequent reception of the sacraments, etc., to fortify themselves for the struggle against loneliness. But ultimately, finding themselves psychologically incapable of leading a solitary life, they marry again, and in their shame depart from their Mother the Church possibly for years, possibly for life.

There are others who, after failure in their first marriage, remarry and find a good life and fruitful union with their second spouse. In humility they conquer the pride that would dissociate them completely from the Church. They attend Mass. They give their children a religious education and as much spiritual encouragement as possible. They dedicate themselves to the service of their parish, sometimes more selflessly than their fellow Catholics who are not banned from the sacraments. Is there not a note of contradiction here? According to the Church, such parents are technically in the state of mortal sin, deprived of grace, and therefore destined for hell. Yet, has not Christ himself proclaimed: "Without me you can do nothing!" (Jn. 15:5). Whence this good, this love, hope, and faith, if not from the grace of Jesus Christ? Still, even the best of those Catholics who have divorced and remarried must live tortured by separation from the sacraments and with the fires of Gehenna flickering about them.

Then, there is the anomaly of the "Favor of the Faith" privilege. According to the present canonical practice, no matter how many times a certain individual has been married, no matter what his past life has been, provided that he has never been baptized, all of this can be wiped away as though it never existed if he desires to be baptized and enter a sacramental marriage. But if both parties to a marriage were baptized, then, regardless of the reasons for the failure of the marriage, regardless of the innocence or virtue of one of the spouses, nothing can be done. Is divine justice really represented by a system that will absolve someone who has several times, perhaps wilfully, failed in marriage, but will do nothing for a person who has made one serious mistake, or has been the victim of another's irresponsibility, simply on the basis of baptism or non-baptism?

But, some will object: plead as you may, and unfortunate as some particular cases seem to be, there is nothing the Church can do. There is simply no possibility of dissolving a marriage between Christians, for God has reserved to himself jurisdiction over the sacramental bond uniting baptized Christians; it lies beyond any and all human authority. Assuredly, at times the innocent must suffer for the sake of the preservation of the law, but has it not always been thus? The few must endure persecution and possibly even be lost, that the many might be saved.

This, however, is the very heart of the question. Has God actually placed the sacramental marriage bond outside of the jurisdiction of the Church? And exactly what is this "sacramental bond" in itself? Is it some kind of entity which begins to have an existence of its own from the moment that two baptized persons unite in matrimony? Not in the least.

The true nature of the sacramental union can be more clearly perceived through a comparison with "natural" union in marriage. In the latter, two persons vow themselves to each other before God. Ideally they become one in will and purpose by virtue of their marriage. Their union is sacred because it is blessed and sanctioned by God as a most excellent participation in his creative plan. Because of the fact that at least one of the spouses is not baptized, however, there is one thing lacking to their marital union, and this is the sacramental grace of Christ by which their love is perfected, rendered more pleasing to God, and more apt to lead them and their children to the side of God. While the partners in a natural bond marriage can be a source of grace to one another, their marriage cannot benefit from the very special personal encounter with our Lord present uniquely in the love of baptized Christians for each other in the sacrament of marriage.

Now, are not the elements constituting *the bond itself* of marriage fundamentally the same in either case? Is not the bond or contract constituted by the intent of the two spouses and the sanction of God? To be sure, when the partners to the marriage are baptized, their union becomes a special source of sacramental grace for them and their offspring, but is there any *intrinsic* reason why the sacramental bond should be absolutely indissoluble? The dignity of the latter is certainly enhanced by its sacramental quality, and it is all the more *fitting* that it should never be shattered by divorce, but this is not the same thing as saying that this bond in itself, by its very nature, cannot be dissolved. It would seem that only an extrinsic factor, a divine decree, could make the sacramental bond untouchable, and as we have suggested above, it may be that so categorical a precept has never been levied by God, not even through the words of Jesus on the permanency of marriage.

It is not our purpose here to assert that the sacramental bond of marriage is dissoluble. We only ask that the matter become the subject of further research on the part of exegetes and reflection on the part of the Church's historians and theologians. The present theological and canonical practice of the Church declares natural bond marriage dissoluble. When such marriages are dissolved, it is for the spiritual welfare of at least one of the spouses who wishes to enter a new marriage, or who has perhaps already "attempted" a new marriage. In some cases it has not even been required that the new marriage be a sacramental union. It is deemed sufficient that a significant spiritual good be attainable through such a marriage. (For example, a non-Catholic woman may originally have been married to a non-baptized husband. This marriage ends in divorce and she remarries, her second husband also being non-baptized. She then decides that she would like to join the Catholic faith, but at the same time desires to remain married to her second husband who refuses to be baptized. In some cases the Church has allowed the first marriage to be dissolved, making it possible for the second marriage to be validated and the interested party to enter the Church.) If, therefore, it can be shown that in certain well defined cases great spiritual good might follow, not only for individuals but for the Church as a whole, from allowing some divorced Catholics to remarry, might this not be an indication that while Christ has willed the permanency of marriage, he has not willed the absolute indissolubility of the sacramental bond?

A New Morality?

At the outset of the present study we commented on the ambiguity of change. We observed that it can be either positive, contributing to the greater perfection of man and the universe, or negative, yielding to the forces of decay always at work in the world. In light of this perspective, how are our suggestions concerned with such questions as those of hell and divorce to be evaluated?

It may seem to the reader that some of our proposals are indeed exemplary of negative change, reflecting the infection of a "new," subjectivist, totally relative morality. For if such absolutes as the eternal quality of hell or the indissolubility of the sacramental bond of marriage are discarded, what is left? What is there that cannot be questioned, doubted, and ultimately set aside?

Perhaps it sounds good to criticize the Church, remonstrating that she has become irrelevant to the world. But is there not

another side to the coin? Could it not also be true that the
world has rejected the true relevancy of the Church? Did not
the Lord demand that his disciples be "in the world but not of
the world"? If the world chooses to turn its back on the authentic
values of the Church, will the Church become more "relevant"
by succumbing to the values of the world?

The dangers which the Church must face in striving to become
relevant to mankind should not be underestimated. On the other
hand, the Church cannot afford to withdraw, in an effort to
keep herself pure. The price of her being "in the world" is that
she must inevitably at times become "of the world." It is her
task to become one with the world, to perfect it and make of it
an offering acceptable to God.

As the Church unites herself with the problems of the world,
she must be at once both strong and flexible. She must be strong
enough to enforce faithfully what is absolute in the Word God has
entrusted to her. But she must be flexible enough to be able
to adapt realistically her absolute principles to the concrete
situation of the world, so that her interpretation and application
of revelation will truly serve the spiritual needs of mankind.

This does not mean that the Church must be ready to make
a clean break with past tradition, nor that she must be willing
to "soften" her doctrinal position. But she has to be open
to *substantial development* of her understanding of the *depositum
fidei,* and she has to be disposed to adjust her discipline accordingly.

Thus, with regard to the doctrine of hell, even if we come
to admit that hell is not everlasting in the sense of absolute and
eternal separation from God and loss of all happiness, this would
not imply a dilution of Christ's warning. He admonished the
Jews that a life of sin merits a terrible punishment, symbolized
by the torment of dwelling in everlasting fire. Does not the
modern conception of "hell" as an existence lived with an ever-
lastingly stunted capacity to love and consciousness of a wasted
life meet the standards of a "terrible punishment"? The "absolute
truth" in the teaching of Jesus was that sin has tragic consequences, both in this life and in the next; our argument is that

the exact nature of these consequences remains in the domain of the problematical.

Nor should the notion of the dissolubility of the sacramental marriage bond be construed as a proposal that the Church lessen her emphasis on the importance of the permanency of marriage. Rather, this emphasis should be increased, and should be implemented through programs to prepare our young people more adequately for marriage, and through marriage clinics to help couples deal more effectively with their marital difficulties.

The fact is, however, that many Catholic spouses have sought divorce and will seek divorce, whether the Church permits it or not. And it is questionable whether the Church's rigid interpretation of our Lord's directive is actually very effective in deterring the faithful from divorce. If, for example, under certain circumstances the Church would permit its members to divorce and remarry — but only after one year of counseling and attempts at reconciliation — might this not save more marriages than an absolute proscription of divorce? Regardless of the pros and cons, of course, the ultimate question is: what does Christ command? and, could he command anything that would be detrimental to mankind as a whole?

But, let us endeavor to focus now on the point we have been trying to make throughout our study of the changing interpretations and applications of the sense of Sacred Scripture. In this frighteningly and yet entrancingly changing world of ours, the Church cannot risk standing aloof. Because her life is the life of Christ, she must remain open to the positive values to be reaped from the dynamism of the new age. The enthusiasm with which she has begun to delve into the potentialities of the modern approach to the Bible shows that while she is cautious, while she does not have the least intention of forsaking the wisdom which pervades her centuries of tradition, neither is she impervious to the pleadings of the contemporary world. She will not close her ears to the call of any of her children, she will not leave unexplored any path which might afford the members of the Mystical Body new opportunities for spiritual growth toward eternal life.

The many changes which have been suggested or debated in the context of the Second Vatican Council have impressed upon the Church as a whole that her position in relation to doctrine, discipline and the world must be rethought. Certain especially perplexing and complicated problems have made her painfully aware of the fact that she does not have a ready answer for every issue to be faced. Her tradition, and even Sacred Scripture itself, cannot furnish the solution to many of the questions raised today. The attempts of the bishops and theologians of the Church to grope their way through such thorny problems as the morality of modern warfare, or contraception, have made this all too evident. The Word of God does not dictate a precise response to man's searching appeal; it simply provides a guideline which it is the Church's mission to pursue under the inspiration of the Spirit.

There should be no illusions about the seriousness of proposals to change such things as the Church's policy on divorce. In the latter case, for instance, much more is entailed than the problem of divorce itself. The question of the value of statements of popes and councils must be taken up. The problem of the application of the principle of infallibility enters the picture. A significant evolution in the sacramental theology of marriage might be required.

In brief, the particular issue of divorce points to a problem which is perhaps the key question in the Catholic Church today, one which very likely will determine the fate of the ecumenical movement and orient the destiny of the Church for centuries to come: how much of the truth is comprehended in "infallible definitions" promulgated by the Church? Is the divine will on any particular matter affecting mankind capable of being contained adequately in any human statement? Can a command issued or a truth revealed by God be so worded by humans that it will never stand in need of further interpretation, no matter how long the race endures, no matter how circumstances change?

Or, if *some* of the eternal truths can be thus expressed, as for example the truth that "God is One," can *all* that God has revealed be treated so simply? What we are asking is basically

this: can the Church in certain instances take a substantial leap
forward? Can she, with regard to at least some of the positions
which she has traditionally defended, radically alter her course,
while at the same time remaining loyal to her tradition and
insisting that insofar as she has proclaimed something infallibly
to be true, she has not erred, she has borne witness to the truth,
but in the measure that the truth has been known to her?

Earlier in our evaluation of the modern approach to the
New Testament, we asserted that there are two attitudes toward
the interpretation of revelation which are to some degree reproachable. Up to this point we have considered but one of these:
the tendency of Catholic theology, and on occasion even the
councils, to be somewhat narrow in interpreting the Sacred Writings,
leaving the impression that it is within the power of the Church,
through its definitions of dogma, to exhaust utterly in a few well-
chosen words the significance for all time of some point of divine
revelation.

There is, however, another attitude subject to reprimand.
While the Church may in some respects fall short of all the ideals
we look for in the Spouse of Christ, she also has her children who
are in some instances rebellious, untowardly outspoken, or shallow
in their faith. Thus, certain of the trends represented in past and
even present attitudes toward the Scriptures, or the Church herself, merit severe criticism.

The emphasis placed by Bultmann and his followers, for
example, on the necessity of demythologizing the New Testament,
although it has its value, is not altogether a salutary symptom.
It bears the traces of scientism, if not pure rationalism, and opens
the way to a pathetic incredulity which can only isolate man from
the reality of the saving acts of Jesus.

The protestations of certain sincere, but excessively cynical
Catholic critics, such as Magdalen Goffin and other contributors
to works or articles of the tone of *Objections to Roman Catholicism,* [21] are also deserving of reproval. It is not so much what
is said that should be challenged as the attitude with which it is

21. As cited above.

said. No one will be motivated to seek reform, no one will be led to believe, no one will be inspired to action by hearing the spiritual mother of souls and the spouse of Christ referred to as "stupid," "ridiculous," "absurd," "corrupt," the bastion of superstition. Criticism, especially that coming from Catholics themselves, when it degenerates to mere invective defeats its purpose. We should indeed view the Church objectively, and not fear to criticize her constructively. But the keenest and most penetrating kind of criticism can be proffered in a spirit of respect and of love. Diatribe has little to offer for the revitalization of the Body of Christ.

* * *

We conclude our study now, however, by returning for the last time to our central theme of the inexhaustible nature of the truth God has entrusted man with the mission of discovering. It would be marvelous if we Catholics could rest content with our traditions and our defined doctrines and announce to the world: "You seek the Truth? You will find it here, in the Church, whole and entire. The Eternal Truth is ours, in its definitive form. Come to us and you will be blessed with the Truth that is not subject to change or revision, that will never stand in need of further interpretation. Come to us, and the Truth is yours!" But this is not the case. Our own sense of the transcendency of divine revelation, which has been considerably intensified by the fruits harvested from recent studies of the Bible, and the endless appeals for guidance coming from an ever-changing world do not allow us to rest content with the past, or with the Church as we find her.

The Modern Age has brought us to realize, more clearly perhaps than any of our human predecessors, that the divine truth does not lie behind us as a deposit to be guarded. *It lies in the future.* It is not an object which the Church possesses and manipulates. It is a Reality which the Body of Christ LIVES, moment by moment, ever more fully, as the Spouse of Christ moves incessantly forward to meet her Bridegroom in eternal glory.

As mankind continues to evolve humanly and supernaturally toward its point of culmination in God, to whom it has been called from the beginning, there are certain things which it knows to be true, but which it must always seek to understand, and there are other truths which it partially grasps, but must always seek to apply in accordance with the needs of the day and the will of the creator.

At all times great faith is required. At all times respect for the Mystery must be upheld before all else, for who can comprehend "the breadth and length and height and depth . . . and the love of Christ which surpasses all understanding"? [22] At all times our hope for the future should suffer itself to be marred by no shadows, for as the experience of the human race in its development has demonstrated, both from the point of view of material and spiritual events, what has often seemed the most improbable, the most fantastic, the most incredible, from the almost unbelievable complex of factors which had to be coordinated to make the appearance of man on earth possible to the much more incredible miracle of the appearance on earth of God in the nature of a man, it is precisely the proposal which is the most difficult to believe that has often had the best chance of being the truth. [23]

---

22. Eph. 3:18-19.

23. A thought suggested by some of the comments of Teilhard de Chardin in *The Future of Man,* as cited above. For further insight into the importance of modern exegesis for the growth of the Church, the ecumenical movement, and the development of theology, cf. John L. McKenzie, "Authority and Power in the New Testament," *The Catholic Biblical Quarterly,* October, 1964, pp. 413-22; for a more thorough scriptural basis for the vision of the Church as a living, changing reality, cf. Rudolf Schnackenburg, *The Church in the New Testament,* Herder and Herder, New York, 1965, particularly "The Mystery of the Church: Unfathomable aspects," pp. 141-49.

POSTSCRIPT

A great deal of theological literature has been focused recently upon the confrontation of Christianity with the secularization of modern man. What significance might this secular trend in theological emphasis have for a contemporary interpretation of Sacred Scripture?

Among the great number of recent works dealing with secularization, to cite only a few (more because of the attention they have drawn than on account of their intrinsic worth), the books of J. A. T. Robinson,[1] Harvey Cox,[2] Paul M. van Buren,[3] T. J. J. Altizer and William Hamilton,[4] Leslie Dewart,[5] and Robert Adolfs [6] have incited more than a little comment and controversy, as these authors have sought by various approaches to render Christianity or the Church relevant to twentieth century man, even if secularization must go so far as to embrace a "gospel of Christian atheism." [7]

---

1. *Honest to God*, S. C. M., 1963; *The New Reformation*, S. C. M., London, 1965.

2. *The Secular City*, MacMillan, New York, 1965; revised edition 1966.

3. *The Secular Meaning of the Gospel*, S. C. M., London, 1963.

4. *Radical Theology and the Death of God*, Bobbs-Merrill, Indianapolis, 1966.

5. *The Future of Belief*, Herder & Herder, New York, 1966.

6. *The Grave of God*, Burns & Oates, London, 1967.

7. Altizer, *The Gospel of Christian Atheism*, Collins, London, 1967.

Much has been written about the inspiration gleaned from the last thoughts of the Lutheran theologian and witness, Dietrich Bonhoeffer,[8] whose genius it was to take special cognizance of the irrelevancy of "religion" to modern man. With ineluctable regularity his proclamation of a "world come of age," his appeal for a " 'religionless' Christianity," (or more frequently and precisely a "non-religious interpretation" of the Bible and Christian faith), have been summoned to the lists.

More than one authority on the theology of Bonhoeffer, however, has dropped a word of caution with regard to the ease with which these expressions may and have been misused.[9] Bonhoeffer undoubtedly owes much of his prominence to the fact that he succeeded in communicating the spirit of an already existing phenomenon through several "catchphrases" — so enticing to "adult" modern man — and above all sealed his Christian convictions with his life-blood. It is unfortunate, nonetheless, that so many "secularizing" authors retain only these few phrases, largely neglecting Bonhoeffer's rich traditional Christology, his deeply Christocentric ecclesiology, his continual emphasis on the primacy and uniqueness, indeed what I would designate the transcendent-immanence of the Word of God, as well as his criticisms of the kind of "worldliness" that is the enemy of God.[10]

The preoccupation of much of today's theology with secularization, however, finds its source ultimately not in the utterance of a Bonhoeffer, but in western man himself and what he has become across the last several centuries of his history. Authors

---

8. *Letters and Papers From Prison,* S. C. M., 1953; revised translation, S. C. M,. London, 1967.

9. Cf. Eberhard Bethge in his foreword to the revised translation of *Letters and Papers*; E. H. Robertson, *Dietrich Bonhoeffer,* Carey Kingsgate Press, London, 1966; John D. Godsey, *The Theology of Dietrich Bonhoeffer,* S. C. M., London, 1960; Martin E. Marty (ed.), *The Place of Bonhoeffer,* S. C. M. Greenbacks, London, 1963; John A. Phillips, *The Form of Christ in the World,* Collins, London, 1966.

10. *The Cost of Discipleship,* revised edition, S. C. M., London, 1959; *Ethics,* Collins (The Fontana Library), London, 1964; see particularly *No Rusty Swords,* Collins, 1965, p. 91, and *The Way to Freedom,* Collins, 1966, pp. 46-48, 239.

such as Cox, C. van Peursen,[11] Colin Williams,[12] etc., give interesting (if rather over-simplified) accounts of this process. In
this respect, within our own century perhaps the concept and
application of *demythologization* of Sacred Scripture, especially
as evidenced in the Bultmannian and affiliated schools, has been
one of the most influential contributing forces in the secularization
of theology.

We have previously referred to demythologization, in particular
while discussing the authenticity of the resurrection, but in
light of current theological developments it would seem opportune
to consider the latter with regard to its effect upon biblical interpretation and related ecclesiastical structures in the context of
secularization. In spite of its limitations, not the least of which
is the tendency to rationalize that which lies beyond reason,
demythologization has unquestionably made a decisively positive
contribution to the twentieth century's revitalized approach to
the Word of God. Stripping away diverse "sacred" barriers,
it has helped to open the way to a truly *living* interpretation of
divine revelation.[13] But how?, one might demand.

The discernment of the presence of "myth" even in the New
Testament has effected a new consciousness of the involved nature
of biblical truth. It was and is, before all else, truth that is
meant to convey and reveal God's concern and will for man in
every *present* moment. In this awareness, the early Christian
community — while determined to witness faithfully to Christ —
was not deterred from transmitting the Word of Jesus through
forms and theologies conforming to the needs of the time. In
an age dominated by a sacral world-view, the first Christians did
not hesitate to "sacralize" the sayings and accomplishments of

---

11. "Functioneel Denken en geloof," in *Gemeente onderweg* (Lochem);
"Man and Reality — the History of Human Thought," *The Student World*,
vol. 56, (First Quarter 1963).

12. *Faith in a secular age*, Collins, Fontana Books, London, 1966.

13. We do not mean to infer that demythologization has played the
only or even the most important role in this domain. Contemporary exegesis, with its concern for literary forms, the life-situation of the composing
author, redactor or community, etc., is much too rich and complex to be
reducible to any one 'most significant" aspect.

their Lord. In the same way, we can only be faithful to the Word
of Jesus today by searching for the meaning which the same
Truth has for secular man. The humanity of the "world come
of age" is secular, and if biblical interpretation is to speak to it,
it too must be secularized, "demythologized." This is no denial
of the divine Word, but rather a confession of its transcendence,
its unique dynamism, the power through which it enables God
to address every man of every age.

But what does such a desacralization signify for modern Catholicism? For its dogmas and traditional structures? Specifically,
what does it mean for the doctrines of inspiration and inerrancy,
for the ecclesiastical offspring thereof — papal authority and infallibility, and for the very survival of the *divine* in the Word
of *God?*

Inspiration and Inerrancy

Traditionally, Catholic theology and the Church's official teaching
have insisted that because Sacred Scripture is inspired by God,
it is free from error. The primary effect of God's intervention in
the formation of the Bible has been to guide man so that those
who believe can be assured of possessing perfect truth.

But is this an adequate view of inspiration? Does it place
the accent correctly? Does it preserve an accurate perspective?
Is it not possibly too "sacred" or "mythological" an interpretation
of what God is doing through his Word?

It cannot be denied that Christ himself placed special emphasis
on the truth: "I am the Way, the Truth, and the Life" (Jn. 14: 6),
"you will know the truth, and the truth will make you free" (Jn.
8: 32). But what was this truth? It was not a body of abstract
doctrines, fixed-timeless-formulas. It was not a system or set
of structures by which man could lay hold of salvation with absolute security and self-satisfaction. Rather, it was the very *Person*
of Christ in his boundless concern for man, man in the concrete
conditions in which he found him.

Is this not the key to the ultimate meaning of biblical truth and the inspiration behind it? Is it not the present action of God seeing to it that his Word speak to man's needs *here* and *now*? Is this not the direction in which we should search for the significance of Sacred Scripture today, rather than striving desperately to protect formulations of the "truth" which simply no longer really matter — except possibly as obstacles to concern for what is actually vital? This does not suggest that traditional doctrines should be shelved, but it does intimate that they vary in importance, in "truth," and it points to a very much needed shift of emphasis.

Papal Authority and Infallibility

Nothing has made it so evident that the authority accorded to papal teaching must be demythologized as the quandry of the Church over the birth-control question. Traditional Catholicism has assumed that the pope, because he is divinely guided by the Holy Spirit, is capable of giving errorless judgments on the most complex of issues, so long as they pertain to the realm of "faith and morals." [14] But with the birth control problem — even though most theologians agree that infallibility is not involved — this traditional conception has reached an impasse.

Catholic teaching on the office of the Holy Father has so situated the pope that he must decide, and his decision must bind all of the faithful in conscience. Yet, all available evidence points to the fact that he cannot reasonably decide, and that if he does — no matter what the decision may be — in the eyes of many it will be unjustifiable. In brief, he has been so positioned by a mythological [15] interpretation of office that he is being called

---

14. Admittedly this is a grossly under-nuanced summation of the concept or doctrine of infallibility, but it is sufficiently acurate to meet the demands of the present context.

15. By "mythological" we in no sense mean "false"; we do mean that the influence of the Holy Spirit has been attributed to the Magisterium in such a way by a sacralizing worldview as to bestow almost magically divine proportions or powers of judgment and teaching on individuals who, even with God's assistance, retain their human limitations.

upon to decide in detail a matter which can only, at best, be decided along very general lines.

The birth control problem is mentioned only as an illustration of a crisis the roots of which go much deeper. The degree of authority claimed by the papacy is the result of a lengthy historical process. It has been supported in part by straining to the utmost the sense of such texts as "Thou art Peter . . ." (Mt. 16: 18), "Feed my sheep . . ." (Jn. 21: 17), etc.; in part it has been seized more or less by coercion; in part it has been freely granted by Christians immersed in a sacral-hierarchical worldview; and in part — it must be admitted and emphasized — it has evolved and functioned under the providential influence of the Holy Spirit for the good of the Body of Christ.

Historical conditions have altered, however, and the authoritative quality ascribed to the papal office must, with history, undergo its own metamorphosis. Whereas in the past it functioned in a sacral world-structure, now it must be adjusted to an order in which "religious man" has become "secular man." The magisterium must be ready to admit its inability to judge every case, to decide every issue. It must acknowledge that there are many problems which the Christian can only resolve concretely by his own responsible decision. The teaching office of the Church can give an orientation, it can no longer define every iota of belief or of moral conduct. It cannot dictate "from the top down"; it must more and more reflect the consensus of the People of God as a unity through which the Lord declares his will for our times.

Demythologization of Certainty

There are many within the body of Catholic Christianity, both clergy and laity, who will not welcome such a change of role, such a secularization of papal authority. For certainly will be undermined, security will be threatened. But is not this very loss of certainty and security essential to the Christian if his faith is to become a genuinely *adult* faith?

Individuals shallow in faith clamor for religion to give them security, certainty. Thus many Catholics have looked *too much* to papal authority and infallibility to provide a bulwark against doubt. "The Church has defined thus and so . . . you can be certain it is true. You can be certain of God, of Christ, of salvation, of resurrection and eternal life. You can be sure of forgiveness and of your righteousness. It is all infallibly defined."

Yet, does not true faith exclude certainty? [16] Certainty may flow from empirical knowledge, but it is not the end-product of faith. Is it not of the essence of adult faith to be willing to risk everything, to dedicate one's life to Christ, but *without certainty,* always with the lingering suspicion that possibly, just possibly, after death there is nothing? Faith does not obviate doubt. Quite the contrary, the Christian who does not doubt, does not authentically believe.

Is not modern secular man acutely aware of this painful aspect of his earthly existence? Is it not everywhere evident that he is no longer "certain" even that life has an ultimate meaning and purpose? Is it not his constant experience that nothing can give him this certitude, not even "religion"? The Christian of another day could take comfort in such things as papal declarations and infallible pronouncements. But no more. The adult Christian must learn to live and to give himself to the last moment, without certainty. This is the narrow gate of real faith — and few there are who enter through it — at least willingly.

On the other hand, this does not mean that modern man must live in total confusion, tortured by doubts on every front, deprived of *confidence* in anything. Through faith he can come to serene confidence in God, in his incarnate Son, in the Church. He can believe, on a rational basis, that he has been graced with the revelation of the most vital Truth, a revelation which continues to unfold even to this day. He can surrender himself

---

16. The distinction of various certitudes, i.e., 'metaphysical," "moral," and "certitude of faith," seems to me invalid. Certitude means *knowledge* which excludes doubt. Faith imports a kind of knowledge, but is a singular form of knowledge in that is by its very nature "uncertain"; it is not and cannot be "vision."

totally to Christ during his life, and go to his death with the quiet hope of a Paul: "I have fought the good fight, I have finished the race, I have lived the faith . . ." (II Tim. 4: 7), or of a Dietrich Bonhoeffer, who after two years of imprisonment, after suggesting the need for a "non-religious" approach to Christianity, on the verge of liberation, went confidently to an outwardly meaningless death of vengeance, with the persuasion that this was "the end — for me the beginning of life."

In this secular age the Church must strive to give men not a certainty — whether dogmatic or moral — that lies beyond her grasp, but through what she is and does she must allow the grace of God to create in his sons a confidence in the meaningfulness of authentic Christian existence in faith.

The Future of the Word

The changes of perspective outlined above are not without their risks. There is obviously the peril of opening the way to the annihilation of all dogma, the subjectivizing of all truth. Hence, it must be retained that there is and must always be supreme teaching authority in the Church, for the offices of Peter, the Apostles, and their successors cannot be reduced to myth. They represent a concrete and permanent commission from Christ. The Church must be appreciated as having from Christ the charge to safeguard and preach his Truth. Illusions about the extent or form of this mission must be dispelled, every sort of magicism must be exorcised, but the mission itself, and the Truth, remain.

Demythologization has its value. But a line must be drawn between what is "myth" and what is the faith of the Church. No doubt it is often difficult to discern such a "line" precisely, still its existence in principle must ever be kept in view. Nor should authority and the force of continuous tradition be underestimated as legitimate limiting restraints upon the tendency to demythologize or secularize.

Perhaps one of the greatest dangers in secular theology is the inclination to bend the Word of *God* so that it says what *we* wish it to say (the next step begin to neglect revealed truth altogether). The "Word of God in the words of men" thus becomes no more than the word of man to men, under the name of "relevancy." In searching for the meaning of God's Word for the secular world we must remember that it is *God's* Word that is in question and not merely that of sociological-economic factors or of urbanized man. The openness of the Word of God signifies that through Sacred Scripture our Lord continues to address himself to us today, but we must strive sincerely — even though without certainty — to discover what *He* wills us to hear.

In attempting to understand the Bible in relation to the contemporary world, therefore, we must scorn the temptation to seek "easy" solutions for our problems. As Bonhoeffer has said so well, we must not cheapen the grace of God, nor must we deny Christ his divinity (which is divinity-for-us) in seeking to heighten our appreciation of his humanity.

In the final analysis, no matter how "secular" our views or "adult" our age, the force that still remains most relevant even to our sophisticated modern world is *martyrdom,* in the sense of self-sacrificing witness on the part of utterly convinced and dedicated individuals, given consistency and effective meaning by being offered within and for the structure of the Church. And only the strength that comes through participation in the living God-Man, Jesus Christ, can make possible such understanding of and commitment to the Word of God.

A SYSTEMATIC BIBLIOGRAPHY

GENERAL WORKS

Bibliography

Moriarty, F. L. S.J., "Boston College Select Bibliography of the Bible," *The Bible Today*, March, 1966.
Steiner, U. J., O.S.B., *Contemporary Theology (A reading guide)*, Liturgical Press, Collegeville (Minn.), 1965.

Bible Dictionaries

Buttrick, G. A. (ed.), *The Interpreter's Dictionary of the Bible* (4 vols.), Abingdon Press, New York, 1962.
Douglas, J. D. (ed.), *The New Bible Dictionary*, Wm. B. Eerdmans Publishing Co., Grand Rapids (Mich.), 1962.
Hartman, L. P., C.Ss.R. (ed.), *Encyclopedic Dictionary of the Bible*, McGraw-Hill Book Company, New York, 1964.
Hastings, J. (ed.) (Revision by F. C. Grant and H. H. Rowley), *Dictionary of the Bible*, Charles Scribner's Sons, New York, 1963.
McKenzie, J. L., S.J., *Dictionary of the Bible*, Bruce Publishing Company, Milwaukee, 1965.
Marijnen, P. A., *The Encyclopedia of the Bible*, Prentice-Hall, Englewood Cliffs (N.J.), 1965.

Introductory and Background Material

To the entire Bible:

Auzou, G., *The Word of God*, B. Herder Book Co., St. Louis, 1965.
Beaucamp, E., O.F.M., *The Bible and the Universe*, Newman Press, Westminster (Md.), 1963.

Bouyer, L., *The Meaning of Sacred Scripture*, Notre Dame University Press, Notre Dame (Ind.), 1959.

Bruce, F. F. (ed.), *Promise and Fulfilment*, T. & T. Clark, Edinburgh, 1963.

Castelot, J. J., S.S., *Meet the Bible* (3 vols.), Helicon Press, Baltimore (Md.), 1960.

Charlier, Dom. C., *The Christian Approach to the Bible*, Newman Press, Westminster (Md.), 1958.

Daniel-Rops, H., *What is the Bible?* Hawthorn Books, New York, 1958.

Dannemiller, L., S.S., *Reading the Word of God*, Helicon Press, Baltimore (Md.), 1960.

Dodd, C., *The Bible Today*, Cambridge University Press, Cambridge, 1960.

Guillet, J., *Themes of the Bible*, Fides Publishers, Notre Dame (Ind.), 1964.

Harrington, W. J., *Record of Revelation: The Bible*, Priory Press, Dubuque (Iowa), 1965.

Hunt, I., O.S.B., *Understanding the Bible*, Sheed & Ward, New York, 1961.

Hyatt, J. P. (ed.), *The Bible in Modern Scholarship*, Abingdon Press, New York, 1965.

Kleinknecht, H., Gutbrod, W., Fichtner, J., Stählin, G., *I. "Law" II. "Wrath": Bible Key Words IV*, Harper & Row, New York, 1964.

Leishmann, T. L., Lewis, A. T., *The Bible Handbook*, Thomas Nelson & Sons, Camden (N.J.), 1965.

Levie, J., S.J., *The Bible, Word of God in Words of Men*, P. J. Kenedy & Sons, New York, 1961.

McKenzie, J. L. (ed.), *The Bible in Current Catholic Thought*, Herder and Herder, New York, 1962.

Maertens, T., *Bible Themes — A Source Book* (2 vols.), Biblica, Bruges, 1964.

Robert, A., Feuillet, A. (eds.), *Introduction à la Bible* (2 vols.), Desclée & Cie., Tournai, 2nd. edition, 1959. (*Introduciton to the New Testament*, Desclée Co., New York, 1965.)

Schokel, L. A., *Understanding Biblical Research*, Herder and Herder, New York, 1963.

To the Old Testament:

Albright, W. F., *The Biblical Period from Abraham to Ezra*, Harper & Row (Torchbooks), New York, 1963.

Albright, W. F., *From the Stone Age to Christianity*, Doubleday & Company, New York, 1957.

Anderson, B. W., Harrelson, W. (eds.), *Israel's Prophetic Heritage*, Harper & Row, New York, 1962.

Anderson, B. W., *The Old Testament and Christian Faith,* S.C.M. Press, London, 1964.

Anderson, B. W., *Understanding the Old Testament,* Prentice-Hall, Englewood Cliffs (N.J.), 1957. (2nd ed. 1966.)

Auzou, G., *The Formation of the Bible,* B. Herder Book Co., St. Louis, 1965.

Bright, J., *A History of Israel,* Westminster Press, Philadelphia, 1959.

Eissfeldt, O., *The Old Testament: An Introduction,* Harper & Row, New York, 1965.

Foerster, W., *From the Exile to Christ. A Historical Introduction to Palestinian Judaism,* The Fortress Press, Philadelphia, 1964.

Gelin, A., *Key Concepts of the Old Testament,* Paulist Press, Glen Rock (N.J.), 1960.

Gelin, A., *The Religion of Israel,* Hawthorn Books, New York, 1959.

Giblet, J. (ed.), *The God of Israel: The God of Christians,* Desclée Co., New York, 1961.

Gleason, R. W., S.J., *Yahweh: The God of the Old Testament,* Prentice-Hall, Englewood Cliffs (N.J.), 1964.

Guttmann, J., *Philosophies of Judaism,* Holt, Rinehart & Winston, New York, 1964.

MacKenzie, R. A. F., S.J., *Faith and History in the Old Testament,* University of Minnesota Press, Minneapolis, 1963.

McKenzie, J. L., S.J., *The Two-Edged Sword,* Bruce Publishing Company, Milwaukee, 1955.

Moscati, S., *Ancient Semitic Civilizations,* Capricorn Books, 1960.

Mowinckel, S. O. P., *The Old Testament as Word of God,* Abingdon Press, New York, 1959.

Paul-Marie of the Cross, O.C.D., *Spirituality of the Old Testament,* B. Herder Book Co., St. Louis, 1965.

Pritchard, J. B. (ed.), *Ancient Near Eastern Texts,* Princeton University Press, Princeton (N.J.), 2nd ed., 1955.

Rad, G. Von, *Old Testament Theology* (2 vols.), Harper & Row, New York, 1963, 1965.

Tresmontant, C., *A Study of Hebrew Thought,* Desclée Co., New York, 1960.

de Vaux, R., O.P., *Ancient Israel: Its Life and Institutions,* McGraw-Hill Book Company, New York, 1961.

Vawter, B., C.M., *The Conscience of Israel,* Sheed & Ward, New York, 1961.

Wallace, R. S., *The Ten Commandments: A Study of Ethical Freedom,* Wm. B. Eerdmans Publishing Co., Grand Rapids (Mich.), 1965.

Wright, G. E., *The Bible and the Ancient Near East* (Essays in honor of W. F. Albright), Doubleday & Company, Garden City (N.Y.), 1961.

To the New Testament:

Ahern, B. M., *New Horizons,* Fides Publishers, (Dome Books), Notre Dame (Ind.), 1965.

Amiot, F., *The Key Concepts of St. Paul,* Herder and Herder, New York, 1962.

Barrett, C. K., *The New Testament Background,* Seabury Press, New York, 1956.

Bonsirven, J., S.J., *Palestinian Judaism in the Time of Jesus Christ,* Holt, Rinehardt & Winston, New York, 1963.

Bonsirven, J., S.J., *Theology of the New Testament,* Newman Press, Westminster (Md.), 1963.

Brown, R. E., S.S., *New Testament Essays,* Bruce Publishing Company, Milwaukee, 1966.

Bultmann, R., *Theology of the New Testament* (2 vols.), S.C.M. Press, London, 1965.

Cerfaux, L., *Christ in the Theology of St. Paul,* Herder and Herder, New York, 1959.

Cerfaux, L., *The Church in the Theology of St. Paul,* Herder and Herder, New York, 1959.

Dibelius, M., *Die Formgeschichte des Evangelismus,* 1919.

Fuller, R. H., *The New Testament in Current Study* Charles Scribner's Sons, New York 1962.

Goppelt L., *Jesus, Paul and Judaism: An Introduction to New Testament Theology,* Thomas Nelson & Sons, Camden (N.J.), 1964.

Grossouw, W. K., *Spirituality of the New Testament,* B. Herder Book Co., St. Louis, 1965.

Harrington, W. J., *Record of The Fulfilment: The New Testament,* Priory Press, Dubuque (Iowa), 1966.

McKenzie, J. L., S.J., *The Power and the Wisdom,* Bruce Publishing Company, Milwaukee, 1965.

Moule, C. F. D., *The Birth of the New Testament* (Companion Vol. I, Black's New Testament Commentaries), London, 1962 .

Ryan, R., C.S.J. (ed.), *Contemporary New Testament Studies,* Liturgical Press, Collegeville (Minn.), 1965.

Schnackenburg, R., *The Moral Teaching of the New Testament,* Burns & Oates, London, 1965; Herder and Herder, New York, 1965.

Schnackenburg, R., *New Testament Theology Today,* Herder and Herder, New York, 1963.

Spicq, C., O.P., *Agapé in the New Testament* (2 vols.), B. Herder Book Co., St. Louis, 1965.

Spicq, C., *Principi della morale neotestamentaria,* Edizioni Studio Teologico Domenicano, Bologna, 1964.

Spicq, C., *Theologie morale du Nouveau Testament* (2 vols.), J. Gabalda, Paris, 1965.
Wikenhauser, A., *New Testament Introduction*, Herder and Herder, New York, 1958.

Commentaries

Black, M., Rowley, H. H., (eds.), *Peake's Commentary on the Bible*, Thomas Nelson & Sons, Camden (N.J.), 1962.
Buttrick, G. A. (ed.), *The Interpreter's Bible* (12 vols.), Abingdon Press, New York, 1957.
The Cambridge Bible Commentary (on *The New English Bible*), Cambridge Book Co., Bronxville (N.Y.), 1965.
The Layman's Bible Commentaries, John Knox Press, Richmond (Va.).
McEleney, N. (ed.), *Pamphlet Bible Series* (*Old* and *New Testament*), Paulist Press, Glen Rock (N.J.), 1960, 1966.
New Testament Reading Guide, Liturgical Press, Collegeville (Minn.), 1965.
Old Testament Reading Guide, Liturgical Press, Collegeville (Minn.), 1965.

Archaeological - Geographical

Albright, W. F., *Archaeology and the Religion of Israel*, Johns Hopkins Press, Baltimore (Md.), 1946.
Baly, D., *Geographical Companion to the Bible*, McGraw-Hill Book Company, New York, 1963.
Grollenbergh, L. H., O.P., *Atlas of the Bible*, Thomas Nelson & Sons, Camden (N.J.), 1956.
Kenyon, K., *Archaeology in the Holy Land*, Frederick A. Praeger, New York, 1960.
Schokel, L. A., *Journey through Bible lands*, Bruce Publishing Company, Milwaukee, 1964.

WORKS MORE SPECIFIC IN SCOPE

On Particular Books or Sections of the Bible

In the Old Testament:

Dahood, M., *Psalms I* (1-50), *The Anchor Bible* 16, Doubleday & Company, Garden City, New York, 1966.

Daniélou, J., S.J., *In the Beginning...Genesis I-III* Helicon Press, (A Challenge Book), Baltimore, 1965.

Drijvers, P., *Les Psaumes,* Les éditions du Cerf, Paris, 1958. (*The Psalms: Their Structure and Meaning,* Herder and Herder, New York, 1965.)

Dubarle, A. M., O.P., *Judith: Formes et sens des diverses Traditions, Tome I:Études, Tome II: Textes,* Analecta biblica 24, Pontifical Biblical Institute, Rome, 1966.

Gunkel, H., *The Legends of Genesis. The Biblical Saga and History,* Schocken Books, New York, 1964.

Hauret, C., *The Songs of the People of God,* Priory Press, Dubuque (Iowa), 1965.

McKenzie, J. L., S.J., *The World of the Judges,* Prentice-Hall, Englewood Cliffs (N.J.), 1966.

Murphy, R. E., O. Carm., *Seven Books of Wisdom,* Bruce Publishing Company, Milwaukee, 1960.

Rad, G. Von, *Genesis,* Westminster Press, Philadelphia, 1964.

Speiser, E., *Genesis, The Anchor Bible,* Doubleday & Company, Garden City (N.Y.), 1964.

Stuhlmueller, C., C.P., *The Prophets and the Word of God,* Fides Publishers, Notre Dame (Ind.), 1964.

Vawter, B., C.M., *A Path through Genesis,* Sheed & Ward, New York, 1956.

Between the Testaments:

Burrows, M., *The Dead Sea Scrolls,* Viking Press, New York, 1955.

Burrows, M., *More Light on the Dead Sea Scrolls,* Viking Press, New York, 1958.

Daniélou, J., S.J., *The Dead Sea Scrolls and Primitvie Christianity,* New American Library, New York, 1962.

Vermes, G., *The Dead Sea Scrolls in English,* Penguin Books, Baltimore, (Md.), 1962.

In the New Testament:

Barreau, J.-C., *The Good News of Jesus,* Newman Press, Westminster (Md.), 1965.

Barrett, C. K., *The Gospel According to John,* S.P.C.K., London, 1962.

Bea, A., *The Study of the Synoptic Gospels,* Harper & Row, New York, 1965.

Bell, H. I., Skeat, T. C., *The New Gospel Fragments,* Manchester, 1935.

Bernard, P. R., O.P., *Le Mystère de Jésus* (2 vols.), Salvatore Mulhouse, Casterman-Paris-Tournai, 1959. (*The Mystery of Jesus*), Alba House, Staten Island (N.Y.), 1966.

Boismard, M. E., *Le prologue de saint Jean*, Lectio Divina 11, Paris, 1953.
Bouyer, L., *The Fourth Gospel*, Newman Press, Westminster (Md.), 1964.
Brown, R. E., S.S., *The Gospel According to John, I-XII, The Anchor Bible* 29, Doubleday & Company, Garden City (N.Y.), 1965.
Bultmann, R., *Die Geschichte der synoptischen Tradition*, 1921.
Cerfaux, L., *La voix vivante de l'Évangile au début de l'Église*, Casterman, Tournai, 1956. (*The Four Gospels*, Newman Press, Westminster (Md.), 1960.)
Cerfaux, L., *La Théologie de L'Église suivant Saint Paul*, Éditions du Cerf, Paris, 3rd ed., 1965.
Dodd, C., *About the Gospels*, Cambridge University Press, Cambridge, 1958.
Dodd, C. H., *The Interpretation of the Fourth Gospel*, Cambridge, 1953.
Dupont, J., O.S.B., *Les Beatitudes*, Bruges-Louvain, 1958.
Dupont, J., O.S.B., *The Sources of the Acts*, Darton, Longman, & Todd, London, 1964.
Feuillet, A., *The Apocalypse*, Alba House, Staten Island (N.Y.), 1965.
Feuillet, A., *Johannine Studies*, Alba House, Staten Island (N.Y.), 1965.
Gutzwiller, R., S.J., *The Parables of the Lord*, Herder and Herder, New York, 1964.
Harrington, W. J., O.P., *A Key to the Parables*, Paulist Press, Glen Rock (N.J.), 1964.
Jaubert, A., *The Date of the Last Supper*, Alba House, Staten Island (N.Y.), 1965.
Knox, R. A., Cox, R. J. C.M., *The Gospel Story*, Sheed & Ward, New York, 1958.
Knox, R. A., Cox, R. J., C.M., *It Is Paul Who Writes*, Sheed & Ward, New York, 1959.
The Modern Reader's Guide to the Gospels (*Libra Books*), Darton, Longman & Todd, London, 1966.
Richardson, A., *The Gospel According to Saint John*, S.C.M. Press, London, 1959.
Roberts, C. H., *An Unpublished Fragment of the Fourth Gospel in the John Rylands Library*, Manchester, 1935.
Windisch, A., *Johannes und die Synoptiker*, Leipzig, 1926.

Eschatology: death, resurrection, heaven or hell

Boros, L., *The Mystery of Death*, Herder and Herder, New York, 1965.
Cornélis, H., O.P., et al., *The Resurrection of the Body*, Fides Press, Notre Dame (Ind.), 1964.
Davies, W. D., Daube, D., *The Background of the New Testament and its Eschatology*, Cambridge University Press, London, 1964.
Durrwell, F. X., C.Ss.R., *The Resurrection*, Sheed & Ward, New York, 1960.
Panneton, G., *Heaven or Hell*, Newman Press, Westminster (Md.), 1965.

Rahner, B., *Le chrétien et la mort,* Desclée de Brouwer, Bruges, 1966.

Ramsey, I. T., Boobyer, G. H., *The Miracles and the Resurrection,* S.P.C.K., London, 1964.

Robinson, W. J. C., *Der Weg des Herrn. Studien zur Geschichte und Eschatologie im Lukas-Evangelium. Ein Gesprach met Hans Conzelmann.* Heidelberg-Bergstedt, Reich Verlag, 1964.

Roper, A. L., *Did Jesus Rise from the Dead?* Zondervan Publishing House, Grand Rapids (Mich.), 1965.

Schmitt, J., *Jesus ressuscité dans la predication apostolique,* Paris, 1949.

Stanley, D. M., S.J., *Christ's Resurrection in Pauline Soteriology,* Pontifical Biblical Institute, Rome, 1963.

Troisfontaines, R., *Je ne meurs pas,* Paris, 1960.

Walker, D. P., *The Decline of Hell. Seventeenth-Century Discussions of Eternal Torment,* University of Chicago Press, 1964.

Evolution and the World of Sin

Bonhoeffer, D., *Creation and Fall,* Macmillan Company, New York, 1959.

Chauchard, P., *Man and Cosmos: Scientific Phenomenology in Teilhard de Chardin,* Herder and Herder, New York, 1965.

Dubarle, A. M., O.P., *The Biblical Doctrine of Original Sin,* Herder and Herder, New York, 1964.

Fraine, J. de., *Adam and the Family of Man,* Alba House, Staten Island (N.Y.), 1965.

Fraine, J. de., *The Bible and the Origin of Man,* Alba House, Staten Island, (N. Y.), 1967.

Francoeur, R. T., *Perspectives in Evolution,* Helicon Press, Baltimore, 1965.

Gelin, A., Descamps, A., *Sin in the Bible,* Desclée, New York, 1965.

Hulsbosch, A., *Die Schöpfung Gottes: Schöpfung, Sünde und Erlösung im evolutionistichen Weltbild,* Vienna, 1965. Lengsfeld, P., *Adam und Christus,* Lugerus-Verlag-Wingn, Essen, 1965.

Hulsbosch, A., O.S.A., *God in Creation and Evolution,* Sheed & Ward, New York, 1965.

Lubac, H. de, S.J., *Blondel et Teilhard de Chardin,* Beauchesne, Paris, 1965.

Lubac, H. de, S.J., *La Pensée religieuse de Teilhard,* Aubier, Paris, 1962.

Monden, L., S.J., *Sin, Liberty and Law,* Sheed & Ward, New York, 1965.

Philippe de la Trinité, O.C.D., *Rome et Teilhard de Chardin,* A. Fayard, Paris, 1964.

Porubcan, S., *Sin in the Old Testament, A Soteriological Study,* Herder and Herder, New York, 1963.

Rahner, K., *Hominsation,* Burns & Oates, London, 1965.

Rideau, E., *La Pensée du père Teilhard de Chardin,* Paris, 1965.

Robinson, H. W., *Corporate Personality in Ancient Israel,* Fortress Press, Philadelphia, 1964.

Schoonenberg, P., S.J., *God's World in the Making*, Duquesne University Press, Pittsburgh, 1964.
Schoonenberg, P., S.J., *Man and Sin*, University of Notre Dame Press, Notre Dame (Ind.), 1965.
Smulders, P., *La Vision de Teilhard de Chardin, Essai de réflexion theologique*, Desclée de Brouwer, 1964.
Smulders, P., *Teilhard de Chardin*, Newman Press, Westminster (Md.), 1965.
Teilhard de Chardin, P., *The Future of Man*, Harper & Row, New York, 1964.
Teilhard de Chardin, P., *The Phenomenon of Man*, Harper & Row (Torch Books), New York, 1961.
Vandenberg, J., S.J., *Christian Evolution*, Newman Press, Westminster (Md.), 1965.

Faith and Reason

Aubert, J. M., *Scientific Research and Christian Faith*, Newman Press, Westminster (Md.), 1965.
Fichtner, J. A., *Theological Anthropology: The Science of Man in Relation to God*, Notre Dame University Press, Notre Dame (Ind.), 1963.
Hauret, C., *Beginnings: Genesis and Modern Science*, Priory Press, Dubuque (Iowa), 1964.
Heaney, J. J., (ed.), *Faith, Reason and the Gospels*, Newman Press, Westminster (Md.), 1961.
Hessler, G., *The Bible in the Light of Modern Science*, Franciscan Herald Press, Chicago (Ill.), 1960.
Lonergan, B., *Insight*, Longmans, London, 1957.
Michalson, C., *The Rationality of Faith: an Historical Critique of the Theological Reason*, Charles Scribner's Sons, New York, 1963.
Smith, R., O.P., "Faith Without Belief," *Paul Tillich in Catholic Thought*, Priory Press, Dubuque (Iowa), 1964.

Inspiration, Revelation

Balthasar, H. Von, *Word and Revelation*, Herder and Herder, New York, 1964.
Benoit, P., O.P., *Aspects of Biblical Inspiration*, Priory Press, Dubuque (Iowa), 1965.
Benoit, P., O.P., *Inspiration and the Bible*, Sheed & Ward, New York, 1965.
Latourelle, R., S.J., *Theology of Revelation*, Alba House, Staten Island (N.Y.), 1966.

Moran, G., F.S.C., *Theology of Revelation*, Herder and Herder, New York, 1966.

Rahner, K., *Inspiration in the Bible*, Herder and Herder, New York, 1961.

Schökel, A., *The Inspired Word. Scripture in the Light of Language and Literature*, Herder and Herder, New York, 1965.

Marriage, Divorce, and Scripture

Alberti, A., *Matrimonio e divorzio nella Bibbia* (Coll. "Il nostro tempo"), Massimo, Milan, 1962.

Bonsirven, J., *Le Divorce dans le Nouveau Testament*, Desclée, Paris, 1948.

Dupont, J., O.S.B., *Mariage et divorce dans l'Évangile-Matthieu 19, 3-12 et parallèles*, Abbaye de Saint-André, Desclée de Brouwer, 1959.

Grelot, P., *Man and Wife in Scripture*, Burns & Oates, London, 1964.

Schillebeeckx, E., O.P., *Marriage: Human Reality and Saving Mystery*, Sheed & Ward, New York, 1966.

Wilkens, E., *Ehe und Ehescheidung*, Furche-Verlag, Hamburg, 1964.

Myth and History

Bultmann, R., and Five Critics, *Kerygma and Myth* (ed. H. W. Bartsch), Harper & Row (Torchbooks), New York, 1961.

Collingwood, R. B., *The Idea of History*, Oxford, 1946.

Dodd, C. H., *Historical Tradition in the Fourth Gospel*, Cambridge University Press, 1963.

Drioton, É., Contenau, G., Duchesne, J., Guillemin, J., *Religions of the Ancient East*, Hawthorn Books, New York, 1959.

Eliade, M., *Birth and Rebirth*, Harper & Row, New York, 1958.

Eliade, M., *Myths, Dreams and Mysteries*, Harper & Row, New York, 1960.

Eliade, M., *The Sacred and the Profane*, Harcourt, Brace & World, New York, 1959.

Frankfort, H. and H. A., Wilson, J. A., Jacobsen, T., *Before Philosophy*, Penguin Books, Baltimore, 1946.

Frazer, J. G., *The Golden Bough* (Vol. I, abridged), Macmillan Company, New York, 1960 (originally published in 1922).

Fuchs, E., *Studies of the Historical Jesus*, Allenson Press, Naperville (Ill.), 1964.

Funk, R. W. (ed.), *The Bultmann School of Biblical Interpretations: New Directions?* Harper & Row (Torchbooks), New York, 1965.

Gaster, T. H., *The Oldest Stories in the World*, Beacon Press, Boston, 1952.

Historicity and Chronology in the New Testament (a collection), S.P.C.K., London, 1965.

McKenzie, J. L., S.J., *Myths and Realities*, Bruce Publishing Company, Milwaukee, 1963.

Malevez, L., S.J., *The Christian Message and Myth,* Newman Press, Westminster (Md.), 1960.

Moule, C. F. D., *Faith, Fact and Fantasy,* Collins, London, 1964.

Robinson, J. M., *A New Quest of the Historical Jesus,* S.C.M. Press, London, 1959.

Van Der Loos, H., *The Miracles of Jesus,* E. J. Brill, Leiden, 1965.

Other Aspects, particularly Ecumenism

Benoit, P., *et al.* (eds.), *The Human Reality of Sacred Scripture (Concilium* 10), Paulist Press, Glen Rock (N.J.), 1965.

Bouësse, H., Latour, J. J., (eds.), *Problèmes actuels de Christologie* (collection), Desclée de Brouwer, Bruges, 1964.

Callahan, D., Oberman, H. A., O'Hanlon, D. J. (eds.), *Christianity Divided,* Sheed & Ward, New York, 1961.

Callahan, D., *Honesty in the Church,* Charles Scribner's Sons, New York, 1965.

Caster, M. van, S.J., *The Redemption: A Personalist View,* Newman Press, Westminster (Md.), 1965.

Cerfaux, L., *Apostle and Apostolate,* Desclée Co., New York, 1960.

Cerfaux, L., *Recueil Lucien Cerfaux* (2 vols.), Louvain, 1954.

Cody, A., O.S.B., *Heavenly Sanctuary and Liturgy in the Epistle to the Hebrews,* Grail Publications, St. Meinrad, (Ind.), 1960.

Cullmann, O., *The Christology of the New Testament,* Westminster Press, Philadelphia, 1959.

Grispino, J., S.M., *Foundations of Biblical Spirituality,* Alba House, Staten Island (N.Y.), 1965.

Häring, B., C.Ss.R., *Christian renewal in a Changing world,* Desclée Co., New York, 1964.

Hooft, W. A. Visser't, *L'Église face au syncrétisme,* Labor and Fides, Geneva, 1964.

Hooft, W. A. Visser't, *No Other Name: The Choice between Syncretism and Christian Universalism,* Westminster Press ,Philadelphia, 1964.

Johnston, L., *Witnesses to God,* Sheed & Ward, New York, 1961.

Jones, A., *Unless Some Man Show Me,* Sheed & Ward, New York, 1960.

Küng, H., *The Council, Reform and Reunion,* Sheed & Ward, New York, 1961.

Niebuhr, R., *The Nature and Destiny of Man, A Christian Interpretation,* Charles Scribner's Sons, New York, 1964.

Oraison, M., *Love, Sin and Suffering,* Macmillan Company, New York, 1964.

Oraison, M., *Une morale pour notre temps* (Coll. Le Signe), Fayard, Paris, 1964.

Rahner, K., *The Dynamic Element in the Church,* Herder and Herder, New York, 1964.

Robinson, J. M., Cobb, J. B., *The New Hermeneutic: New Frontiers in Theology Discussions among Continental and American Theologians,* Harper & Row, New York, 1964.

Schnackenburg, R., *The Church in the New Testament,* Herder and Herder, New York, 1965.

Schnackenburg, R., *God's Rule and Kingdom,* Herder and Herder, New York, 1963.

Spicq, C., O.P., *Charity and Liberty in the New Testament,* Alba House, Staten Island (N.Y.), 1965.

Stanley, D. M., S.J., *The Apostolic Church in the New Testament,* Newman Press, Westminster (Md.), 1965.

Swidler, L. J. (ed.), *Scripture and Ecumenism,* Duquesne University Press, Pittsburgh, 1965.

Vorgrimler, H. (ed.), *Dogmatic vs. Biblical Theology,* Helicon Press, Baltimore, 1965.

ARTICLES

Papal Documents

Humani Generis (Pius XII), 1950, English edition, Catholic Truth Society, London, 1957.

"Sul Domma del peccato originale" (Paul VI), *La Civiltá Cattolica,* Aug., 6-20 1966. Also in *Acta Apostolicae Sedis,* vol. 58, Sept. 30, 1966, no. 9.

General

Ahern, B. M., "The Book of the People of God," *Clergy Review,* no. 50, 1965.

Hunt, I. J., O.S.B., "Recent Biblical Study, 1960-63," *American Benedictine Review,* no. 14, 1963.

McKenzie, J. L., S.J., "Pastoral Apologetics and Modern Exegesis," *Chicago Studies,* Fall 1962.

The Old Testament

Buit, F. M. Du, "Comment lire le livre de Josué," *Bible et Terre Saint,* no. 56, 1963.

Childs, B. S., "Interpretation in Faith. The Theological Responsibility of an Old Testament Commentary," *Interpretation,* no. 18, 1964.

Duprey, A., "Le Livre de Judith," *Évangile*, no. 47, 1962.
Hay, L. S., "What Really Happened at the Sea of Reeds?" *Journal of Biblical Literature*, no. 83, 1964.
Liver, J., "The Literary History of Josue 10," *Journal of Semitic Studies*, no. 8, 1963.
Soggin, J. A., "Giosué 2 alla luce di un testo di Mari," *Rivista degli Studi Orientali*, no. 39, 1964.

Gospel Studies

Ahern, B. M., "The Gospels in Light of Modern Research," *Chicago Studies*, Spring 1962.
Braun, F. M., "L'arrière-fond du quatrième évangile," *L'Évangile de Jean*, Desclée de Brouwer, Bruges, 1958.
Montague, G. T., S.M., "The Emergence of the Gospels," *The Bible Today*, Nov. 1964.
Quispel, G., 'L'Évangile de Jean et la Gnose," *L'Evangile de Jean*, Desclée de Brouwer, Bruges, 1958.

New Testament Theology

Keck, L. E., "Problems of New Testament Theology. A Critique of Alan Richardson's 'An Introduction to New Testament Theology,'" *Novum Testamentum*, no. 7, 1964.
McKenzie, J. L., S.J., "Authority and Power in the New Testament," *The Catholic Biblical Quarterly*, Oct. 1964.

Faith and Contemporary Theology

Pittenger, N. A., "A Contemporary Trend in North American Theology: Process-thought and Christian Faith," *The Expository Times*, no. 76, 1965.
Runia, K., "Dangerous Trends in Modern Theological Thought," *Concordia Theological Monthly*, no. 35, 1964.
Scheffczyk, L., "Die Erbschuld zwischen Naturalismus und Existentialismus," *Munchener Theologische Zeitschrift, no.* 15, 1964.
Sikora, J. J., "Faith and the first Moral Choice," *Sciences Écclésiastiques*, no. 17, 1965.

Eschatology

Bailey, R. E., "Is 'Sleep' the Proper Biblical Term for the Intermediate State?" *Zeitschr. Neutest. Wiss.*, no. 55, 1964.
Cross, H., "Eschatology in the Old Testament," *Theology Digest*, no. 12, 1964.

Cullmann, O., "The Resurrection: Event and Meaning," *Christianity Today*, no. 9, 1965.

Feuillet, A., "Les origines et la signification de Mt. 10:23b," *Catholic Biblical Quarterly*, 1961.

Flor, M., "O Inferno," *Igreja Luterana*, no. 24, 1963.

Goffin, M., "Reflexions on Superstition and Credulity," *Objections to Roman Catholicism*, J. B. Lippincott Co., Philadelphia and New York, 1965.

Key, A. F., "The Concept of Death in Early Israelite Religion," *The Journal of Bible and Religion*, no. 32, 1964.

Mitton, C. L., "Life after Death. VII. The After-Life in the New Testament," *The Expository Times*, no. 76, 1965.

Pinnock, C. H., "In Defense of the Resurrection," *Christianity Today*, no. 9, 1965.

Robilliard, J. A., Lefèbvre, G., "Reflexion sur l'enfer." "L'enfer, mystère d'amour," *La Vie Spirituelle*, no. 108, 1963.

Schubert, K., "Resurrection in Pre-Christian Times," *Theology Digest*, no. 12, 1964.

Taylor, V., "Life after Death. I. The Modern Situation," *The Expository Times*, no. 76, 1964.

Unnik, W. C. van, "The Newly Discovered Gnostic 'Epistle to Rheginos' on the Resurrection," *The Journal of Ecclesiastical History*, no. 15, 1964.

Wilson, R. J., "The Hope of Life Hereafter in the Old Testament," *The Expository Times*, no. 76, 1965.

Marriage and Divorce

Ascoli, L., "Si parla di divorzio," *Democrazia e Diritto*, 1964.

De Naurois, L., "Le problème du divorce en France," *Revue de Droit Canonique*, no. 15, 1965.

Dubarle, A. M., "Mariage et Divorce dans l'Évangile," *L'Orient Syrien*, no. 9, 1964.

Emmet, C. W., Paterson, J., "Divorce," *Dictionary of the Bilbe*, Charles Scribner's Sons, New York, 1963.

Huizing, P., S.J., "Actus excludens substantiale matrimonii. Crisis doctrinae et Codicis" (Part II), *Gregorianum*, no. 45, 1964. "Should the Church's Marriage Laws be Revised?" *Concilium*, Vol. 18, Paulist Press, Glen Rock, N.J., 1966.

Lepp, I., Doherty, D., O.S.B., "The Problem of Divorce and Remarriage," *Marriage*, July 1966.

"Les tendances récentes du droit anglais en matière de mariage et du divorce," *Revue International Droit Comparé*, 1964.

O'Rourke, J. J., "A Note on an Exception: Mt. 5:32 (19:9) and I Cor. 7:12 Compared," *The Heythrop Journal*, no. 5, 1964.

Peter, A., "St. Paul and Marriage. A Study of I Corinthians Chapter Seven," *African Ecclesiastical Review*, no. 6, 1964.

Piola, A., "Fondamento costituzionale dell' indisssolubilità del matrimonio," *Diritto Ecclesiastico*, no. 76, 1965.

Vaccari, A., "O Divórcio nos Evangelhos," *Revista de Cultura Biblica*, no. 7, 1963.

Myth and Historicity

Bedenbaugh, J. B., "The First Decade of the New Quest of the Historical Jesus," *Lutheran Quarterly*, no. 16, 1964.

Borchert, G. L., "Is Bultmann's Theology a New Gnosticism?" *Evangelical Quarterly*, no. 36, 1964.

Bourke, M., "The Gospels as Theologically Interpreted History," *Studies in Salvation History*, C. L. Salm, Englewood Cliffs (N.J.), 1964.

Bourke, M., "The Historicity of the Gospels," *Thought*, Spring 1964.

Brown, R. E., S.S., "The Problem of Historicity in John," *Catholic Biblical* Jan. 1964.

Brown, R. E., S.S., "The Problem of Historicity in John," *Catholic Biblical Quarterly*, Jan. 1962.

Cahill, P. J., "Rudolf Bultmann and Post-Bultmann Tendencies," *Catholic Biblical Quarterly*, April 1964.

Chapman, G. C., "The Hermeneutics of Hermann Diem: A Renewed Conversation between Existentialist Exegesis and Dogmatic Theology," *Dissertation Abstracts*, no. 24, 1963.

Curtis, J. B., "A Suggested Interpretation of the Biblical Philosophy of History," *Hebrew College Annual*, no. 34, 1963.

Fitzmyer, J. A., "The Biblical Commission's Instruction on the Historical Truth of the Gospels," *Theological Studies*, no. 25, 1964.

Grabau, R. F., "The Necessity of Myth: An Answer to Rudolf Bultmann," *The Journal of Religion*, no. 44, 1964.

Hay, E. R., "Demythologizing and the Postsupernatural Era," *Canadian Journal of Theology*, no. 10, 1964.

Hill, E., "Remythologizing: the Key to Scripture," *Scripture*, no. 16, 1964.

"Instruction on the Historical Truth of the Gospels," *Catholic Biblical Quarterly*, July 1964.

McKenzie, J. L., "*Rudolf Bultmann. A Catholic Survey*," The Month, no. 32, 1964.

Mahoney, M., "History and the Gospel, Literary Forms and Inadequate Apologetics," *Tablet*, no. 218, 1964.

Roberts, J. S., "The Old Testament and the Historicity of the Gospels," "Instruction on the Historical Truth of the Gospels," *Catholic Biblical London Quarterly and Holborn Review*, no. 35, 1965.

Witmer, J. A., "The Authority of the Words of Jesus," *Bibliotheca Sacra,* no. 122, 1965.

Original Sin and Evolution

Alszeghy, Z., Flick, M., "Il peccato originale in prospettiva evoluzionistica," *Gregorianum,* no. 47, 1966.

Alszeghy, Z., Flick, M., "Il peccato originale in prospettiva personalistica," *Gregorianum,* no. 46, 1965.

Beis, A. H., "Some contributions of anthropology to ethics," *Thomist,* no. 28, 1964.

Boné, E., "Un siècle d'Anthropologie prehistorique," *Nouvelle Revue Théologique,* July-Aug. 1962.

Boyer, C., "Le Péché Originel," *Théologie du Péché,* Desclée & Cie., Tournai, 1960.

Bruna, M., Schoonenberg, P., "Tweegesprek over het ontstaan der zondigheid (Summary: The Origin of Sin)," *Tidsskrift for Teologi og Kirche,* no. 4, 1964.

Flick, M., "Peccato originale ed evoluzionismo. Alla ricerca di una soluzione," *La Civiiltà Cattolica,* July 2, 1966.

Flick, M., "Peccato originale ed evoluzionismo. Un problema teologico," *La Civiltà Cattolica,* July 2, 1966.

Flick, M., "Problemi teologici sull'ominizzazione," *Gregorianum,* no. 44, 1963.

Flick, M., "Theological Problems in 'Hominisation,'" *Theology Digest,* no. 13, 1965.

Michel, A., "Monogénisme, polygénisme et péché originel," *L'Ame du Clergé,* no. 75, 1965.

O'Rourke, J., "Some Considerations about Polygenism," *Theological Studies,* no. 26, 1965.

Pendergast, R. J., "The Supernatural Existential, Human Generation and Original Sin," *Downside Review,* no. 266, 1964.

Porter, J. R., "The Legal Aspects of the Concept of 'Corporate personality in the Old Testament,'" *Vetus Testamentum,* no. 15, 1965.

Schoonenberg, P., "Erbsunde und Welt,'" *Orienterung,* no. 26, 1962.

Theurer, W., "Monogenismus und Erbsünde," *Theologie de Gegenwart,* no. 8, 1965.

Revelation and Interpretation

"Basic Issues in Modern Theology: Revelation as Truth," *Christianity Today,* no. 9, 1965.

Cahill, P. J., "Miscellanea Biblica — Rudolf Bultmann's Concept of Revelation," *Catholic Biblical Quarterly,* July, 1962.

Ebeling, G., "Word of God and Hermeneutic," *The New Hermeneutic,* Harper & Row, New York, 1964.

Edwards, G. R., "The Present State of New Testament Interpretation," *Interpretation,* no. 18, 1964.

Foley, G. E., "Interpretation in Contemporary Theology. IV. Paul Tillich and the Bible," *Interpretation,* no. 18, 1964.

Moran, G., "What is Revelation?" *Theological Studies,* no. 25, 1964.

Murnion, P. J., "Sensus Plenior and the Progress of Revelation," *Dunwoodie Review,* no. 2, 1962.

Schnackenburg, R., "Biblical Views of Revelation," *Theology Digest,* no. 13, 1965.

Other Aspects of Biblical Theology

"The Place of the Bible at the Council," *Journal of Biblical Literature,* no. 83, 1964.

Etienne, J., "Théologie morale et renouveau biblique," *Ephemerides Theologicae Lovaniensis,* no. 40, 1964.

Demythisation et morale (a collection), Éditions Montaigne, Aubier, Paris, 1965.

Kasper, W., "The Church under the Word of God," *The Church and Ecumenism* (*Concilium* 4), Paulist Press, Glen Rock (N.J.), 1965.

Leroy Long, E., "The Use of the Bible in Christian Ethics. A Look at Basic Options," *Interpretation,* no. 19, 1965.

Mooney, C. F., "Teilhard de Chardin and the Christological Problem," *Harvard Theological Review,* no. 58, 1965.

Outler, A. C., "The Sense of Tradition in the Ante-Nicene Church," *Journal of Ecumenical Studies,* no. 1, 1964.

Rahner, K., "Christology and an Evolutionary World View," *Theology Digest,* no. 13, 1965.

Spicq, C., "I tratti principali della morale neotestamentaria," *Sacra Doctrina,* no. 9, 1964.

Thils, G., "Le choix d'un critère," *La "Theologie Oecumenique,"* É. Warny, Louvain, 1960.

RECENT PUBLICATIONS OF SPECIAL INTEREST

General

Albright, W. F., *New Horizons in Biblical Research,* Oxford University Press, New York, 1966.

The Church in Tension

Kavanaugh, James, *A Modern Priest Looks At His Outdated Church,* The Trident Press, New York, 1967.

"A Modern Priest Looks At His Outdated Church," critiques by Bishop T. D. Roberts, G. Baum, and others, *Continuum,* vol. 5, no. 2, Summer 1967, pp. 329-360.

Thielicke, Helmut, *The Trouble With The Church,* Harper & Row, New York, 1965.

Van Bilsen, B., *The Changing Church,* Duquesne University Press, Pittsburgh, 1966.

Vanhengel, M.C., O.P., and Peters, J., O.C.D., "Signs of the Times," *Concilium,* vol. 25, 1967, pp. 143-152.

Marriage

Bauer, J. B., "De conjugali foedere quid edixerit Matthaeus? (Mt. 5, 31s.; 19, 3-9)," *Verbum Domini,* vol. 44, 1966, pp. 74-78.

Beaupère, R., O.P., "Propositions pour un dialogue oecuménique," *Lumière et vie,* vol. 16, no. 82, May-June 1967, pp. 121-129.

Charland, R., "Le pouvoir de l'Église sur les liens du mariage," *Revue de Droit Canonique,* vol. 16, 1966, pp. 44-57.

Civisca, L., S.J., *The Dissolution of the Marriage Bond,* D'Auria, Naples, 1965.

Crouzel, H., S.J., "Séparation ou remarriage selon les Pères anciens," *Gregorianum,* vol. 47, 1966, pp. 472-494.

David, J., *Nouveaux aspects de la Doctrine catholique du Mariage,* Desclée, Tournai, 1966.

Gibson, Elsie, "Rethinking Marriage" (a review of three recent works on marriage), *Cross Currents,* vol. 17, Winter 1967, pp. 70-74.

Hewett, W. A., "A Possible Link in the Development of St. Paul's Teaching on Marriage," *Bellarmine Commentary,* vol. 4, 1966, pp. 23-31.

Journet, Charles, "Matrimonio indissolubile," *La Famiglia,* vol. 1, Jan. -Feb. 1967, pp. 7-22.

Lener, S., S.J., "Ancora un fermo e consapevole 'no' al divorzio," *Civiltà Cattolica,* vol. 2, 1966, pp. 209-215.

Pospishil, V. J., *Divorce and Remarriage. Towards a New Catholic Teaching,* Herder & Herder, New York, 1967.

Simons, Francis, "The Catholic Church and the New Morality," *Cross Currents,* vol. 16, 1966, pp. 429-445.

Snoek, J., C.Ss.R., "A pastoral dos divorciados que se casaram novamente," *Revista Eclesiastica Brasileira,* vol. 26, 1966, pp. 397-401.

Van der Marck, W., "De recente ontwikkelingen in de theologie van het ruwelijk (Summary: Recent developments in the theology of marriage)," *Tijdschrift voor Theologie,* vol. 7, 1967, no. 2, pp. 127-140.

Original Sin

De Lavalette, H., "Théologie dogmatique. — I. Péché originel. — II. La justification," *Recherches de Science Religieuse,* vol. 55, April-June 1967, pp. 226-251.

Grelot, P., "Réflexions sur le problème du péché originel," *Nouvelle Revue Théologique,* Nos. 3-5, 1967.

Koch, R., *Grâce et liberté humaine. Réflexion théologique sur Genèse I-XI,* Desclée, Tournai, 1966.

Labourdette, M. - M., "L'Eurve du Pere Teilhard de Chardin," *Revue Thomiste,* April-June 1967, pp. 263-290.

Lyonnet, Stanislaus, S.J., "Das Problem der Erbsünde im Neuen Testament," *Stimmen Der Zeit,* vol. 7, July 1967, pp. 33-39.

Murray, G. B., S.J., "Teilhard and Orthogenetic Evolution," *Harvard Theological Review,* vol. 60, 1967, pp. 281-295.

Rahner, K., "Evolution and Original Sin," *Concilium,* vol. 26, 1967, pp. 61-73. (All of vol. 26, *The Evolving World and Theology,* is relevant to this issue.)

Reese, J. M., O.S.F.S., "Current Thinking on Original Sin," *The American Ecclesiastical Review,* vol. 157, no. 2, Aug. 1967, pp. 92-100.

Webb, Dom Bruno., "The Species Adam," *The Downside Review,* July 1967, pp. 295-312.

The Resurrection of Christ

Bergquist, J. A., *The Resurrection of Jesus in the New Testament: An Exegetical Study,* Dissertation University of Southern California, 1962.

Bieri, H., *Die Auferstehung Jesu als historisches und als theologisches Problem,* Kirchenblatt für die reformierte Schweiz, vol. 121, 1965, vol. 121, 1965, pp. 178-182.

Fuchs, E., *Die Auferstehung Jesu Christi und der Anfang der Kirche,* Glaube und Erfahrung, J. C. B. Mohr, Tübingen, 1965, pp. 49-69.

Hooke, S. H., *The Resurrection of Christ as History and Experience,* Darton, Longman, and Todd, London, 1967.

Lampe, G. W. H., and MacKinnon, D. M. *The Resurrection,* William Purcell (ed.), Mowbray, London, 1966.

Pannenberg, W., "Did Jesus Really Rise from the Dead?," *Dialog,* vol. 4, 1965, pp. 128-135.

Ponthot, J., "Les traditions évangéliques sur la Resurrection du Christ. Perspectives Theólogiques et problème d'historicité," *Lumen Vitae*, vol. 20, 1965, pp. 649-673.

Von Campenhausen, Hans Frhr., *Der Ablauf der Osterereignisse und das leere Grab*, Carl Winter-Universitätsverlag, Heidelberg, 1966.

INDEX